D0959129

The Gospel of
Sustainability

The Gospel of Sustainability

Media, Market and LOHAS

MONICA M. EMERICH

University of Illinois Press

URBANA, CHICAGO, AND SPRINGFIELD

© 2011 by the Board of Trustees
of the University of Illinois
All rights reserved
Manufactured in the United States of America
C 5 4 3 2 1
∞ This book is printed on acid-free paper.

Library of Congress Cataloging-in-Publication Data
Emerich, Monica.
The gospel of sustainability : media, market, and LOHAS /
Monica M. Emerich.
p.   cm.
Includes bibliographical references (p.) and index.
ISBN 978-0-252-03642-2 (alk. paper)
1. Green marketing—Religious aspects.
2. Sustainable development—Religious aspects.
I. Title.
HF5413.E47   2011
658.4'083—dc23   2011028784

Contents

Preface

How are we to live? This deeply spiritual, moral, and ethical question of the ages is the heartbeat of the LOHAS—the Lifestyles of Health and Sustainability—marketplace. The question forces us to think of ourselves in relation to one another as well as to a higher consciousness. By its nature, it compels us to think about the purpose of our lives, about the substance of our communities, about the rights of the nonhuman, and about boundaries of respect and tolerance. The answer (more likely the "answers") to the question shape and inform our understanding of "truth," of the sacred.

The question doesn't limit itself to matters of our survival (as in "how are we going to get enough to eat?"), but rather it also embraces the thorny problem of ethics (as in, "is it really fair that we eat that?"). These concerns have historically been understood as the provenance or the problem of church, elder, shaman, or other moral leader. In the LOHAS marketplace, they've been also entrusted to the hands of the local grocer or the pages of your favorite magazine; they are articulated in very public, mediated, and commodified ways. Business, as they say, is booming in LOHAS, and while the endgame is still profit it's no longer acceptable at any price.

Australian market researcher Andy Baker put it well in his article, "The Growth of LOHAS Internationally," featured in the spring 2008 issue of *The LOHAS Journal*. He wrote, "Businesses the world over are leveraging LOHAS as a way to understand the consumption preferences of a growing number of people who care deeply about personal, community, and planetary health and well-being, and are willing to spend accordingly."

Baker captured three key facts about LOHAS. First, even though the word "LOHAS" only entered the pubic lexicon in 1999 via a small publishing firm in Broomfield, Colorado, the concept has managed to go global. Second, LOHAS designates a marketplace of goods and services, one immersed in an intricate web of deeply meaningful personal values about the "self" and about the social and natural worlds. Third, Baker's assertion obfuscates issues of class—about who can pay to play in LOHAS—and frames it instead as an issue of personal choice, as an issue of *willingness* to spend rather than an *ability* to spend.

While LOHAS is an intriguing example of an innovative business strategy, this book isn't a marketing text; instead it treats LOHAS as a window onto processes of social change, as a certain kind of appeal for a moral and spiritual reordering of the world that comes through media and market organizations. Before going further, a little history of LOHAS is in order.

LOHAS was the brainchild of eco-goods and healthy-living products retail giant, Gaiam Inc., owned by Jirka Rysavy, once a runner-up for *Inc.* magazine's prestigious Entrepreneur-of-the-Year award and an Olympic-level athlete from the Czech Republic. Rysavy coined the term "LOHAS" with a hand-picked group of advisors and investors in the mid-1990s and it was circulated within that circle as an "in-house" market strategy. This changed a few years later when Rysavy approached the small publishing firm Natural Business Communications with the idea of creating a business magazine based on LOHAS.

Natural Business Communications was a young company. It had only recently launched its first publication, *Natural Business*, a financial newsletter for executives in the natural and organic products industry. Nonetheless, co-owners Steven Hoffman and Frank Lampe were eager to expand. They agreed with Rysavy that the market for healthy goods in the United States and around the world was undergoing dramatic growth. With investment support from Rysavy, Hoffman and Lampe subsequently launched the four-color trade magazine *The LOHAS Journal* and produced the first LOHAS Forum, a trade conference and exhibit. With these, the concept of LOHAS was officially released into public distribution in the spring of 2000.

LOHAS was a smart marketing move. After all, natural and organic products were selling like ice on a hot summer day. Throughout the 1990s the natural and organic products industry had mushroomed, making millionaires out of former back-to-the-land hippies who had become manufacturers and retailers of natural, organic and ecologically friendly products. Thanks to a convergence of forces in the culture, including an aging U.S. population and an eroding healthcare system, consumers were flooding small mom-and-pop health food stores around the United States. They were in search of food and dietary supplements marketed as healthier than "mainstream" fare. They were eager to try the alternative medicine products in these stores, such as homeopathy and herbal medicines; they were demanding products that didn't harm the environment.

Wall Street, always looking out for the next big thing, noticed the shifts and soon began happily extending investment dollars to the natural marketplace. Capital seemed to be suddenly falling from the skies. Entrepreneurs scurried to integrate, merge, innovate, and market so they, too, could get a piece of the healthy-living pie before it vanished from the public-funding plate.

At the time, the natural and organic products industry was a highly fragmented, fiercely entrepreneurial amalgam. While dietary supplements were the traditional money makers of the industry, that was changing as the offerings of packaged natural and organic foods and personal care categories expanded and new "periphery" departments such as fresh produce, refrigerated, frozen, food service, and housewares appeared. You could find anything from apples to bamboo yoga tights.

These architectural changes to the marketplace were driven by undercurrents in the culture. Suddenly consumers and producers were talking about values, about morality and social responsibility, about the ethics of living on a small planet. The marketplace for alternative, healthy, natural, organic, and environmental goods had become the socially responsible marketplace. It was a sprawling market, and that represented a potential problem that could create consumer confusion.

Enter LOHAS. Rysavy and Natural Business thought LOHAS could serve as a conceptual canopy or a system of logic to help consumers and producers understand why this diverse and global field of goods and services, organizations and individuals, ideals and beliefs was really a single, unified entity. Not only that, but LOHAS investors banked on their belief that a more integrative notion of health and wellness was brewing in the culture, one that didn't just stop at personal health but that also extended to ecosystems, cultures, workers, nations, communities, and more.

These early LOHAS producers also believed consumers didn't want to just plug in the odd product here and there to express "healthfulness" but instead were searching for an comprehensive "lifestyle," one that reflected their deepening concerns about a dirty planet, disgruntled and exploited workers, fading cultures, and frayed communities. Market researchers understood that individuals were increasingly losing faith in governmental and social institutions to solve the mess and were ready to take matters in their own hands.

When LOHAS was introduced, it was defined as "a market segment focused on health and fitness, the environment, personal development, sustainable living, and social justice" (http://www.lohas.com). It was a new way to sort out the natural and organic marketplace, and *The LOHAS Journal* defined this different ordering through six key market segments:

- Personal Health (including alternative and complementary or integrative medicine; natural and organic products; mind/body/spirit goods and services; dietary supplements)
- Natural Lifestyle (including eco-goods and social change philanthropy)
- Green Building
- Alternative Transportation
- Eco-Tourism
- Alternative Energy

In 2003 LOHAS received the ultimate validation when it was the subject of a first-section, full-page article in the *New York Times*. And, for the record, no one since has put forth a more entertaining definition of LOHAS than the *Times* article's author, Amy Cortese: "LOHAS sounds like a disease, but may be the biggest market you have never heard of, encompassing things like organic foods, energy-efficient appliances, and solar panels, as well as alternative medicine, yoga tapes, and eco-tourism."

Many, no doubt, shared a good chuckle with the *Times* at the lumpish name of "LOHAS," but investors and business mavens were smiling politely—the silly sounding word had managed to stick—and spread. Market research put the LOHAS market in 2009 at $215 billion in the United States and more than $500 billion globally. If you Google LOHAS, you'll read that 40 million Americans are considered to be "LOHASians," the word *Newsweek* magazine and beliefnet.com use to describe people who buy "healthy" and "sustainable" products and services. Natural Marketing Institute estimates that nearly 20 percent of Americans are LOHAS consumers, while *Newsweek* declares "LOHASians" comprise 17 percent of the population (Waldman and Reiss).

It's clear that ideas of sustainability have purchase even in "mainstream" U.S. society, even though it wasn't that long ago when the way in which these ideas are framed in the LOHAS marketplace—such as with the phrases "mind, body, and soul," "natural foods," and "spirituality"—were equated with hippies and New Agers. Now the term "sustainability" links to a kaleidoscope of concerns facing Americans, including the furor and frustration over American dependence on foreign oil; the plummeting of global economies; the collapse of the healthcare system; climate change; exposure of social injustices; and new research on health hazards posed by chemicals, industrial processes, and pharmaceuticals. Entire supermarkets are devoted to healthful products; First Lady Michelle Obama planted an organic vegetable garden on the south lawn of the White House; and Al Gore won the Nobel Peace Prize. In 2008 Discovery Communications launched its Discovery Home Channel—"a 24-hour channel focused on eco-friendly living"—because, as Discovery's chief executive, David M. Zaslav opined, "the time is ripe to push into the rising environmental movement" (Siklos). "To be able to rebrand an existing channel and launch with over 50 million homes in 2008 is a big statement to where the world is today . . . five years ago, people would have said 'who are those lefties talking about green?'" Zaslav said, adding, "Today, green means responsible" (Siklos).

The election campaign of U.S. President Barack Obama incorporated a strong health and sustainability platform that included a commitment to the development of alternative energy, sustainable development, healthcare reform, and various social responsibility programs. Along with his commitment came government development money—$60 billion in his Energy and Environment platform alone, and these were dispersed through state and federal agencies to promote product innovation, production, and partnership.

On Earth Day 2009, the Obama administration announced the details of its new renewable energy project located in the waters of the Outer Continental Shelf that will produce electricity from wind and ocean-wave currents. In his speeches on renewable energy, the president situated these new projects within a history of American leadership and courage. As the White House connected sustainability issues to national security, economic solvency, and international stature, environmental projects were represented as innovations made possible by American mind and muscle. More than twenty-five years after pulling Carter-era solar panels off the White House roof, the Recovery and Reinvestment Act has become this administration's salvo over the hydra-headed legacy left to it by former administrations.

How was it that cultural peace was made between the culture and associated ideals once labeled as "alternative" and their counterparts, known as the "mainstream"? LOHAS gives us a window onto the evolution of key cultural conversations that have informed the current narrative about "health and sustainability." These include the global movement for environmentalism; the American tradition of therapeutic work on the "self"; individualism and other prized tenets of liberalism; and the spirit of the 1960s social movements.

While these histories are key to the development of LOHAS, LOHAS itself is positioned (as are most market-based phenomena) as "new," progressive and forward-looking. LOHAS discourse carries an air of the "can-do" rally cry of candidate Barack Obama, who said in a stump speech in Newton, Iowa, "We've got to have some imagination and we've got to be bold. We can't be looking backwards, we've got to look—we've got to look forward." If it had been available back when LOHAS began, it would have made a perfect pitch for the budding LOHAS market. If nothing else, LOHAS is represented as visionary, progressive, and transformative.

Whether it is those things, one thing is certain: LOHAS is a perfect product of late modernity, which has bequeathed us a razor-sharp awareness of how connected people, environments, nations, and organisms really are. We're no longer in need of experts' projections about pending social and environmental crisis—most of us can see actual changes, for better or worse. No matter our location—culturally and physically—most people have come up against the forces of globalization defined as "the compression of the world and the intensification of consciousness of the world as a whole" (Robertson 8). We've come to recognize the fragility of our situations, stoking concerns about how we are going to remain a viable planet with a future that does not resemble something out of a post-apocalyptic *Terminator* movie. So widespread is the discourse about and the portrayal of pending chaos and even disaster for people, animals, and environments that even if the term "LOHAS" is unfamiliar to you, you are likely very familiar with the products and services it encompasses.

But as Amy Cortese's *Times* article captured, it isn't the contents of LOHAS that are so intriguing—they already existed in the marketplace—but rather why and how they've been tossed together in the same sustainability salad, so to speak. What links this miscellany of goods and services, beliefs and practices, spheres and organizations to one another in LOHAS? What is the substance of their urgency and appeal?

One clue is in the title to Cortese's article: "They Care about the World (and They Shop, Too)." LOHAS sets out to answer how we should care about this world, and in the LOHAS market the word "spirituality" is freely invoked as part of that. But beyond the substantive mentions of the word "spirituality," the term would still be my choice to describe the aggregate of ideas, references, practices, and products circulating in the LOHAS marketplace and media. One reason for that is LOHAS carries the same sort of symbolic language and imagery that is the currency of religion—including references to transcendence (intuition, for example, or a numinous dimension of beingness that goes beyond the empirical world), eschatology (death or destiny of the planet), soteriology (salvation of self, society, and planet; karma), theology (the beliefs of specific traditions), and often some combination of these. But even though it has these elements, what LOHAS doesn't employ is the word "religion." And that means there must be a way to account for these "religious" sentiments when the word itself is avoided and even denied by practitioners.

Health and sustainability have become metonyms for spirituality in LOHAS. And by spirituality I mean something different from religion with its formalized infrastructures and doctrines. While spirituality can carry much of the content of religion (for example, delineating between good and evil), it isn't beholden to religion's context (for example, authorities, buildings, objects, rituals, or dogma—although spiritual practices *could* also have these things). Spirituality hasn't been "branded" to the degree that religion has, and I'm thinking here of brands as specific denominations of religion such as Catholicism, Lutheranism, or Judaism, for example (see Einstein). Instead, spirituality has an openness to it (some might say a relativism) that lends, indeed requires, customization by the individual or group to give it shape and form (see Heelas and Woodhead).

The rise of a spiritual quest culture was elucidated by Wade Clark Roof in his seminal work on spiritual seeking among baby boomers in the United States and also in work on new spiritualities and the New Age by such scholars as Stephen Sutcliffe, Marion Bowman, Ursula King, Catherine Albanese, Paul Heelas, Linda Woodhead, Dick Houtman, Stef Aupers, Chris Ellison, and Wouter Hanegraaff.

But spirituality has now become a megabusiness and chief marketing strategy for businesses, and that means it's all about positioning (see Einstein; Badaracco). As an example of what I mean, Claire Hoertz Badaracco, writing about the nature of media in the construction of ideas about health and medicine in America, says, "Positioning is not just a matter of medical marketing, but is also about changing the spiritual story behind the cultural lens, feeding the collective and individual imagination of consumers about self, health and disease" (160). LOHAS is a positioning of sustainability as a spiritual endeavor.

The terms "health" and "sustainability" reflect both the *pragmatic* and *integrative* aspects of spirituality in LOHAS. By pragmatic I mean that the ideas, practices, products, and services that constitute the LOHAS marketplace are positioned as correctives for a.) the exploitation of people, environments and animals; b.) the imbalance of mind, body, and spirit, particularly in highly industrialized societies; c.) the deterioration of healthcare structures; and d.) the rampant poverty and environmental destruction around the world. These are practical and urgent considerations.

By integrative, I refer to the way in which the solutions posed in LOHAS attempt to bridge space and time, the roles we occupy in everyday life, and the spheres of experience. The end result is a map of the world—the landscape upon which our lives are played out—and the dimensions of space and time in which we are situated. Like any map, LOHAS marks the paths and byways, the points of interest, and the distances between what we have (or where we are) and what we want (or where we're aiming to go). It is a representation of the world as it is and the world as we want to imagine it.

Perhaps more than anything, though, the map attempts to represent the world as cohesive and logical, and as such it is meant to help consumers and producers resolve contradictions and to reconcile inconsistencies in the world rising from capitalism and their place within both it and a globalized world. In that way, the LOHAS discourse aims to help us understand how to be simultaneously local and global (how we exist with relationship to space), how to understand histories with an eye to making midcourse corrections to protect future generations (our relationship with time), and the various roles we play during our lives (our relationship with culture and structure).

The endgame is to achieve "health." Most commonly, health is understood as the absence of sickness or disease, but what constitutes *those*? The waters get murky here, because certainly in LOHAS at least sickness and disease are understood very broadly, far beyond common physical complaints. Instead of limiting the discussion to those, LOHAS speaks instead to a *holistic* idea of health, one that intertwines our own individual health with that of ecosystems and environments and with that of institutions, of communities, and of cultures. These elements form an interdependent, inclusive picture of health in the LOHAS discourse. Each is a composition of the other; each is dependent on the optimal functioning of all.

But optimal functioning or health relies on *sustainability*. Sustainability comprises the processes by which this holistic model of health will be attained and maintained. The concept of sustainability commonly refers to an amalgamation of methods and practices that replenish and nourish rather than extract and deplete the raw materials that compose and support a human body, a culture, an organism, or an ecosystem. In LOHAS, sustainability can as easily refer to the inner realms of spirit as it can to the global battlegrounds of poverty and environmental destruction.

The porosity of these terms—health, sustainability, and spirituality—is extremely useful to the promulgators of the ideals of LOHAS: media and market organizations. The goal of this book is to explore the ways in which these secular, transitory, and everyday organizations have been legitimated as purveyors of deep values, to speak so seriously about the sacred and to speak so spiritually about commodities and consumerism. To that, this book is keenly interested in LOHAS because of its mediated and commodified creation and distribution.

Considering those market organizations, media in particular have been often treated like bicycle reflectors or mirrors with regard to culture, establishing where we are as a society and where we are heading to or coming from. But media are more intimately involved in the running of the social and cultural machinery than that metaphor implies. That is, beyond simple reflection of culture, they also construct and generate culture. They do this by providing symbolic resources from which we weave our identities and make our meanings. Through these resources, we come to understand the world and our place in it. Along with the market, media *mediate* social conscious-ness—representing, rearranging, and circulating the values and beliefs by which we define our societies, others, and ourselves. So rather than regard them as simple transmitters of information and social mores, it's more use-ful to think of them as the actual sites where raw materials, or symbols, are processed and where meaning making and action can occur.

To that point, media, religion and culture scholar Stewart Hoover (*Religion*) says we live in a *media age,* while others claim capitalism has become a new *metaphysics* of existence (Colin Campbell, qtd. in Bauman). Given these sets of circumstances, it is difficult to see how the sacred could manage to stand apart from media and market, despite the fact that they have traditionally been held up as the *profane* polarities to spiritual life.

Along with their symbolic manufacturing and distributing, we also have to remember that media and market organizations are ideological forma-tions and ideology-forming structures as well. While media and market can't impose meanings on consumer minds as if they were cultural chalkboards, these organizations *do* have determining power—editors of magazines, for example, have the power to select or reject material for their publications. The reach into the social world and the public nature of these organizations give them an authoritative presence, a legitimacy. Through the constancy of their production, images and concepts can become *normativized*, forming a worldview that becomes so familiar it elides other competing views and voices. This is particularly worrisome with regard to the ongoing consolida-tion of media and market organizations and the power of their reach that is fueled by massive budgets and the social and political influence that imparts.

In late capitalism, the market has become the measure of who we are and what we can become; we may think of ourselves as independent operators in a world awash with material goods and that each choice we make in this matter reflects something deeply revealing about who we really are or who we want to be, when in fact, desire and notions of identity are also created by market organizations, including the media, and done so to serve their in-terests of profit and expansion (Fjellman). The consumer model has become the overlay, or as Colin Campbell puts it, the "template by which citizens of contemporary Western societies have come to view all their activities" (qtd. in Bauman 41–42).

I propose that LOHAS is represented as a way to open up space within capitalism using media and market organizations to reshape consumerism as a force capable of promoting collective conscience and moral social order via a "lifestyle"—one that doesn't overemphasize "consumer sovereignty" or engage in a negative critique of "consumer-as-dupes" (Jackson 210). The aim in LOHAS is finding a place in materiality where consumers, adorned in all their individualized glory, can find some solid ground from which to consider the morphing world they find themselves in and from which they can reflexively view themselves as empowered to generate change, to be, if they so wish, intentionally and successfully oppositional (McDannell 12).

With the narratives and symbolic resources offered up by media and market, consumers learn how to construct a *lifestyle*, and identity through which they are able to plot their future, understand their past, and situate their present (see Hoover and Clark 17). These institutions are capable of sensing even minor notes of discord and discomfort among their audiences; and they are able to respond with head-spinning speed to counteract disgruntlement and to offer up a different set of products or resources as solutions. In the case of LOHAS, we can see the market was created to address the rising social concerns consumers were having about market capitalism itself.

If Westerners are left in a place where they cannot act outside of media and market, then LOHAS's posing of ethical and moral possibilities and deliberation through those sites is liberating as well as practical. LOHAS in this sense becomes the creative work of populations working within their own political, social, or economic constraints to find avenues of resistance, in this case media and market, but it isn't quite the same sort of resistance we saw in, say, the 1960s. This time there is an appeal being made to your very soul, to your spiritual beliefs and, without hesitation, the media and the market are happily offering themselves up as the site, the voice, and the tool of spiritual practice (see Hoover and Venturelli 258). While "religion is a product, no different from any other commodity in the consumer marketplace," as Mara Einstein says (4), LOHAS is using religious sensibilities in a different way, melting away the fibers of individual institutions of religion in a stew of global faith practices and serving up a universal dish of spirituality, where we all know the right thing to do if we just listen closely enough to our inner voice.

This book is going to examine the processes through which LOHAS attempts to integrate two sites of labor: where we externally labor for wages and where we internally labor for transcendental meaning. I'm asking how, why, and where LOHAS does this, but in doing so, I'm also asking what this discourse, culture, and marketplace: a.) reveals about the nature of the evolution of religion in American culture; b.) adds, for better or worse, to global exigencies regarding the meaning and content of beliefs and practices of "sustainability"; and c.) lends to our insights into the dynamics among media, religion, and culture in late modernity.

In closing, I would like to thank the people who made this book possible, starting with those workers and consumers in the LOHAS market who allowed me into their lives during the course of ten years of research to share their ideals and thoughts. To my informants who must remain anonymous to protect their competitive edge in the marketplace, thank you for your perseverance even in times when our government was penalizing you for your beliefs. Thank you for sharing words and visions in a spirit of cooperation and in the belief that average people realoly can make a difference in the world.

I am indebted to the Center for Media, Religion and Culture at the School of Journalism and Mass Communication, University of Colorado. As a doctoral student there, I received unparalleled research experience and generous funding support. I want to thank Professors Stewart M. Hoover and Lynn Schofield Clark for their mentoring. It was a privilege to continue my research as the center's Post-Doctoral Fellow. My deepest gratitude to Dr. Hoover and Dr. Clark for their support and friendship through the years.

I was particularly fortunate to also study at the University of Colorado with brilliant scholars who shaped my thinking: Andrew Calabrese, Marjorie McIntosh, Tim Oakes, Janice Peck, Elizabeth Robertson, and Michael Tracey. You opened new worlds to me. To Marion Bowman and Garry Tregidga at the Open University and the Institute for Cornish Studies respectively, thank you for your direction, advice, and support. My sincere thanks to the Center for British and Irish Studies at the University of Colorado, which awarded me the Ogilvy Travel Fellowship that generously enabled me to pursue research into spirituality and sustainability at the Institute for Cornish Studies, in Truro, Cornwall.

During the years of research and writing I was blessed with the support and love from many friends who served as sounding boards, editors, and shoulders. A special thank you to Yuri Obata and Richard Khleif for impeccable advice and seemingly endless tolerance for confused comrades. To my parents, Clara and John Emerich, your love and respect of animals and plants rooted my interests in sustainability. Most importantly, to my husband Frank Lampe Jr., thank you for your vision of health and sustainability that inspires me every day to do better by the planet and its people and creatures. Thank you for spending hours tirelessly reading this manuscript; it produced a better book by far and your patience with the ups and downs of the writing life ensured there was any book at all.

*The Gospel of
Sustainability*

The Business of Consciousness

"The focus on spirituality has become so pervasive that it stands as
today's greatest megatrend. Its impact on personal lives is
spreading into institutions. And spirituality in business is
converging with other socioeconomic trends to foster a moral
transformation in capitalism."

—Patricia Aburdene, coauthor of *Megatrends;* author of
Megatrends 2010: Conscious Capitalism.

The futurist and author Peter Russell sat on the dais looking relaxed as he
waited for the crowd filing into the seminar room to take their seats. He
was the sole speaker at a special session entitled "Consciousness: The Next
Frontier," held at the 2007 LOHAS Forum, a business conference serving the
international marketplace known as Lifestyles of Health and Sustainability,
LOHAS for short. It was a concurrent session, and clearly the conference
organizers had underestimated Russell's appeal. With the seventy-five chairs
in the room taken, the overflow of attendees stood along the walls of the
seminar room and sat in the aisles. When the room quieted at last, Russell
said in a soft voice, "We are going through a global spiritual renaissance for
the first time. Humans are now in an evolutionary period of consciousness,
whereby we can move away from a narcissized consumer culture toward a
more collective understanding of the nature of life, as self dissolves into a
universal awareness."

Narcissized consumer culture? Spiritual renaissance? Dissolution of the self?

Could Russell say *that* at a conference attracting some titans of American
industry, including Intel, Dell, and Ford Motor Company, and a few of Hollywood's more recognizable faces, including Raquel Welch's and Daryl Hannah's?

"Consciousness is our greatest untapped resource and it is never more in
need than now because the world is undergoing a major worldview shift," he
said. "This is a shift that has been predicted for ages by many of the world's
religious faiths and metaphysical traditions." The audience was hushed and
intent upon his words. Russell had just linked consciousness with religion

and spirituality, but he did not provide any references from world religions to illustrate his point. Instead he chuckled and said, "religion is what spirituality looks like when put into human hands; they are two different things." People began to laugh and nod. Someone exclaimed, "Yes!" For a brief moment, the venue seemed more akin to a revival tent than an upscale business conference. Russell waited for the stir to subside before adding that the paradigm shift to a different, more spiritual consciousness was "a leaderless movement" attributable to the rise of the globalized media. "We've never had a global media before and now we can access traditions and information anywhere," he said.

Russell seemed relaxed about his frequent juggling of the word "consciousness," and the more he used it, the more it appeared to serve as a sort of code for a constellation of practices and beliefs on the "self," the social world, and the natural world that were being ethicized and moralized.

A year later, at LOHAS Forum 2008, Russell was again speaking on consciousness. As he had the previous year, he spoke about the power of the free market to change the world for the good—and he called it "conscious capitalism." As businesses develop "consciousness," he said, they will cease to be just market entities, evolving into servants to the world and ushering in the new paradigm of health for the planet that Russell called sustainability. "The real root of unsustainability," Russell declared, "is the unsustainability of consciousness. The old way of consciousness that has worked for a long time—that materialistic consciousness—doesn't work any longer."

The concept of consciousness in LOHAS is an overarching theme. It is used in that marketplace in ways that carry the deepest questions of the ages, about survival, quality of life, compassion, and duty. In fact, the words "spirituality" and "consciousness" are used so often in LOHAS that they are treated normatively—without much explanation as if the receivers of these messages understand at a deep level the inherent meanings. Testing this hypothesis, I recognized in Russell's 2007 LOHAS Forum seminar an editor who had worked in the natural and organic products industry for more than twenty years. After the seminar, I asked him whether he had found it surprising to hear Russell marshal terms such as "consciousness" in a business setting. He shrugged. If anything, he said, he found Russell's use of the word almost passé. "Everyone is tuned into the changing consciousness field," he said. Later that evening at the event reception I posed the same question to a group of attendees and received much the same response.

It is surprising that these two terms that appear to be signposts to a new world vision of sustainability do not ignite livelier discussions about their definitions, if for no other reason than so we know when we've arrived at the goal of sustainability. Certainly no one in either of Russell's seminars in 2007 and 2008 debated or argued with his notion of consciousness or even that of sustainability. And, clearly, his weaving of spirituality with consciousness within the sphere of business seemed to be well received. The crowd had been appreciative of his deliberate opposition of spirituality to religion.

Russell's treatment of spirituality situated it as a universal, supra-categorical phenomenon. If it surprised them, the audience of Rust Belt manufacturers, Silicon Valley entrepreneurs, and natural "foodies" didn't show it. They seemed overwhelmingly supportive of the ideas, and this in itself is a bit astonishing because it wasn't so long ago when the idea of "spirituality" conjured up images of chilled-out New Agers with crystals and incense. Just a decade earlier, it would have been tough to envision Ford Motor Company executives sitting through Russell's talk on the dawn of a new age of consciousness, which was the provenance of the "alternative" lifestyle crowd and the butt of jokes for the "mainstream." But the term "spirituality" has become pervasive, enough so to allow this diverse crowd to place themselves on the same map if even for just a few days of a conference. The term was being used by Russell to remonstrate religion, to give it a bit of a public flogging, and the audience loved it.

He could do that because the word "spirituality" is malleable, readily adopted and adapted by individuals to fit in with any manner of values they might hold. Its fluidity allows it to be attached variously to different artifacts, practices, people, or beliefs without causing much of a stir, because while it is understood that even though it is customizable it denotes some sort of common human experience (U. King 7). Sutcliffe and Bowman say its pliability "represents not only a pragmatic, but also a strategically powerful resource for mobile individuals in the modern world," and that it operates as a sort of "halfway house" between formal religion and the "variegated lifestyles and niche cultures of modernity" (10). This certainly seems to fit the manner in which it operates in LOHAS.

The word "spirituality" as it is used in LOHAS is interchangeable with "consciousness." I've questioned my informants about how they interpret both words, and I've analyzed LOHAS texts with the same question in mind. In both cases, the terms serve as metonyms for righteousness, truthfulness, and "natural" ways of being. As adjectives, they are the identifying marks of change-agents—those people such as "conscious consumers" whom my informants believe will lead the charge toward planetary sustainability, and for whom the phrase "conscious capitalism" is their rallying cry, indicative of the assumption in LOHAS that a new worldview is being birthed through a reformed capitalism. And, those who see this transformation are people who have somehow awakened from the stupor of consumerism.

To that, Russell said in his 2008 seminar, "deep within us we know it is not true, this belief that having more will make us feel better." This might be considered a surprising statement in a conference held in a hotel where rooms go for four hundred dollars a night and where no one would be sitting if their companies weren't successfully selling more of something, be it hybrid cars, energy bars, or yoga mats. But Russell went on to say, "This is where the shift to spirit comes in—all teachings question that material mind set and show we have choice about how we feel. In LOHAS, we see a shift in values and a shift in caring and questioning of the materialistic attitudes hypnotized into us from birth."

Consciousness in LOHAS is both a state of existence and a process, whereby we come to recognize the very *essence* of our humanity, a nugget lying dormant within us, silenced by the cacophony of late modernity, late capitalism, globalization, and more. This essence is uncorrupted and incorruptible, almost as if it has somehow been lying outside the mundane world all this time just waiting to be rediscovered by LOHAS. It's an ethical, moral place that answers to a higher authority that isn't called God in LOHAS texts but which certainly points to something beyond our sensory cognition, something *like* God.

And through all of this, through the silencing of our essential consciousness through the decades, through our rediscovery of it and our subsequent enlightenment, the media and the market are showing us the way. The print, digital, broadcast, and visual media have always had a strong presence in the LOHAS phenomenon. They've been solemnly charged with sowing the seeds of "consciousness" into public culture. *Utne Reader* CEO Nina Utne, at her panel presentation at LOHAS Forum 2007, described the role of the media as "acupuncturists, trying to douse and scan what is important to the future of society and what is happening now."

This is the essence of LOHAS: the manner in which it has brought spirituality into dialogue with business and sustainability. The mere existence of LOHAS is revealing of the creative ways in which people can transfer ideas that are normally assigned to the sphere of "sacred" to the materials and environments at hand, including to those relegated to the "profane" side of the equation, particularly pertinent here, to markets and to media (see Einstein; Hanegraaff, "New Age"; Heelas and Woodhead; and Pike).

Created by two market organizations, one a retailer and one a publisher, and embraced by many of the entities it seeks to describe as a way to reorder the marketplace for alternative, natural and environmentally friendly goods and services, LOHAS continues to take shape through market and media through various "texts." By texts I refer to commodities, advertising, events, regulatory policies, marketing efforts, market organizations, lectures, conversations, and agencies that align with the term (see Murphy 399).

LOHAS bridges the alternative and mainstream, the sacred and profane, capitalism and sustainability by using the power of the media and the marketplace. At LOHAS Forum 2006, Barbara Harris, executive editor of Weider Publications, then the publisher of *Natural Health* magazine, said in her presentation on the role of media in LOHAS: "Media is a dialogue that reflects society." Indeed media *are* involved in the "dialogue" of culture, but that's only half of the story. Harris's comment leaves out the very generative role that media play in *making* culture, but those I interviewed who work in the media did not want to go that far even though they accepted that media should reveal truths and provide leadership in ways other institutions could not.

One way in which to think about this productive role of media is to reflect on media as dealers in symbols. They form a sort of global cultural bazaar, where the world's symbols, rituals, traditions, people, goods, and practices are arrayed. As users of media, we shop there for symbolic resources in order to construct identities, values, opinions, and goals. But the selection and presentation of symbols is just part of the media's work. The media can also re-sort these symbols into new arrangements, taking them out of one context and reinserting them into another, changing their meanings in the process. By doing so, the media create competencies. One example of this is the ways in which we access mediated knowledge and which requires we learn the vagaries of media technologies. These competencies, in turn, have their own structuring effects on the realm of culture. Both of these processes deeply engage media in the acts of meaning making, and "[a] focus on meaning," says Stewart Hoover, "gets to the heart of the relationship of media to culture" (*Religion* 36).

Religion, one of the central sites and forces of meaning making, hasn't stayed immune to media influence. Religious and spiritual "competencies" are also included in the work of media and market. Spirituality is part of the ordering and locating work we humans do to situate and understand ourselves and others, but we can only engage in constructing our various spiritualities because we're to some degree autonomous, that is, we regard ourselves as individuals who are legitimate sources of information and meaning making. "If the purpose of spiritual seeking is the development of an evolved sense of identity and selfhood, media provide a major resource that grounds the individual rather concretely and directly in contemporary lived culture," Hoover says ("Visual" 154).

Methodology

Terminology: LOHAS as Marketplace, Culture,
Movement, and Discourse

A few notes on methodology and terminology are in order. Throughout the
book, LOHAS is referred to as a marketplace, as a discourse, and as a culture
and a movement.

LOHAS AS CULTURE AND MOVEMENT   Gaiam, the company that currently
owns (at press time) both the *LOHAS Journal* and the LOHAS Forums, calls
LOHAS a movement. It bases that claim on various market research studies
that say LOHAS goods, services, and concepts appeal to nearly one-quarter
of the American adult population, the people the mass media call "LOHAS-
ians" (Ray and Anderson; Waldman and Reiss). LOHAS is no longer, if it ever
was, a label that demarcates certain "healthy" goods and practices; rather,
LOHAS is a "socially intentional process," to borrow cultural geographer
Don Mitchell's definition of culture.

I think about culture as a "map of meaning"—as the way in which people
make sense of the world, how they describe forms and processes, and how
they handle the raw material of their social and material existence, as Peter
Jackson has said. Culture is a way to denote difference and concerns how we
turn those "differences into something orderly, mappable and controllable,"
Don Mitchell says (107). In the case of LOHAS, difference is captured in the
concepts "healthy" and "sustainable." They sit opposed to the unhealthy and
unsustainable aspects of society and set LOHAS apart from competing markets.

As to LOHAS being a "movement," it might be in the vested interest of
those who are in the business of promoting a LOHAS product to frame it
as a movement in order to convey a sense of growing excitement and rising
membership, but I use the term a bit differently here. I rely on Hanegraaff's
("Spectral" 44) very useful delineation of the New Age as a movement (also
helpful because the New Age, as I will show, is important to the development
of LOHAS). His key elements of a movement have been modified here to
address the LOHAS phenomenon:

- "They are not membership organizations." This is true for LOHAS businesses in the United States (Japan has consumer-based LOHAS clubs, however). There is no central committee approving membership, only events,
  media, and commodities that are open to those who can pay and, in some
  cases, meet the product or ingredient requirements and restrictions.

- "They come to be perceived as movements mostly because the popular media find a certain term that seems useful to them as a general label." I find this to be the case with LOHAS, a term that was created through and with various market research that was useful to the organizations adopting the term.
- "Once this happens, many people begin to associate themselves, their ideas and their activities with the 'movement' identified by that label." The term LOHAS has caught on globally and is especially strong in the Pacific Rim countries. Its appeal among consumers now as an identity (LOHASians) has been interesting to watch considering that the term itself is quite porous with regard to what can and cannot be considered LOHAS in nature.
- People do not self-identify with a LOHAS movement and most likely have a number of other self identities in operation as well. The diversity of industries that participate in LOHAS and the range of social movements it encompasses attest to this.
- Nonetheless, people's association with LOHAS can be demonstrated through their actual behavior and participation.
- "The 'movement' of people implicitly associating themselves with a certain label may be analyzed by scholars, who may invent various etic definitions based upon their perception of what the participants in the 'movement' have in common."

LOHAS AS DISCOURSE   LOHAS is a "hard" market of goods, services, and organizations. But how do these material things become designated as "LOHASian"? What makes a Toyota Prius LOHASian and a Hummer not, for example? This sort of labeling occurs *discursively*, which means that objects, goals, ideas, and practices become identified in some way through a series of logical connections that we make about them, based on any number of factors about the way in which they are used, grown, sold, or consumed, for example. We rationalize and understand things through their relationships to each other, to us, to cultures, to environments, and to other points in social life. All of this is to say that we socially construct some things to be LOHASian "by virtue of [their] place within a system of relations which have an undeniable signifying element," says Murphy (400–401).

Thus, when I refer to LOHAS as a discourse, I am describing it as a set of relational systems. John Dryzek says this another way: discourse refers to a "shared set of assumptions and capabilities embedded in language that enables its adherents to assemble bits of sensory information that come their way into coherent wholes" (134).

If you look at the marketplace that the word "LOHAS" was meant to embrace, you can see why its organizers had to find a common denominator to convince potential participants to come together at the forums or as readers of the *LOHAS Journal*. What did yoga, cars, and fair trade coffee beans have in common? They weren't just about greening the environment; they didn't solely support physical fitness; and they weren't only about social responsibility or compassion. They engaged each of these points, and a new language was needed to bring these them into a logical partnership. The construction of health as a three-pronged holism of self, society, and natural world did just that.

Treating LOHAS as a discourse has five key advantages for a scholarly investigation such as this one, because it also opens up space through which to regard LOHAS as an expression of power and authority. First, a discourse emphasizes the *mediation* of LOHAS. The concept and construction of LOHAS occurs through the "ongoing practice of its various and multiple articulations" (Murphy 401) among market organizations, media, and consumers. However, I've chosen to focus here on the first two—on market and media organizations as *producers* of the concept of LOHAS. There are a few reasons for why I chose to analyze these institutions: a.) these organizations originally created the term; b.) these organizations are the most public of efforts to refine the term "LOHAS"; and c.) these organizations have the means to broadly circulate definitions and meanings through society, which gives them a notable cultural power in the processes of meaning making.

A note needs to be made here: The division that I make in this book between the concepts of producer and consumer is, I admit, a troubled one. Producers are also consumers of goods and cultural tropes, just as consumers also produce meanings beyond those that social institutions such as media organizations promote. My focus on LOHAS *producers* is not meant to imply that consumers are dupes or blank slates, inscribed with predetermined meanings by retailers, manufacturers, and publishers in the LOHAS industries. Quite the opposite, in fact, is true. The agency of consumers is what LOHAS producers are counting on, after all. That is, consumers' freedom to choose is what generates and supports "niche" markets, and LOHAS is one of those specialties on offer to them.

The early mass communication theories ("magic-bullet" theories) were awash in ideas about media power to disseminate propaganda and brainwash the masses into behaving and thinking in certain ways, and these theories have since been countered by audience reception theories that maintain people have other ways through which to access and weigh information. Still, that said, it remains important to plumb the ways in which social institutions such as media and market organizations are involved in the generation of cultural assumptions and the processes by which individuals make meaning. Consumers may not be dupes, but neither are they sovereign (Goodman and Cohen). While media and market organizations may not inject us with pre-formed meanings and ideas, that doesn't preclude that these institutions are simply passive mirrors of culture, capable only of reflecting back to us the activities of the cultures in which they sit.

Under these conditions, then, arises a second key benefit from regarding LOHAS as a discourse. It also enables us to think of it in terms of how and why it generates a worldview, an ideology. Ideology concerns issues of power—who or what is represented or excluded in the discourse and with what impacts on whom or what? We all hold and express power in various ways; it isn't a phenomenon confined to politics. In fact, Stuart Hall defines ideology as the "mental frameworks—the languages, the concepts, categories, imagery of thought, and the systems of representation—that different classes and social groups deploy in order to make sense of, define, figure out and render intelligible the way society works" ("Problem" 26).

LOHAS is curious in that it champions capitalism, a global power structure operating through wealth, ownership, and labor, and as such, *sustains* the hegemony of capitalism (and democratic liberalism in general). But LOHAS also *contests* its form. For example, on the host site for the *LOHAS Journal* and LOHAS Forum (http://www.lohas.com), Dan Montgomery, host of the Internet talk radio show *Sustainable Leadership*, condemns the current mode of business as disastrous. "With this worldview, we've created unprecedented wealth, knowledge and communication," he says. "And, we've created environmental toxicity, cheap throw-away products, denatured industrially produced food, and a culture of low self-esteem and spiritual poverty."

With that in mind, then, is LOHAS what John Thompson describes as contestatory discourse—as "challenging, disrupting interventions" that serve as incipient forms of the critique of ideology (*Ideology* 68)? There are plenty who would say no, arguing that a discussion among strains or variants of liberalism is hardly resistance and, I imagine, these scholars, such as Ernst Laclau and Chantalle Mouffe, would place LOHAS in that fold. It is a good argument and one I have sympathy for, but it's worthwhile to examine LOHAS on its own terms—the claim that capitalism can be commanded to shed its historical forms and to take on different ones that will be able to address multiple social concerns in new ways.

Maybe that new form should be called socialism, but LOHAS isn't about to go *there*. That would hardly be good business with America's renewed McCarthyism and the charges of socialism leveled at the Obama administration. Instead LOHAS nurtures a new sort of consciousness aiming to rein in the deleterious impulses of capitalism (such as we have seen in the colossal bank

and business bailouts). The texts of LOHAS say capitalist market organizations can voluntarily reorder and recontextualize their *habitus*—or their field
of products, practices, industries, and beliefs—and do so before a(nother)
global calamity looms.

Thinking of LOHAS as a discourse also forces us to consider other factors
in play in the articulation of "lifestyles of health and sustainability" including class, gender, age, domicile, and race. LOHAS is an idea premised on
the assumption that consumers and producers in a capitalist economy are
able, through their market labor, to bring about global social change. There
are some mighty assumptions inherent in that, about who can participate
and who can't and who is affected by the market demands of elites. While
this book cannot manage to give adequate analysis to all of these serious
concerns, it does mean to generate enough questions about these issues so
that we have a place to begin a hopefully continuing study of LOHAS. In
this investigation, the goal is to paint the landscape into view so that we can
consider the contents of its worldview and its expression of power.

Thirdly, the word "discourse" emphasizes that LOHAS is first and foremost
a *concept* that is socially constructed, despite the acronym being attached to
real products and people. Fourthly, the notion of discourse presupposes the
contribution of various historical narratives. In the case of LOHAS, we will
be exploring those histories including the environmental and human rights
movements, self-healing practices in America, and neoliberalism.

Lastly, treating LOHAS as a discourse underscores its permeable nature,
both in the sense of its content (what is actually accepted as part of LOHAS)
and its contexts (where the term LOHAS is used). To this last point, LOHAS
is now used across global markets. The term "LOHAS," although branded in
the United States, can be disseminated and used in nonexclusive ways (for
example, a company could not market *the* "LOHAS" shoe but could market
a shoe saying it is in line with LOHAS values). This means that the term has
an appealing fluidity to it, attractive to the needs of capitalism because it can
be adapted to the flavors of the cultures in which it finds itself.

Methods

The data for this book comes from my ten years of fieldwork in the LOHAS
marketplace and eighteen years' experience as a journalist, market researcher,
and communications consultant in the natural and organic products industry and, later, in the LOHAS marketplace. This study is based on qualitative
research methodologies: participant observation, auto-ethnography, in-depth
interviews, and textual analysis. And a note is due here on the nature of
these methodologies.

My methods reflect an interpretivist paradigm, meaning that they accommodate the idea that the world is socially constructed, or interpreted, by organizations and individuals. This, of course, says that there is no objective reality "out there" somewhere, waiting to be discovered. We peer into LOHAS culture to understand what it is the people who compose it believe they are doing. Morley and Silverstone have put this into perspective nicely: There is no "correct scientific perspective which will finally allow us to achieve the utopian dream of a world completely known in the form of indisputable facts," but there is, rather, a richly varied world where social actors and structures involve in struggles for meaning, power, and identity (161). Let me expand on my methods briefly.

A. Participant observation: I attended numerous trade and consumer conferences and exhibits in both the natural and organic products industry and in the LOHAS marketplace since 1991, when I first signed on as an associate editor for *The Natural Foods Merchandiser,* a leading trade journal in the natural and organic products industry. These events include the annual trade shows Natural Products Expo East and Natural Products Expo West (these are the two largest trade shows in the world for these products, attracting 53,000 attendees at the West show in 2009); the annual LOHAS Forums; a two-day conference on the film *What the Bleep Do We Know!?*; the two-day Sustainable Opportunities Summit in Denver in 2009; and many related industry fundraisers and receptions for non-profits and for-profits.

My data analysis reflects the conversations and observations made at these events.

I would like to touch here on the subject of researcher subjectivity. As the phrase "participant-observer" connotes, I am more than an observer of LOHAS. First, I have all the attributes that go into making a LOHASian—I eat organic foods, take vitamins, and invest in green mutual funds. I support farmer's markets and I try to buy products from fair trade companies. I take the bus when I can and I recycle. I happen to enjoy exploring world spiritualities. And, I really do believe that my choices in the marketplace can affect the social world.

Second, I worked for many years in the natural and organic marketplace as a journalist. My husband, Frank Lampe, cofounded Natural Business Communications (publisher of *The LOHAS Journal* and producer of The LOHAS Forums) in 1996 with Steven Hoffman. They were also journalists with extensive experience in the natural and organic products marketplace. As the nascent company's consulting research director, I helped to quantify the size of the original LOHAS market-size research report, which included deciding what products and practices should be included in a "LOHAS" marketplace.

As an academic in the doctoral program in Media Studies at the University of Colorado, I wanted to explore the relationship between the media and ideas about sustainability in the LOHAS industry. Ultimately, this research led me to reconfigure my hypothesis about LOHAS and to investigate the expression of spirituality there. I became an affiliate researcher with the university's Center for Media, Religion and Culture, under the direction of Stewart Hoover and Lynn Schofield Clark.

My positionality as an *insider* to LOHAS has required certain methodological rigors, but perhaps no more than what an "outsider" would also have to adopt. Fears of the "unreflexive subjectivism of the insider" are matched fear for fear by concerns of the "objectification" of the phenomenon from the outsider, to paraphrase a quote from Denis Cosgrove (1998).

On the one hand, an insider must control for potential "blindness" to normative constructions: familiarity breeds complacency, if you will. But, on the other hand, the outsider's due diligence comes in the form of careful and thorough background research of the history of the "other" whom she is studying. This is necessary in order to avoid interpreting another's culture through the researcher's personal filters. In either case, insider and outsider positions come with their own particular and peculiar challenges. There is a tradition in scholarly research to regard insider vs. outsider as competitive approaches, with the insider role usually coming up short-strawed. This is, I think, a great shame because the two approaches can be quite complementary, leading to a well-rounded analysis (see Denzin, "Performing"; Foley; Georges and Jones; Lindlof). Each approach provides a different perspective onto a phenomenon, and, as such, each contributes to the scholarly pursuit of knowledge.

As an insider to the LOHAS phenomenon, I've been keenly aware throughout the study that the advantages and the disadvantages of my study spring from the same seed—that is, from my knowledge of the field. While I bring a historical perspective and insight to the origination of the term "LOHAS" that an outsider might not so easily discover, or might present differently, this could also be my proverbial blind spot. An outsider might also choose to track the evolution of LOHAS differently, for example, through its roots in the "green" movement rather than use my approach to the phenomenon as a convergence of various industry histories. In any case, I've had to be careful throughout the study to be attentive to two avenues of my knowledge about LOHAS: through my "experiencing self" and through my "analytic self" (Lindlof, 254).

B. Textual analysis: I analyzed hundreds of print, digital, visual, and broadcast media aligned with the LOHAS marketplace. My texts included magazine and journal editorial, radio programs, websites, promotional and marketing materials, advertising, discussion forums, presentations and lectures, and products exhibited at trade shows. These mediated texts serve as cultural artifacts and compass points to the values and beliefs of LOHAS.

The criteria I used to select various texts to study were based on the producing organization's relation to the term LOHAS, which I judged across four categories:

- Organizational materials such as media kits that name a target audience or consumer described as the "LOHAS consumer," "the conscious consumer," or "Cultural Creative";
- The organization emphasized one or more of these values in the mission statement: "holism," "interconnectedness," "natural and organic," "green or eco," "socially responsible," "social justice," "mind, body and spirit," "sustainable," or "alternative" or "integrative medicine;"
- The organization is represented (either as speakers or in product exhibitions) in natural products stores such as Whole Foods Markets, catalogs such as Co-op America (now Green America) Green Pages, and trade shows including but not limited to LOHAS Forums, Natural Products Expos, Whole Life Expos, and Green Festivals.
- The company self-identified as participating in the "LOHAS" marketplace, through company mission statements, marketing materials, or interviews with upper management.

C. Interviews: I interviewed twelve upper management professionals (CEO, founder, director, editor-in-chief, editorial director, or president) from the leading media in the LOHAS space. I also informally spoke over the years with many market professionals who were in upper management in the LOHAS marketplace.

I chose media with the largest circulations in the LOHAS marketplace, again identifying them through the criteria named above. As to the identification of my informants, I've used pseudonyms in order to protect their privacy, particularly for reasons of marketing competitiveness. LOHAS media comprise a small circle of organizations, and their identities could easily put them at a marketing disadvantage.

D. Personal experience: While this book is not an auto-ethnography, I have incorporated my own experiences as a journalist in the LOHAS industries and as a market researcher in the LOHAS marketplace during the early days of its conception. I note in the text when I am using my recollection of events such as in the recounting of the history of the LOHAS-related industries.

A Short Tour of the Book

Chapter 1 examines LOHAS as a bridge between the two poles of the American marketplace—the "alternative" market and the "mainstream" or conventional market. This market-based binary shaped and informed many of the industries now considered part of the domain of LOHAS. These were companies and industries that once purposefully positioned themselves as *alternative.* "Alternative" defined their intended consumer base, their company missions, and even, in many cases, the founder's personal values. Today, however, LOHAS organizations regard this alterity as more of a handicap than an advantage. Not only that, but the so-called *mainstream* is actively adding LOHAS products and services to product inventories and marketing materials, blurring the boundaries even further. Chapter 1 historicizes this, following the emergence of *The LOHAS Journal*, the first truly public and mediated circulation of the word.

We travel a history of LOHAS to learn why these LOHAS industries have found a new relevancy in the world that has encouraged them to try and dismantle their once favored "fringe" status. The popularity of the LOHAS ideals in the world has come about through a chain of events in food safety, environmental concerns, and the exposure of human rights violations, but all of these events are closely tied to media and mediation, to a rise in the mediazation of culture. These cultural conversations about social and environmental change have been circulated, reinterpreted, and recontextualized in media and market, and this book treats those sites and processes as producers of meaning.

Chapter 2 examines how LOHAS salvages its "New Age" focus on self-development or actualization. The idea that we even have a self to develop is a fairly recent invention of modernity, informed by the processes handed down to us from the Enlightenment that enabled individuals to consider themselves, to varying degrees, as autonomous creatures and as sources of authority or decision making in transcendental and pragmatic matters. The autonomous self has been nurtured and groomed by late capitalism; the self is a product and a raw material to sculpt, enabling it to fulfill its highest potential. This is a deeply therapeutic conceptualization of the self that emerged along with consumer culture in the late nineteenth and early twentieth centuries; a self was something that could be objectified, healed by its own efforts and made a perfect vessel to receive happiness, as the culture understood that. LOHAS is in the lineage of the American healing narratives of Mind Cure, New Thought and the New Age.

Examining these movements in terms of their relationship to capitalism, I'll show how LOHAS extends and expands these movements through the LOHAS category of Personal Development (also referred to as the Mind/Body/Spirit market). In Personal Development goods and services, physical and spiritual self-healing reflects a moral pragmatism by linking self-healing work with that of healing the world. Threaded through the LOHAS discourse is a popular American theme—the power of positive thinking—and this healing modality is put to use in what I've called the quantum spiritualities, the latest incarnation of the American therapeutic tradition. At the end of the chapter, we'll see how the LOHAS texts use examples of healed selves as testimonials to show that it is indeed possible for individuals to transform themselves to social warriors.

In chapter 3 the LOHAS vision of health is articulated as a three-part holistic model of self, society, and the natural world. In turn, "holistic" has been described in LOHAS more through Eastern perspectives rather than Western religious traditions in that it presupposes a state of interconnectedness of all phenomena—mind and matter, animal and human, global cultures and ecosystems.

Interestingly, the holistic worldview of Buddhism (a frequently called-upon tradition in LOHAS literature), for example, understands that interdependence means that "humanity is only one actor" in the environment and that all actors must remain in balance for the system to be healthy (Gunaratne 60). But this flies in the face of late consumer culture, where the individual reigns supreme, and where LOHAS is predominantly lodged. In the last section, we examine how that problem is overcome, how Mother Nature becomes intertwined with the healed self as part of the healing and a vital component of the model of holistic health. I'll show how healing the self becomes exonerated from the "narcissism" of the New Age and instead becomes reframed as the stepping stone to a collective good, capable of initiating global transformation based on the notion of holistic health.

Throughout the book, I'll be concerned with the manner in which meanings are made, legitimated, and circulated, and toward this end, I set the stage in this chapter for the examination of "ideology" and the media and the market's roles in meaning making processes. As part of that, I'll be looking closely at the articulation of "health" in LOHAS texts. Health is a concept built upon ideas of what is "natural"; chapter 3 will tease out the ways in which the LOHAS discourse treats the idea of "natural" and of "Nature," including looking at a LOHAS keyword "authenticity." This, I argue, serves as a metonym for "natural." But these are problematic concepts, made so by their prescriptive status in LOHAS. What is natural is what is good, or so the discourse claims, and while this might actually be the case, for our purposes here authenticity is a construct and truth claim that serves as the beacon for a LOHAS cosmology that we are attempting to understand.

In chapter 4 we have the healed self, contextualized as united with the natural world, moving toward its reconciliation with the third arm of the holistic model of health—the social world. First, there are apologies and confessions to be made by industrialists and consumers who have recognized the "Consequences of Modernity" (Giddens, *Modernity*) and their own roles in those results. LOHAS is a capitalist endeavor but also attempts to position itself as resistant to those processes, and as such it must articulate "LOHASians" as ultimately powerful in themselves to change the course of late capitalism and consumer culture. There are instructions here for how to say you're sorry and move on to the real work of mopping up the mess. As part of this, LOHAS narratives tell us to remain positive, of course, but also that older notions of desire and ideals of happiness afloat in the culture were off course. By situating individual consumers and producers as capable of bringing about sweeping social transformation, LOHAS not only sustains consumer culture, but also contextualizes it as the locus for the healing of the world.

Chapter 5 takes up with the healed self, the newly "conscious" change-agent, now interpellated as global "citizen" as he and she move from inner work to externalized work in the world. Chapter 5 is concerned with social reform and the idea of "good capitalism" in LOHAS narratives. Capitalism must be exonerated in LOHAS culture, and to do so means that certain perceptions and practices that have been treated as economic and cultural axioms need to be reworked. LOHAS begins with the idea of success. We'll investigate how the texts attempt to juggle a new meaning of success that entails doing with less—but better things—while still promoting the interests of capital. It does this by creating two capitalisms: a good and a bad version. Delineating these is a key part of the discourse because upon it hangs the claim that business can revolve around a new set of values. LOHAS is the instruction manual for putting those values to work, not only in organizations but also within individuals.

Values are the foundation of a LOHAS version of good capitalism. Values are articulated here as the deeply meaningful codes by which we navigate our understandings of ourselves in relation to the world, including our relationships with others, certainly, but also in relation to transcendent meanings. The ethicizing of capitalism through the application of historical and global traditions of faith and healing is analyzed as part of what Heelas and Woodhead have called the "subjective turn," whereby we are left to look for authority in ourselves rather than in external agents. "Spirituality" is open-ended, and LOHAS gives us a way to consider how populations adapt the term to cultural forms and pressures—even within domains often considered inhospitable to the pursuit—and to the process of forming deep values about how one should live.

Despite its roots in business, the LOHAS phenomenon is situated as a deeply spiritual question for participants. I'll historicize LOHAS discourse to reveal how it is informed by various social movements including early American Christian Reform, the European Green Party of the 1960s, and the social movements occurring in the 1960s in the United States, including environmentalism, feminism, and civil rights.

Chapter 6 follows the trail of LOHAS texts in the infusion of consumption and production with spiritual meaning. Consumption has somehow been disentangled in LOHAS from the charges of greed, mindlessness, and self-interest. "Mindful" or "conscious" consumerism heralds the reformed economy that can supposedly be put to work on solving the most persistent and challenging questions of our existence. This is an examination of the relationship between money and morality, looking at the manner, too, in which this expanding marketplace is also attracting those who would green-wash and spiritual-wash their products, making them seem more environmentally and socially conscious than they really are.

LOHAS texts spend a great deal of time explaining the tangled path between consumption and social change and how we are to achieve our goals. There is a middle way, we're told, and on its path, you must travel slowly. Enter the Slow Movements: from Slow Food to Slow Thinking, these practices celebrate traditional life and rituals as ways of being that were, in the long run, healthier.

But LOHAS is, chiefly, a bridging narrative among contradictions—between slow and fast, sacred and profane, alternative and mainstream. While celebrating the slowing down of everything from our eating rituals to our conversations, LOHAS walks a fine line between sensuality (consumerism) and asceticism (minimalism). LOHAS has no choice but to square off with this binary so that it can speak seriously about creating sacred space through commodification. LOHAS is a progressive, forward-looking discourse, and the last thing participants want to do is sound old-fashioned. I'll explore how LOHAS tries to depict sustainability and health as hip and fun, crafting "slow" into "sexy" and sexy into spiritual.

I examine here how LOHAS is evangelized and the manner in which participants see themselves as carriers of the truth, sent to build bridges among people, industries, nations, and the spheres of our lives. Integration is the endgame in LOHAS. To do that requires that media and market craft particularly appealing *positive* messages; I'll show how these are framed within broader cultural conversations about what it means to be "spiritual" in the context of environmentalism and social activism.

Chapter 7 deals with LOHAS in the context of "community-building" and the formation of a collective conscience. LOHAS is ultimately a narrative about how to change the world using consumer culture. This is a global vision, and I use the lens of globalization to examine how LOHAS attempts, on the one hand, to overcome a legacy of anthropocentrism, Eurocentrism, cultural and economic imperialism, and Westernization in capitalism, while, on the other hand, self-consciously reinforcing the capitalist imperative to sell more and different things to more people. As a market-based movement and as a claim to a reformatory effort, LOHAS is only as successful as the quantity of consumers and producers that support its premises.

With its sweeping global agenda, LOHAS texts try to position the concept as a nonpartisan movement, one based on commonalities rather than differences. This chapter is a study of the rise of community and collectivity in LOHAS culture, which is chiefly occurring through mediated means, particularly through social media. I'll historicize LOHAS within social movements, examining the importance of media and the central role of communication in democratic efforts. This prepares the stage for a closer look at the ways in which media and market enable and disable participation in the communication process. An important part of this is the working of ideology in the construction of truth claims.

We'll look closely at the media's role in the construction of truth, particularly as it forms through claims about *taste* and *style*. Because of its focus on consumer culture, important class issues are raised in the articulation of products and practices as the path to social reform. Using the work of such social theorists as Pierre Bourdieu and Michel Foucault, I raise questions about the relationship between power and knowledge that is made manifest through the way in which LOHAS narratives treat the ideals of "happiness," "health," and "success." These are also linked up to the idea of being "authentic," but this word has become normative, meaning it can actually conceal the ways in which knowledge about what is or is not authentic is legitimated. As expressions of power, these representations may seem benign and egalitarian, particularly in context of specific populations, but when decontextualized and framed within other segments of the population than the targeted LOHAS consumer or within other cultures, the restraining, contradictory elements of LOHAS become clear. If LOHAS seeks to be an egalitarian movement, these are concerns that go directly to the heart of the movement, to its "truth" and whose voices are represented in that construction and whose are not.

In the concluding chapter, I propose that LOHAS represents a "spirituality of sustainability," an integrative and pragmatic ethical system that seeks to help participants overcome the dissonance of modern life that has failed, in many ways, to deliver the promised goods of happiness and security. LOHAS juggles an enormous variety and number of concerns facing people around the world. While I focus on the expression of LOHAS in the United

States—the term's country of origin but not necessarily of its ideals, goods, and practices—I want to be clear that LOHAS is a global phenomenon and that there is little doubt that LOHAS will express differently in different societies and cultures. For now, those necessary investigations must wait for other minds and pens.

This is a first attempt to theorize LOHAS, as a matter of ideology and as a social movement. I have posited questions about the inherent ideological work going on so that we can more thoroughly and carefully assess what LOHAS may or may not be able to offer the world as a resistance movement. LOHAS texts make claims about the power of market organizations, including media, to operate within the restraints of profit and expansion, while still being innovative, creative, and contestatory to the status quo. This is not always an easy relationship in LOHAS, and the texts reveal a self-conscious awareness on the part of producers about the possible contradictions between capitalism and sustainability.

To quell these points of tension, spirituality has become a useful tool for LOHAS, as it has for other narratives and practices of sustainability. It can serve as an inner disciplining gaze that may be the only logical higher authority left to appeal to in LOHAS due to its faith in laissez faire and in self-regulating economies.

The logic of LOHAS serves as a map to help modern populations negotiate the pressures bearing down on them: how to be local and global at the same time, how to resolve the promises and failures of the American Dream, and how to be both material and spiritual. In doing so, I hope to bring to light certain potential pitfalls for LOHAS culture and to contribute to the debate already going on there. In the end, I believe LOHAS may point to new directions and possibilities in the study of contemporary culture and the awakening of a newer, globalized spirituality based on recognition of the frailties of the small planet we share.

1. Neither Mainstream nor Alternative

LOHAS at the Crossroads

In spring 2005 the ninth annual LOHAS Forum (interestingly christened as the ninth when the first LOHAS Forum was advertised as such in 2000) opened in a swank Los Angeles hotel within easy batting distance of Hollywood and a long way from its birthplace in Broomfield, Colorado. It had come a long way in more than just distance, too; where once the program at a typical "Lifestyles of Health and Sustainability" Forum comprised mostly researchers, manufacturers, and retailers of such goods as natural dietary supplements, hemp clothing, biodiesel, and organic baby food, LOHAS 9 boasted a star-studded cast that included Joan Baez and Raquel Welch along with the actors Ed Begley Jr., Daryl Hannah, Wendie Malick, Mariel Hemingway, and Amy Smart. They too, as it turns out, were interested in herbs, hemp, hybrid vehicles, and healthy babies.

Perhaps more surprising than the attendance by this celebrity muscle was the sheer industrial star power on the program. Office Depot hosted one of the evening receptions (dishing up a luscious banquet of organic food). Just a couple of years previously the closest Office Depot would have come to one of these conferences would have been the use of its recycled copy paper products by attendees. Also present was a gaggle of representatives from Ford Motor Company. They seemed to move through the conference as a pod: where one went, there were bound to be the others. But sitting side-by-side with them were officers from Celestial Seasonings and Horizon Organic dairy, the nobility of the natural and organic products kingdom.

When it came time for the opening speech, actress and yogi Mariel Hemingway confidently strode onto the stage, her lithe frame fashionably garbed in stilettos, blue jeans, and a tunic top that just might have been made from hemp.

She took her place at the speaker's podium and got right to the point. "Why isn't consciousness out in the mainstream more?" she demanded. "We need to get the message out there; we must lead by example. We are a small group, but we need to carry a big message and do a lot of work to make change and I know all of you are incredibly smart and successful."

Suddenly, Hemingway was our interlocutor and we, the LOHAS audience, were conjoined with her in revolutionary fervor. Not only that, we were leading the charge, apparently, to shepherd our generalized, nonconscious brothers and sisters toward the goal—to live sustainably. She received loud applause and even some cheers among the suited crowd, most of whom who had just paid upwards of eight hundred dollars to get into this three-day event. Here we were—people who hailed from Rust Belt heavy industry, natural foods supermarkets, big-box retailing, medicine, agriculture, communications, the press, Wall Street, Hollywood, and all manner of spiritual traditions. And we had just been interpellated as holding a common ideology.

A few years ago, this team would not have been sitting in the same room, much less running on the same ticket, so to speak. We would have been ignoring one another across the ideological chasm of the American marketplace known as the "alternative" vs. "mainstream" markets. In truth, however, even then, those of us on the "alternative" side of things were casting furtive glances across the border. As journalists for the natural and organic products industry press throughout the 1990s, we watched with a sort of mesmerized horror as the "mainstream" supermarkets started tossing into their mix the odd organic carrot (they were almost always wilted) or the sad, lonely little box of unsweetened Cheerios-pretender cereal. They'd never get it right, we sniffed. We had our values, after all. Would "they" ever understand the complexity of what "we" stood for? Meanwhile "they" were chuckling over their morning Folgers with nondairy creamer at our itsy five-thousand-square-foot grocery stores, which we considered nigh to nirvana. They stopped stirring and sipping, however, when they realized that they hadn't seen Whole Foods Market marching up on their flanks, on fire with organic and fair trade caffeine and full of the vim of the socially responsible.

That got their attention.

The fact was that sales of natural and organic foods and products, dietary supplements, mind/body/spirit goods, and New Age books were skyrocketing. Wall Street had caught the scent of success and was happily pumping millions of investment dollars into these tiny "alternative" industries. We now had the momentum of a tsunami. The mainstream market had no choice but to respond. Flooded by investment capital, the natural, alternative, and eco-markets expanded, sold, and merged faster than we journalists could publish the news. But it was a topsy-turvy world: the new consumers in the "healthy living" space still wanted some conventional product choices. Natural foods supermarkets started to bend to their wishes. I can still recall the day when a staff member at *Natural Foods Merchandiser* came in shaking his head telling us he had just seen Heinz Ketchup in the local Whole Foods store. Meanwhile, the mainstream stores were carrying on their own subterfuge by providing unheard of monstrous-sized orders to natural foods manufacturers (and offering along the savings of these economies of scale to consumers) in ways that made the mom-and-pop health food storeowners wring their hands in despair.

By 2000, when *The LOHAS Journal* was first published and the term went "public," the alternative and the mainstream were not just sharing market space; many had merged operations. Still, the old binary was tenacious. Quoted in the *Washington Post*, Steve Case, the cofounder of America Online and a LOHAS Forum speaker said: "There's an uneasy courtship going on between corporate America and the diverse, sometimes idiosyncratic collection of companies that make up the 'sustainable lifestyle' movement— firms that promote their products as healthy and easy on the environment. Wal-Mart Stores Inc. has begun buying organic cotton; Colgate-Palmolive Co. owns natural products pioneer Tom's of Maine; prominent organic food brands have become subsidiaries of major agribusinesses" (Shin).

Case said his new company, Revolution LLC, was "trying to pick through the miscellany for products and services that might succeed in the *mainstream*" (my emphasis). The *Post* article about the 2005 LOHAS Forum said Case's $20 million investment in yoga and Pilates products was made as "part of his ongoing bet that activities once associated with a New-Age lifestyle are going mainstream" (Shin).

Interestingly, despite the article's thrust that alternative and mainstream were converging, the *Post* still seemed to have a fairly solid idea about their differences; it delegated Case to the mainstream side while assigning other LOHAS attendees to the "fringe," a group that included, the *Post* stated, "the inventor of an organic herbal throat spray, the maker of an immune-boosting tea and a psychic healer who talks to dogs." Yet, with the exception of the psychic (and even that if you allow for books) all of these products could be found in lots of mainstream grocery stores.

A year later at the LOHAS Forum 9, the audience of eight hundred or so sat expectantly waiting for the Ford Motors Hydrogen Engines Chief, Vance Zanardelli, to begin his presentation. Against a back-drop of a curtained wall decorated with hanging "signifiers"—small placards bearing the words Eco, Global, Conscious, Green, Authentic, Balance, and Organic—Zanardelli walked on stage and made a confession. "This morning," he declared, "I attended my first yoga session." The crowd applauded enthusiastically, breaking into laughter when he admitted, "My biggest fear was walking into the room—I couldn't find any of my colleagues, but I survived." On a more serious note, he added that he was pleasantly surprised by the hard-edged realism of the LOHAS audience. "I feared that coming here I would see a group of people with a Pollyannaish view of the future."

This was a familiar salvo: healthy and sustainable equals liberal, Birkenstock-shod, longhaired idealists. I decided to follow up on this reasoning. How would one define a "Pollyannaish" view, I asked "Richard," a journalist with twenty-plus years in the LOHAS or healthy living press and currently working as the vice president of a consumer lifestyles magazine. Richard was there to report on the conference and he said he supposed Zanardelli had in mind people "holding hands and singing Kumbaya." Richard was joking, but I pointed out that there was indeed a drumming circle at LOHAS 9, one led by the son of Joan Baez, no less, and I asked him if that wasn't rather along the lines of a Kumbaya circle. He laughed. Yes, he said, probably Zanardelli would think so, and probably we could bet that the gentleman would decline to attend. I asked Richard if he planned to attend the drumming circle; he said he wouldn't miss it.

Similarly, later that evening a shot was fired from the "alternative" side to the mainstream. It was an evening event featuring singer and songwriter Ricki Lee Jones. The hotel ballroom had been transfigured into a candlelit bistro, with small café tables covered in black cloths. Jones, always a quirky performer, suddenly stopped midtune to peer across her baby grand piano at the audience where I was sitting right in front of the stage with Richard and Lou, a marketing consultant. "So, are you all rich?" she asked with a smirk. There was a ripple of laughter. It wasn't an outlandish assumption to make, even of a group attending the "lifestyles of health and sustainability" conference, because we *were* in the tony Marina del Rey Ritz-Carlton Hotel, after all. She stared at us for a while before shrugging and turning back to her instrument. Her fingers tapped out an arpeggio. "I was rich once," she said as she pounded out a chord before telling us about a house she once built out of sustainably harvested timber. Pausing, she looked us over, lowered her head, and sang her famed croaky music. After some time, she glanced our way again, telling us that while she believed in sustainable and healthy living, the products were simply too expensive. She asked the crowd to do something about that.

The next day, the 1960s activist and performer Joan Baez, in her brief address to the conference, said, "In the 1960s, we thought so much in common," she said, peering out at the audience and pausing. She then acknowledged the

diversity of the composition of the audience before her—retailers, manufacturers, entertainers, health professionals, reporters, activists, and NGOs—and
she reminded us that we were, after all, a community of some sort. That's the
type of bonding LOHAS producers encourage.

Still, the cultural divide between alternative and mainstream is alive and
well, enough so that it can provoke a good laugh. For example, at LOHAS
Forum 12 in 2008 (which had returned to its Colorado roots and was held
in the all-things-natural city of Boulder), at a seminar titled "Talks with
Whole Foods Market and Wal-Mart," then–Whole Foods Southwest Regional President Michael Besancon shared the stage with Wal-Mart's Rand
Waddoups, Senior Director of Corporate Responsibility. When asked how
he started in sustainability, Besancon laughed and said, "It's really interesting the juxtaposition between Rand and I. Rand started out as a hard-assed
businessman and got to, er, another place. But I started out as a hippie and
became a hard-assed businessman." The audience erupted into laughter and
applause at this nod to a familiar discourse: there are those who have spent
decades toiling for an alternative lifestyle dedicated to organic agriculture
and environmentalism and there are those who are still initiates. Many of
these latter "greenhorns," such as the world's largest retailer Wal-Mart, wield
such vast bankrolls that their power in the marketplace to create change is
regarded with awe, but also with suspicion.

The New Battleground of Values

In the spring 2008 issue of *The LOHAS Journal*, John Rooks, president of
Dwell Creative, wrote: "LOHAS consumers have been identified as having an
emotional connection to sustainability." He then adds, "What happens when
the authentic language of the fringe is borrowed by the mainstream?" (49).

The alternative/mainstream divide becomes rearticulated in another dubious and ephemeral signifier, *authenticity*, which seems to stand in for consciousness that in turn comprises an enormous laundry list of attributes. The
fear that the language of health and sustainability can be lifted and co-opted
points to the belief or the fear that consumers won't be able to see past words
and images and will be duped into thinking a company is deeply committed
to those issues when it is not. And, when I say committed I am speaking
about a host of concerns that extend far beyond offering a green product
here and there and instead address issues such as how the company treats
employees, what holdings it might have in foreign lands and with what effect
on those cultures and environments, and its support of local communities
and environments, for example.

In the Wal-Mart/Whole Foods Market seminar, Besancon made a point of saying he had worked for thirty-eight years in the natural and organic foods industry and that during that time he had seen his dream come true of expanding the market for organic so that it became available to more consumers. He eyed Rand Waddoups seated next to him, and he said, "People say, 'Oh, my God, Wal-Mart is in the organic cotton business—they're going to be the largest grower of organic cotton in the world.' Or, 'Wal-Mart is the biggest seller of organic produce in the world.' And, I say, 'damn, my life has been successful. I won.'" Here the audience again broke into cheers and loud applause.

Besancon was citing one side of the common argument about what happens when the mainstream lifts the "authentic language of the fringe." Is it a good thing or a bad thing that the giant retailers and manufacturers of the mainstream have decided to join the ranks and sell "alternative" goods? On the one hand, people argue that it is a good thing because it expands the market, meaning more acres will be put under organic agriculture or that more consumers will have access to less expensive organic foods, for example. On the other hand, the argument goes, the mainstream's entry into the LOHAS industries comes with serious trade-offs. This argument says that the mainstream stores such as Wal-Mart are only in it for the money, not because of deeply held values that are "holistic." The problem with not having such values, continues the counterargument, is that sustainability is a complex process. In the case of food, for example, it stretches from the type of seed one puts in the soil (and a LOHAS seed is a nongenetically engineered or GMO-free seed that isn't stomping on someone's or something's intellectual property rights), to the growing methods, to the treatment of farm workers, to the distance of distribution, to the type of fuel used in transport, and on to the environmental friendliness of the building in which the product is eventually sold. And this is only a partial list of sustainability concerns, but you get the picture.

Another way to illustrate the argument is this: Wal-Mart may be able to offer organic foods at lower prices than natural foods stores because Wal-Mart forces vendors and especially farmers into cutting their profit margins. As farmers' profits erode, other players in the supply chain are squeezed as well, such as crop pickers who are already occupying the lowest salary rung on the organic ladder. Or, maybe some other bottom line gets squeezed and products will be bagged in cheaper, nonrecyclable petroleum-distillate bags. There are a lot of stops on the way from seed to table.

Here's the view on the argument from best-selling author and *New York Times* columnist Michael Pollan in his opinion piece titled "Wal-Mart Goes

Organic": "Cheap industrial food, the organic movement has argued, only seems cheap, because the real costs are charged to the environment (in the form of water and air pollution and depletion of the soil); to the public purse (in the form of subsidies to conventional commodity producers); and to the public health (in the cost of diabetes, obesity and cardiovascular disease), not to mention to the welfare of the farm- and food-factory workers and the well-being of the animals."

While LOHAS producers might enjoy imagining that the market binary between alternative and mainstream is extinguished, another binary has crept into its place, and this time it's one based on the distinction between those who are "conscious" of the urgent need to reform capitalism and its modes, goals, and organizations and those who are not *awakened* to such a need. This is a distinction based on *values*. Certain types of values are legitimated and celebrated in LOHAS, and they're all caught up in the word "conscious."

It's a complex word, but the discussion among Waddoups (who admitted to being new to the ideals of sustainability), Besancon (who underlined his nearly four-decade-long commitment to sustainability), and the moderator Simran Sethi, an award-winning environmental journalist, make clear there are a few shared assumptions about the nature of conscious consumption and production.

- Making money is both contested and contradictory. On the one hand, LOHAS is a discourse promoted by market organizations to generate more sales for healthy and sustainable goods and services. It is capitalist. It is about profit. On the other hand, there are highly charged sensibilities around how that profit is made.
- Jumping on the sustainability bandwagon without paying due diligence to the complexity of the practices and beliefs of sustainability (referred to in LOHAS as the triple bottom line of people, planet, and profit) will garner you a lot of criticism. Some of that could be made very public and hence become very dangerous to a company's reputation and bottom line. "Green-washing," for example, is a charge aimed at companies that market their products as eco-friendly when, in truth, some or most of the ingredients are not at all environmentally friendly. That, or, the company indulges in environmentally unfriendly practices either during the manufacture of the green product or in another part of company operations.
- Convincing the LOHAS community that you are conscious is accomplished partly through what you do in your business (how you treat your employees, how you construct your buildings, or what products you choose to sell, for example), but also through your own declaration of commitment, effort, and beliefs. The tension in LOHAS between profit and values isn't isolated to the "mainstream" newcomers to sustainability

such as Wal-Mart. In an interview with me, for example, "Brian," a board
member of a national natural products trade association, scowled when I
asked about a large company in the natural dietary supplements industry.
The CEO, he said, was notorious for his cynical attitude about many of the
"deeper principles" that were "endemic to our industry." Brian bemoaned
the way this person did business, "eviscerating companies that had passion
and taking the heart out of them."

Measuring consciousness as a commitment to sustainability across the
various social and environmental dimensions is not a finite science. Often,
the charisma of the company's representative can tilt the balance of public
opinion about the firm within the LOHAS culture, particularly if the company appears willing to take responsibility for past mistakes and to share
their strategies for becoming more sustainable.

In the Waddoups–Besancon seminar, Rand Waddoups responded to moderator Sethi's question, "What is your role in Wal-Mart?" saying, "I like to
call myself a sort of a reformed businessman." Evoking a grim image of Wal-
Mart that has been widely circulated through the media, including the news
program *60 Minutes*, he explained that he was once the sort of Wal-Mart "guy
you read about who is across the table from the supplier and beating them
up, saying 'cost, cost, cost'" (Waddoups slapped his hand into the opposite
palm for effect). After letting that soak in, he grinned and said, "I didn't really
do that." But Waddoups said both he and Wal-Mart had made a central shift
in their "values," and this, he said, occurred because of Hurricane Katrina.

After seeing firsthand how his team members took the initiative to go
the extra mile to help their customers deal with the crisis, he was deeply
affected. "Across all of that affected region, we saw our company act the best
it had ever acted before, more efficient, more powerfully, for the betterment
of society in a way we didn't know we could do," he said. Katrina was his
"wakeup call" that showed him that "doing business as the largest company
in the world wasn't just about making money. It's about doing business, and
in every day of your life, being as good as you were when you were at your
best." If he was looking for leverage to pole-vault his way into LOHAS hoi
polloi, he found it.

Waddoups admitted that his company wasn't perfect and had a long way to
go, but he added, it *was* trying to do the right thing. "Its funny how you grow
with your company," he said. "I went from being a young punk—just out of
college, with more power than I knew what to do with—to realizing that I
had a real opportunity to make a huge difference with an enormous company
with tremendous ability to make change in the world." This emotional narrative is not uncommon among companies new in the LOHAS marketplace,

but it seems to be one that people never tire of hearing. It carries a popular redemption theme similar to what Janice Peck has called the "talking cure," whereby we publicly declare our failures and are healed and accepted back into the community.

Throughout the seminar Waddoups and Besancon had been complimentary of each other's firms, even to the point of camaraderie, pointing out the commonalities between the two. At one point, after Sethi had prefaced a question to him saying that Whole Foods had sustainability deeper in its "DNA" than did Wal-Mart, Besancon said, "If Wal-Mart isn't green then Whole Foods isn't green," referring to the fact that both companies were "imperfect" with regard to sustainability, but underscoring the importance of being on the path. It was a formidable statement of alliance.

Besancon's generosity toward Wal-Mart, allowing it equal footing with Whole Foods Market, the nation's largest natural foods supermarket, would have been highly improbable even a few years previous. But, in 2008 even Whole Foods Market was being questioned about the depth of its commitment to sustainability. Two years earlier, Michael Pollan had sharply criticized Whole Foods. In his book *The Omnivore's Dilemma*, Pollan accused Whole Foods Market of misleading consumers into thinking that more foods in the store were from local vendors, pasture-based farms, and artisanal sources than was actually the case. Pollan has long been a vocal critic of industrial farming. He notes that buying locally produced food is socially, economically, and environmentally more sound than buying organic food from foreign sources such as China, which, he says, Wal-Mart does. Pollan's charges reverberated around the world, raising questions among consumers about Whole Foods' core values: Was Whole Foods *selling out* to make money? Was the company guilty of deception?

Stung by Pollan's comments, Whole Foods Market cofounder and chairman and CEO John Mackey ("Past") retaliated, saying Pollan had not interviewed Mackey or other top management at Whole Foods for the book and that his comments had cost Whole Foods dearly. In his blog on the Whole Foods website, Mackey quoted Michael Strong, CEO of Flow, a nonprofit that Mackey cofounded. Strong said it was possible that Pollan's comments had wounded Whole Foods, contributing to a $2 billion loss in stock market capitalization suffered by the company between the time Pollan's book was published in 2006 and 2007.

The outcry and economic impact to his company were serious enough that Mackey had earlier challenged Pollan publicly. The two enjoined in a series of letters via their public blogs and then met face to face before an audience of two thousand in Berkeley, California, in 2007. According to the

UC Berkeley News, Mackey, a self-proclaimed vegan Buddhist libertarian, gave a hard-hitting forty-five-minute presentation that showed the journey of human society through its food stages (Powell). Mackey acknowledged Pollan's argument that the industrial era had brought greater amounts of food to more people, but did so at a high cost that resulted in environmental disaster, social injustice, and animal cruelty. As the *News* pointed out, even though industrial agriculture increased productivity and lowered costs, "it recognizes no values beyond those two" (Powell).

The *News* reported that "Although Whole Foods almost singlehandedly developed the mass market for organic food, [Mackey] said the company recognizes that organic no longer means what it originally did to consumers, and thus plans to lead the charge into the next phase, or 'beyond organic.' The beyond-organic buzzwords: local, ethical, sustainable, and humane" (Powell).

What is important about Pollan's critique for our purposes here, though, is the manner in which it illuminated the new battleground of "alternative" versus "mainstream" where companies vie for consumers and market share—that is, the territory of values. His accusations aimed at Whole Foods and Wal-Mart essentially found both firms guilty of short-circuiting the holistic "value" chain that the LOHAS discourse promulgates as "consciousness." Values are cultural capital in LOHAS; they are currency upon which exchange is based. But the question must then be asked: How did values come to be the new line of demarcation, culminating in LOHAS?

A Look Back at Events: The History of LOHAS

During the first half of the twentieth century, the idea of food became a scientific interest. Interested in the role of nutrition on health, researchers broke food into components to analyze the roles individual nutrients played in particular functions of the human body, such as the vitamin thiamine and its relationship to the sickness known as beriberi. By the 1930s the specific nutrients had been named and classified, resulting in the creation in the mid-1940s of the daily minimal intakes or recommended daily allowances (RDAs). (These were later modified to the current recommended daily intake or RDI, also called the daily value or DV as seen on food and supplements labels.)

But scientists wondered if the RDA established the bare requirements for survival, what else might be possible to expect from the human body in terms of quality of life and even longevity by manipulating specific nutrients and their doses? Was there a difference between avoidance of disease states and optimal functioning, and if so, could certain nutrients be taken in larger doses or paired with other nutrients to target specific genetic proclivities toward a disease? One of the first of these studies on the effects of higher dosages on optimal functioning involved vitamin C. Linus Pauling believed vitamin C could be used therapeutically to intervene in genetically related health conditions, to prevent age-related deterioration, and to protect the body against environmental toxins.

As these early nutrient-specific studies were beginning, other concerns were surfacing about the relationship of health to food. Foreshadowing the modern natural foods movement that would come decades later, early health activists in the United States were wary of the effects of modern agricultural and food-processing technologies on overall health such as the milling of whole grain whereby the nutritious, but tough, outer husk was removed in order to produce a silkier and whiter, but less nutritious flour. In their research on organic agriculture Georgiana Holt and Matthew Reed write: "Organic agriculture was global from the very beginning; the first association of organic enthusiasts was formed in 1940 in New Zealand, whilst by the mid 1940s Ehrenfried Pfeiffer, a follower of Rudolph Steiner, was introducing biodynamics to the USA. Books, journals, lecture tours and personal letters helped spread the word in the early years. The Soil Association, which was formed in London in 1946, aimed deliberately to have a global membership; after all, they argued, the entire planet was at peril" (14).

These nascent voices for organic had to compete with the well-funded and growing American food manufacturing sector and its national advertising campaigns extolling to housewives everywhere the virtues of white flour and refined, white sugar, marketing them as symbols of an upwardly mobile American lifestyle. In a period ad for white sugar that ran in *LIFE* magazine on October 3, 1955 (p. 45), a happy couple enjoys their time together at the dinner table, cups of coffee and a bowl of sugar between them. The husband eats an apple and admonishes his wife that while he loves sugar, he's watching his weight, to which she replies, "You need sugar for energy! And even 3 teaspoons of Domino Sugar contain fewer calories than your apple." The new processed foods appealed to war-weary Americans ready to leave frugality behind and join in The American Way (see Marchand).

J. I. Rodale, founder of the Rodale Press Company and a heath-food pioneer, wasn't one to be taken in by the advertising. Concerned about compromised nutrient levels in food crops, caused by industrial agricultural methods, Rodale set out to educate Americans about how organic agricultural methods could serve up more nutritious meals and lessen the health threats posed by modern agricultural methods that were highly dependent upon petroleum-based chemical pesticides and herbicides. His work spawned Rodale Publishing, the mouthpiece of the organic movement, and which produced a series of books about organic agriculture and the advantages of using homegrown compost over synthetic chemicals to improve soil health and to boost crop yields. By 1948 he had founded the precursor to the now legendary *Organic Gardening* magazine. In 1950 Rodale added another magazine to the company, *Prevention* magazine, which, as its name implies, focused on healthfulness through nutrition and fitness. Today, more than 10 million Americans read *Prevention* each month.

The advent of World War II proved to be an unlikely ally for organic gardening. Americans responded to their government's edict to support the war effort by planting home vegetable gardens, enabling the government to redirect public food supplies to feed the troops. Popular in urban and rural settings alike, these "victory gardens" received the hearty endorsement of manufacturers of seeds and farming equipment. As the war ended, however, so did the interest in victory gardening, and the American industrial complex shifted from the production of armaments to consumer goods, as consumerism scholar Lizabeth Cohen points out: "The United States came out of World War II deeply determined to prolong and enhance the economic recovery brought on by the war, lest the crippling depression of the 1930s return. Ensuring a prosperous peacetime would require making new kinds of products and selling them to different kinds of markets" (236).

The idealized "good life" became urbanized and privatized. It wasn't only that consumer goods represented a reward for the hardships the country had endured and a symbol of American ingenuity, it was also that shopping for mass-produced consumer goods became a civic duty (Cohen). Nonetheless, organic agriculture and the link between good health and safe environments had taken root in the popular imagination and would go on to inspire a new generation. By the 1960s the *good* life was suspected of deteriorating *good* health.

In 1962 a scientist specializing in zoology and genetics wrote the book that would spawn the modern environmental movement. Rachel Carson's *Silent Spring* attacked the chemical-based agriculture that had expanded during the post–World War II years, with what she felt were with disastrous results. Seeing firsthand the detrimental effects of chemical pesticides and herbicides on ecosystems during her fifteen-year career with the U.S. Fish and Wildlife Service, Carson shared Rodale's concerns about the impact of modern technology and science on human and environmental health.

Time Magazine named Carson one of the one hundred most influential people of the twentieth century for informing new ideas about our relationship to the natural world. Her book established a new lexicon, a new vision, and a new argument with regard to living in harmony with the planet. Her pro-environmental ideas went on to spawn nonprofit organizations, media, and federal regulations, even contributing to the designation of Earth Day celebrated every April 22 since 1970.

Just prior to the time that Carson was railing against chemical-intensive farming, nutritionist Adelle Davis authored a popular book titled *Let's Eat Right to Be Fit* and generated a mantra for the 1960s: you are what you eat. Davis had been writing on the subject of nutrition since the 1930s publication of her book *Optimum Health*. She had become the famous (infamous, some might say) proponent of unprocessed, natural, whole foods then as now known as "health foods." Her vehement opposition to food additives and the food industry in general had a spiritual fervor to it, one noted by *Time Magazine* in a 1972 article about Davis: "As the high priestess of a new nutrition religion, she preaches a gospel that many scientists and academicians find heretical. According to Davis, who holds a master's degree in biochemistry from the University of Southern California School of Medicine, malnutrition is at the root of most of America's health, emotional and social problems, and only proper nutrition offers the populace a chance for salvation."

As the 1960s wore on, legions of youth were taking to the streets to protest the Vietnam War and to take part in civil rights marches. New concerns rising through these two social movements moved from the peripheral outliers of the culture into the center of American culture, and more surprisingly, even into its far right-leaning branches of conservative evangelicalism (Eilperin).

As a product of those tumultuous and promising times, author Frances Moore Lappé wrote *Diet for a Small Planet*, again underscoring the pitfalls of modern agriculture. But Lappé's book opened up another chapter in the debate about food; her book pointed out the role of political economy in global hunger and poverty. The book's premise was simple. Global hunger was less the result of food shortage than it was the way in which food resources were managed in unequal distribution and inefficient systems that produced cheap and unhealthy food and fluctuations of scarcity and abundance that were based on wealth rather than need. Lappé examined the social costs of food production, arguing that raising animals for meat gobbled up an exorbitant quantity of resources such as tillable land and water that could be better used to grow foods with higher nutrient-to-resource expenditure ratios. The book took up the cause of vegetarianism as a social commentary and as a method of civic engagement.

These same ideas were fermenting down in Deaf Smith County, Texas, where a man named Frank Ford had invested his small savings in an organic-grains and natural packaged-goods company that he called Arrowhead Mills.

Ford agreed with Carson and Rodale on the dangers of modern agrichemi-
cals, but he was also concerned about how agriculture was linked to community solidarity and to his Christian faith. In the preface to the 1972 *Deaf
Smith County Cookbook: Natural Foods for Family Kitchens*, coauthored by
his former wife Marjorie and two other women, Ford wrote:

> A phenomenon that might best be described as a revolution of renewal is hap-
> pening in this land and it is causing amazing things to happen. A new pioneer-
> ing spirit is developing and this time, the frontier is within us. Our technology
> has conquered mountains, oceans, and space, but many of us are empty and
> unsatisfied. We have mined our soil, polluted our water and air, often taken
> unfair advantage of our fellow human beings, and now we have begun to pause
> and ask ourselves a simple question—"why?" Having defined the question in
> our minds, we have begun to seek out the answers. It is a very hopeful begin-
> ning. In these days, the Holy Spirit is truly being poured out upon all those
> who seek, and the right relationship with God, which begins with faith, can
> logically be extended to the methods used in farming and food preparation as
> well as our relationship with each other. (xi)

Ford regarded his promotion of natural foods as *explicitly* spiritual because
it honored community and good health for all people and all creatures and
thus followed God's will. Arrowhead Mills became a leader in the young
U.S. health food industry and emphasized not only alternatives to mass-
produced goods and industrialized agriculture, but also an alternate way of
doing business. Ford stressed the need for partnerships among local vendors
and growers as a way to both reduce strain on the environment caused by
long-distance transportation of products and materials and to promote the
health of the local community.

Throughout the ensuing decades, the young men and women who had
matured during the 1960s social movements were joining the work force, but
they were doing so in ways that aligned with their values forged during those
tumultuous times. They still wanted to change the world, even though that
meant doing it from the office instead of from the protest marches. Among
these alternative-economy pioneers was Mo Siegel, who cofounded the international tea company Celestial Seasonings by working shoulder-to-shoulder
with his friends picking wild herbs in the foothills west of Boulder, Colorado.

Another health-food pioneer, Steve Demos, wanted to merge his Buddhist
beliefs with his work. Inspired by his faith, he hoped to encourage people to
eat more healthfully and mindfully by eating lower on the food chain. With
a shoestring budget, he started a deli and tofu shop in Boulder. Little would
he have guessed then that in twenty years the company he cofounded, White

Wave, would evolve into an international manufacturer and produce the fresh soy beverage Silk, one of the most popular soy products to ever hit the market.

Around the same time in northern California, Michael Funk was driving a garbage truck past hillsides of fruit orchards and noticed trees bearing ripening, unpicked, and imperfect fruit. Instead of letting it go to waste, Funk backed up his pickup truck and started harvesting. Mountain People's Co-op was birthed in the bed of his truck, where he sold the fruit at a reduced cost. Today, he is the CEO of United Naturals, the nation's largest natural foods distributorship, which was formed from the 1990s merger of a conglomerate of companies (including Mountain People's). In 2009 the company reported a record $3.45 billion in annual sales.

Back in Boulder, in 1979 two followers of Guru Maharaj Ji opened a small natural foods store called Pearl Street Market, which became predecessor and the incubator for the larger Alfalfa's Markets four years later. Alfalfa's, along with Whole Foods, became one of the nation's first natural-foods supermarket chains. One of Alfalfa's creators, Mark Retzloff, went on to cofound the nation's largest organic dairy, Horizon Organic Dairy with its famous flying cow logo.

Back in 1968 in Ann Arbor, Michigan, a group of friends, including Retzloff, opened a natural foods co-op called Eden Foods, based on the principles of macrobiotics—dietary guidelines set forth by George Ohsawa, born Nyoichi Sakurazawa, in Japan. Designed as a relational system where humans live peacefully with the natural world (the environment should be as little manipulated as possible), a macrobiotic diet excludes meat and processed food, although it is shifted to adjust to dietary needs brought on by pregnancy, individual genetics, and aging. The principles of macrobiotics guide not just what you eat but also the way in which food is prepared and eaten as well as the types of foods one consumes. In 1969 the company opened a retail store and a manufacturing plant, producing one of the top-selling brands of natural and organic foods that still endures today, Eden Foods.

As products rolled off the conveyor belts of these new food companies, retail stores found themselves pinched for shelf space. Until the 1980s, the average health-food store rarely extended beyond fifteen hundred square feet. For the most part, these stores focused on packaged groceries and dietary supplements, with a few venturing into natural body-care lines and offering limited refrigerated and frozen foods sections. Some of these stores even carried small organic-produce sections, but very few had "peripheral" departments such as fresh meats and seafood, delis, and bakeries. These fresh foods had yet to be fully developed as natural and organic.

When former teacher Sandy Gooch opened the first Mrs. Gooch's Natural Foods Store, a five-thousand-square-foot, full-service grocery in West Los Angeles, California in 1976, she rang in a new era of *natural-products* stores. As opposed to health-food stores, the natural products store carried a deeper and broader inventory of goods, including fresh foods, housewares, and body care. But mostly Gooch became famous for her store's strict rules regarding the products it carried. By doing so, she set the standard for the growing natural and organic products industry. Gooch defined natural products as those that were as close to their original state in nature as possible—with minimal processing and containing no unnecessary or chemical preservatives and dyes or synthetic ingredients and fillers. This seemingly direct definition was about to become much more complicated into and through the 1990s, thanks to a sweep of new trends, studies, research reports, and media exposés. These events included:

- The baby boomers, the "Baby Huey" of generations, were aging. Boomers wanted to stay healthy and vibrant into old age, something their parents' generation had never considered or been able to achieve;
- Pesticide fears fueled by the use of Alar on apples and the subsequent media blitz in 1989 had moms on the march. Oscar-winning Actress Meryl Streep was hired for Public Service Announcements that warned moms about the dangers of pesticides, earning her the nickname Meryl Creep in Agricultural Extension offices. The entertainment industry was lending "face and name" celebrity to specific causes, raising awareness of the effects of war, hunger, development, worker exploitation, pollution, and more;
- The nation's health care system was collapsing;
- Decades of environmental disasters including Bhopal (India), the Exxon Valdez spill (United States), Chernobyl (Russia), Sevesco (Italy), Love Canal (United States), and the oil and chemical spills during the first Persian Gulf War, were accompanied by new research showing the alarming facts about dying oceans, vanishing species, and toxic overloads in soil, water, and air.
- Sweet-faced American TV icon Kathy Lee Gifford claimed she was shocked when media revealed that minors in Honduran sweatshops produced her clothing line, working for seventy-eight cents an hour. It kicked off a national exposé of exploited garment workers both domestic and foreign, and the subsidizing of their misery by American industry and the need for cheap labor brought about by consumer demand for inexpensive goods.
- The cattle industry took a major hit when reports surfaced about the possible link between bovine growth hormones (rBGH or rBST), which are injected into food animals, and human cancers. Adding to the concern

about industrial farming, Mad Cow Disease made international headlines when more than a hundred people in the United Kingdom died from eating meat from infected animals, igniting a global scare and the slaughter of more than 4 million cows. Investigations showed the disease resulted from factory-farming techniques where cattle were forced to eat food that included the flesh and other parts of mammals, some which were diseased and considered unfit for human consumption.

- In 1990 David Eisenberg of the Center for Alternative Medicine Research and Education at Beth Israel Deaconess Medical Center in Boston, conducted a survey on the use of alternative medicine in America. He found that 33.8 percent (60 million people) of the U.S. adult population used at least one form of alternative-medical therapy during 1990.

- Dietary supplements and health-foods manufacturers, retailers, and consumers joined forces to lobby lawmakers for a legal definition of dietary supplements and continued access to these products in the marketplace. The result, the Dietary Supplement Health and Education Act (DSHEA), passed by Congress in 1994, was one of the most successful grassroots movements in history.

- Still to be rigorously tested for safety to humans, animals, and ecosystems, genetically modified organisms (GMOs) are also an agricultural bungle, having dramatically failed to produce hoped-for crop yields, which has cost the economy billions of dollars in lost revenue. Additionally, pesticide inputs have increased, and once planted, GMOs are nearly impossible to contain due to natural cross-pollination, causing transgenic contamination in non-GMO crops. Similarly, genetic engineering of plants such as tomatoes raises fears about adequate research on long-term effects in the ecocycle. Critics say that crafting what are essentially new species and hybrids by altering genetic codes is unethical and unsafe. In the case of gene splicing, for example, it is possible to inject genes from animals into vegetable crops, violating vegetarian dietary restrictions. Additionally, common allergens such as nuts can be genetically spliced into non-allergen products, raising serious health safety concerns for those with allergies.

- International legal warfare over intellectual property rights asks whether transnational companies should be allowed to patent indigenous products and technologies of other countries, products used by local populations for healing, farming, ritual or spiritual purposes, and economics. "Biopiracy" is the accusation leveled at powerful multinationals that attempt to do this. Biopiracy, says activist Vandana Shiva, disables populations who have used their native products, seeds, and plants for millennia from availing themselves of these plentiful healing sources in ways that particularly harm the poor. Not only that, but farmers are no longer allowed to retain the seeds of their crops, forcing them to buy patented seeds from multinationals instead. This has not only raised costs for farmers but it prevents farmers from protecting themselves against crop failure through the saving and planting of different strains of seeds to accommodate shifting climatic conditions, an ages-old tradition in India. Reliance on specific patented seed types has led to the widespread suicide of Indian farmers whose crops have failed because they were inappropriate plants for the specific climate conditions.

These and other similar issues accompanied the meteoric increase in sales of natural products during the 1990s. In the United States, the fast-growing industry not only got the attention of conventional food and drug manufacturers but also, and perhaps directly related to that, it attracted the suspicion of U.S. Food and Drug Administration (FDA). Dietary supplements, in particular, came under FDA fire. These products were caught in a regulatory limbo; because there were no rules that specifically defined vitamins, herbs, and natural medicines, it was unclear exactly what could legally be said about them in marketing materials. This uncertainty proved to be dangerous for the natural products industry—FDA started to raid health-food stores during the 1990s, seizing products on charges that varied case by case.

It bordered on the surreal to hear of armed FDA agents bursting through the doors of small health-food stores to confiscate dietary supplements such as the now very popular Coenzyme Q-10. In some cases, shoppers were forced out onto the streets while storeowners were handcuffed and led off the premises as their inventory was carted away. Following a number of high-profile raids on stores, manufacturers, and medical clinics by gun-toting agents, a popular natural pet-food store was raided on the grounds that the owner had distributed in-store literature claiming that vitamins were good for pets. It seemed the industry could not escape the cross-hairs of the U.S. government.

As much as those of us working in the natural and organic products industry hated to admit it, the FDA's attention was not entirely misplaced, even if its zealous patrol and quasi-guerilla warfare tactics were dubious. Rising sales had attracted unscrupulous entrepreneurs eager to turn a quick profit by selling products of shoddy quality and effectiveness, accompanied by false or misleading labels and advertising. After the media reported that a number of deaths were possibly connected with the ingestion of the herb ephedra, it again looked like the sales ride enjoyed by natural products might be over. But how could the industry police itself without the legal framework in place to guide regulation?

The passage of DSHEA in 1994 was an industry-led campaign and considered a watershed event. DSHEA established clear guidelines regarding what was and was not a dietary supplement, and this led to the development of standardized label claims on products. DSHEA ensured that a.) dietary ingredients were not considered as food additives; b.) dietary supplements' labeling and advertising could contain certain health claims (structure/function claims) without FDA's prior approval (it was believed these claims such as "calcium can help prevent osteoporosis" enabled consumers to better understand how to properly use the products as part of a healthy lifestyle); and c.) the burden of proof with respect to the safety of dietary ingredients fell onto FDA rather than on manufacturers.

However, critics of DSHEA said that the act also effectively barred the U.S. government from being able to control health-claim fraud or ban possibly dangerous dietary supplements. They claimed the lobby for the health-food industry successfully frightened consumers into believing that FDA was considering the passage of regulation that would remove citizen's rights to buy vitamins, herbs, and supplements. (For more information on opposition to DSHEA, see http://www.quackwatch.org; http://durbin.senate.gov/; or http://www.FDA.gov.)

The natural and organic products industry patched one problem only to find others. Now it was organic products that were also adrift in a regulatory no-man's land. The term "organic" was widely used on natural products, including on vegetables, packaged grocery items, and body care products, but it had not been nationally defined, which meant that dozens of private and state agencies were certifying products as organic using variable criteria. This raised havoc with international trade as well as with domestic trade across state boundaries. And consumers were becoming increasingly frustrated with the products because of the variability.

In 1990 Congress passed the Organic Foods Production Act (OFPA). Regarded as a major achievement within the organic industry, the act created uniform national standards for the growing, manufacturing, labeling, certification, and distribution of organic food products. Both DSHEA and OFPA were important factors in the continuing expansion of the natural products industry because standardization encouraged more investment money to flow into the natural products industry as a whole.

By 1992 investments—both private and public equity funds—poured into the industry. In 1996, an excess of $200 million flowed into the U.S. natural products industry. It was in 1992 that Whole Foods Market went public, trading shares on the NASDAQ Stock Market. This was shortly followed by a succession of some of largest names in the industry.

Natural products supermarket chains (i.e., Whole Foods Market, Wild Oats Markets and Nature's Fresh) and national dietary supplement chains (GNC, for example) were staking out prime metropolitan real estate while engaged in merger and buyout frenzies of established health-food stores.

Mainstream companies such as Lipton, Worthington Foods, Quaker Oats, Hain, and American Home Products were turning large eyes toward the smaller natural-products industries. "Veteran" natural products manufacturers were sold, including Solgar (to American Home Products), Cascadian Farms/Kashi (to General Mills), Horizon (to Dean Foods), and Celestial Seasonings (to Lipton). The rampant consolidation was changing the face of the industry by providing economies of scale that meant more funding for product research and innovation, marketing, and educational outreach. It seemed there would soon be a natural counterpart for every mainstream product on the market, rivaling mainstream packaging, product selection, and price.

The types of venues that offered natural products multiplied as well. From the small mom-and-pop health-food stores and food co-ops to the natural products supermarkets, the field expanded to include mainstream grocery stores; pharmacies; medical professionals; e-tailers; gourmet shops; direct marketers (catalogs, community-supported agriculture clubs, farmers' markets, and multilevel marketers); convenience stores; mass merchandisers and club warehouses; and health, fitness, and weight-loss centers. Companies that were household names in middle America were now producing foodstuffs culturally assigned to "granola heads," "New Agers," "tree-huggers," and Californians. In a new Birkenstocks-meet-briefcases world, natural and organic or "healthy living" products were appearing in regular grocery stores, causing no end of confusion among management as to where to stock the stuff on the shelves—should "alternative" products be segregated from or integrated with traditional or mainstream products?

New advocates for natural medicines and foods arrived from allopathic medicine. Medical doctors such as Larry Dossey, Christiane Northup, Bernie Siegal, Deepak Chopra, and Andrew Weil were also trained in alternative forms of health management including Ayurveda, acupuncture and nutrition. They produced books, newsletters, and seminars educating consumers about Eastern and integrative approaches to medicine, approaches they claimed addressed the whole human being as a balanced system of mind, body, and spirit. Instead of addressing symptoms of disease, the holistic approach emphasized prevention of disease. Chopra, Northrup, and Weil alone sold millions of books and developed some of the most popular websites and seminars in the business. In due course, in 1998, Congressional mandate created the Office of Complementary and Alternative Medicine within the National Institutes of Health.

The idea of *wellness* had migrated far beyond the concern with the human body, however, thanks to authors and activists in the environmental and social justice arenas. Consumers were demanding that their natural products not only be good for them but also good for social and environmental health, and not just locally either. Consumers wanted to know if growers in developing countries received a fair price for their crops, which would allow them to sustain their cultures and protect their environments. And, consumers didn't want any part in supporting sweatshop labor. They boycotted products tested on animals and those made, distributed, or sold by companies with interests in unsavory, unsustainable, and unjust regimes and industries. They wondered: How did a product contribute to the diversity of the economy in the grower's region? Were small companies, family farms, and co-ops better suited to support workers and to provide a higher quality of life than were large-scale factory farms and corporations? These types of questions spurred the rise of social-cause marketing.

Finally, in the late 1990s, the Wall Street firm Adams, Harkness & Hill (now Canaccord Adams) trademarked a phrase, "Healthy Living," as a way to help define the burgeoning marketplace of health and wellness. It was also a branding move for the company: they created the *Healthy Living Index*, an arbitrary reference point and a small version of the Dow Jones 500 that tracked the financials of selected companies—mostly those producing or selling natural foods, dietary supplements, and body care products.

The natural and organic products industry overall was struggling to accommodate merging markets, entrepreneurial spirits, and, most of all, mainstream businesses that had an accomplished grip on the operations side of production but were fledglings in understanding the nuances of Healthy Living. And, there were still concerns among industry members about unscrupulous marketers who managed to squeak around regulations and accepted industry standards to introduce sketchy products. Everyone, it seemed, was eager to hawk the naturalness of his or her product, and this could potentially bring even more government scrutiny and regulation.

Industry associations, manufacturers, retailers, and media alike decided the time had come to self-police beyond the regulation provided by DSHEA and the new national organic rules. New Hope Communications in Boulder, Colorado, producer of the world's largest trade shows for natural and organic products—Natural Products Expos East and West—issued product standards as a way to monitor and to ensure the quality of the goods exhibited at the trade shows and advertised in New Hope's trade and consumer magazines.

This self-regulation wasn't easy, largely due to the fact that the basic consumer of natural and organic products had changed; more and more "mainstream" shoppers had turned to natural products stores for healthful products, such as meat alternatives or organic produce, and these shoppers also wanted the convenience of being able to purchase at the same time some common "conventional"—non-organic, nonnatural—staples. The natural foods stores were eager to comply.

Everyone in the industry struggled to sort out this growing consumer base, and soon a picture began to emerge of this new consumer—labeled as "the Cultural Creative." The name had come about as a result of a 1997 *American Demographics* magazine article titled "The Emerging Culture" by sociologist Paul Ray, who claimed that he had identified a new breed of American—which he called the Cultural Creatives. This group, Ray said, comprised 24 percent of the adult population, or 50 million Americans, across every conceivable cross-sector of the demos. The Cultural Creatives wanted to integrate their social, political, and economic values with their overall lifestyles, including their interactions with a perceived global village. The "Creatives" were concerned about not just their own health, but also that of the social and natural worlds as well. They were skeptical about the legacies they were leaving to their children and grandchildren in a world contorted by war, poverty, hunger, global destruction of ecosystems, racism, ageism, and sexism. Their reformative values formed a rootstalk of beliefs about the sanctity, meaning, and balance of life, and this appeared to inform even the mundane aspects of their lives: from the clothes they wore to the foods they ate. These were people who had "made a comprehensive shift in their worldview, values, and way of life—their culture, in short," say Ray and coauthor Sherry Ruth Anderson in their book *The Cultural Creatives: How 50 Million People are Changing the World* (4).

The idea of the Cultural Creatives hit a nerve among trade members in the natural products industry, a.k.a. the Healthy Living marketplace. For some time, industry members had discussed the idea that the products and practices converging in the Healthy Living marketplace—housing, clothing, food, medicine, community, environmentalism, and social activism, for example—were linked in consumers' minds in more complicated ways than previously thought. Ray's research drove home the idea that the move toward health, sustainability, social responsibility, and environmentalism should be examined in terms of an evolving nexus of *values* distilled from the 1960s social movements.

Ray's research caught the interest of Gaiam, Inc., and Natural Business Communications. Both companies saw Ray's research as a possible signpost to the future of the natural products industry: The "culturally creative" might also be the materially frustrated. That is, perhaps these consumers were being forced into a sort of scavenger hunt for products and services that could produce the integrated, values-based lifestyle they craved. Ray's research showed that Creatives wanted more from the marketplace than ample, convenient, low-priced goods and services; they longed for lifestyles that were interconnected in purpose, vision, and practice, from the foods they ate to the causes they supported, and from the cars they drove to the jobs they held.

Borrowing the term "LOHAS" from Gaiam and consulting with Paul Ray, Natural Business Communications in 2000 launched *The LOHAS Journal* and the LOHAS Forum conference. LOHAS would, they believed, appeal to the Cultural Creative, now reworked as the LOHAS consumer, or the Cultural Creative in the marketplace. And, they hoped that LOHAS could become a new market concept that would encourage businesspeople from different but converging industries such as alternative medicine and organic products to think across market boundaries and to develop new partnerships.

LOHAS was, essentially, a term and concept created by the trade for the trade, as a way to reorder the natural and organic products or Healthy Living marketplace. I served as a research consultant for Natural Business Communications. I was charged with quantifying this new conceptual LOHAS market that encompassed literally hundreds of industries, from hybrid cars to intentional housing communities to organic foods. How did we decide what was in and what was out? Without a doubt, it was in our best interests as an organization to make the market a large one, but it would only hurt the project's credibility if there were not clear guidelines about how we decided to include the things we did. Toward that end, we developed five broad market categories: Sustainable Economy (a business-to-business category comprising sales of raw resources to manufacturers); Alternative Medicine (includes non-allopathic healing modalities and natural and herbal medicines); Healthy Lifestyles (includes natural and organic foods and products and dietary supplements); Personal Development (includes tools for the development of mind, body, and spirit such as self-help books, yoga tapes, and religious or spiritual materials and services); and Ecological Lifestyles (includes a wide range of goods considered environmental). Today, these categories and breakdowns have been slightly altered by various LOHAS marketers including *The LOHAS Journal* and the Natural Marketing Institute, based in Harleysville, Pennsylvania, but most of the products and practices are still included.

By way of company history with regard to LOHAS, in 2002, a LOHAS-focused multimedia company in Colorado, Conscious Media purchased Natural Business Communications. Gaiam then bought Conscious Media, but the LOHAS-based division of the company was separated and made part of a nonprofit entity called Conscious Wave. Today, Gaiam wholly owns the original LOHAS products—the LOHAS Forum conferences and *The LOHAS Journal*. And, of course, the term "LOHAS" has spread beyond its country of origin. Internationally, the word is used to describe what researchers believe are growing numbers of people concerned about health, social justice, and the environment. Estimates of the number of "Cultural Creatives"—that core group of consumers for Healthy Living and LOHAS—in Western Europe alone fall between 80 and 90 million adults (Van Gelder and Ray).

Around the world, media and market organizations use the word variously to describe their own mission, goals, and audiences or consumers. But the word symbolically points to a set of commonalities. A general taxonomy for LOHAS discourse comprises:

- Global interconnectedness. The discourse includes examples of the relationships of cultures, societies, environments, and species and shows how actions can affect all in the chain, not only in the present, but also in the future.
- The environment. Examples of concerns include air, soil, and water pollution caused by manufacturing, transportation, consumer waste, automobiles, oil spills, conventional agriculture methods, deforestation, lack of biodiversity, and some types of mineral or resource extraction. It also includes the preservation of ecosystems and the treatment of animals.
- Social justice. Issues include sweatshops; commodity market pressures on indigenous populations; child labor; worker rights and safety; hunger; poverty; and lack of attention to intellectual property rights, including biopiracy and prior informed consent.
- Personal health and development. This category includes:
  - Complementary and alternative medicine (integrative medicine) that relies on a holistic conception of the body and that encourages the body's own healing properties through the use of natural products such as herbal medicines, homeopathy, naturopathy, nutritional medicine, and Reiki and energy healing modalities. The focus is on nutrition, prevention of disease, and noninvasive treatment of health complaints.
  - Products and practices aimed at balancing the mind, body, and spirit.
  - Natural and organic food and body care.
  - Self-help media.
- Community. Issues include concerns about urban decay, social isolation, recognition and respect of cultural difference, education, and community infrastructure such as access to health care and nutritional food.
- Socially responsible business/fair trade. This overlaps with social justice issues. The concept speaks to controlling the exploitive tendencies of capitalism and ensuring that each individual in the supply chain earns fair and living wages as well. It is concerned with the protection of environments and cultures.

"No More New Age!"

The 1990s was a crucial transition time for American ideas about health—incorporating early twentieth-century concerns about the links between industrialized agriculture and food processing with nutrition, environmental fears, and spiritual or ethical concerns. As to this latter, another shift had occurred in the bedrock of the 1990s natural products industry—its relationship to what has been called the New Age. Wouter Hanegraaff referred to a "New Age movement" and defended that term against charges he had reified the messy, sprawling practices and discourses by saying "my critics might have skipped my methodological introduction, which in fact insists that any concept of New Age or of a New Age movement is necessarily an etic theoretical construct and no more than that" ("Spectral" 43).

In general, it is safe to say that scholars have situated the New Age as a conglomerate of practices performed on the self with an eye to making an impact in the public sphere, carrying visions of a better way of life on the planet (See Hanegraaff, "Spectral"; Heelas, "New Age in Cultural Context" and *New Age Movement*; Sutcliffe and Bowman). The New Age is about *spirituality*, but interesting work by Flere and Kirbiš reveals a strong pattern of connection between ideals of the New Age and traditionalism, or the moorings of formal religion. Useful for purposes here is Eileen Barker's description of the New Age movement in which she identifies six themes: a.) forging integration of religion with science; b.) finding correspondences between spheres of life; c.) emphasizing holism or interconnectedness; d.) seeking to reenchant the world; e.) emphasizing "spiritual" experience; and f.) acknowledging the authority of the "Spiritual Self" (Paul Heelas's term) (Barker).

These themes are also regnant in LOHAS discourse, even though LOHAS media and market organizations have an allergic reaction to the term "New Age" and have valiantly tried to avoid explicit association with it. When the venerable *New Age Journal* changed its name in 2001 to *Body+Soul,* for example, it was quite clear readers were gently being asked to "move on." After Martha Stewart Omnimedia purchased *Body+Soul,* the firm again renamed the publication, this time to *Whole Living* drowning any last gurgle that could possibly be identified as "religion." Even though this grande dame of the healthy living marketplace now features more mainstream advertising and editorials, it is still considered the leading consumer magazine in that market, and the publication and staff maintain a presence at LOHAS Forums.

In 2004, *Body+Soul's* then-editor-in-chief, Janesse Bruce, wrote a telling editorial:

For three decades, originally as *New Age* and now as *Body & Soul*, this magazine has heralded the trends, the philosophy, and the science behind the holistic culture that has shaped today's healthy lifestyle. Those of us who have been living that lifestyle have watched the evolution. Ideas from the counterculture—yoga, meditation, organic foods, and environmentally friendly consumption—were, well, fringe 30 years ago. Now they are the culture. They—and we—have changed the way people live today. More of us embrace natural eating, balanced fitness, a more natural, integrative approach to health, healthy homes, and spiritual practices. How did this happen? (Bruce)

As we've seen, the "how it happened" is a complex collision and maturation of a great many undercurrents in American culture, but Bruce's quote nicely points out just how the term New Age became unserviceable to the broad field of health and sustainability. Ray and Anderson, too, say that while the Cultural Creatives might have been the force behind the New Age, the term has little relevance for them any longer (Ray and Anderson 188). It's not that the sentiments, ideals, practices, and objects that defined a New Age have gone away, but rather, they've just been repackaged. As Mara Einstein explains, turning away from the term "New Age" provided marketers with heaps of fresh customers, by appealing to a younger population who didn't want to follow mom and dad but were more in tune with the "health-oriented" spirituality of mind/body/spirit (205).

The media professionals I interviewed held varying views about the term, but each agreed that it no longer held meaning for their audiences. Not only that, but they were also convinced that the term's odor still lingered in the culture to the degree that it could conceivably alienate new, mainstream consumers and prevent them from venturing into the healthy and sustainable marketplace. The spirituality was just too visible and too laden with specific images. Nonetheless, they did acknowledge the legacies of the New Age.

"Charlotte," editor-in-chief of a consumer magazine, told me that the term was dated but did "represent a period of time in the dawning of the human-potential movement." She told me that "New Age" was tainted because it meant "far-out mystical practices, and people make judgments about those things." She added that she would disagree if someone tried to label her magazine as New Age. Similarly, Richard said "New Age" was "much less relevant [in the LOHAS marketplace] than it was even five years ago." So, what does it even mean, I asked him? He replied, "When I hear New Age, I think of people who have recently discovered these concepts about a society based on sustainability, health and spirituality." He added, "As Paul [Ray] says, it's really more of a transition phrase to describe people who are finding their way to this area. The New Age is more about what happens on a personal level, even though LOHAS, too, has its emphasis on personal transformation."

A CEO of a consumer lifestyles magazine, "Paloma," told me that many of the old labels—New Age; mind/body/spirit; natural and organic; and alternative—carried "baggage." We need a new language!" she cried. "I mean, New Age? I still think of crystals. I've been hearing that term since I was a teenager and resenting it. There are parts of it that are just negative." "Margo," the CEO and founder of a national "alternative" magazine, not only shared these views on the New Age, but she exclaimed, "No more New Age!" That term, she said, along with the phrase "mind/body/spirit"—which she called another "tired tripartite"—are "fuzzy."

Clearly my informants found these phrases old-fashioned, unclear, and geared more toward the 1960s hippie movement than the demographics of current media audiences who were interested in sustainable living. Charlotte told me that her staff "hated being called an alternative publication," which surprised me because, in reality, the content of her magazine is focused on a particular lifestyle participated in by less than 10 percent of the U.S. population—"that isn't mainstream," she admitted, but she added that "advertisers won't look at you if you are alternative, so we try to package our material so that we look mainstream so we can attract advertisers." She added, "We try to present alternative material in a mainstream way by showing how these practices can fit into mainstream lives."

To that point, Wouter Hanegraaff writes, "there are indeed clear signs that New Age religion is losing its status as a countercultural movement and is now increasingly assimilated by the mainstream of society" ("Spectral" 48). Apparently that assimilation is happening under a different name. LOHAS producers still recognize the term as having a fringe, countercultural tone that can scare off more conservative, religious, patriotic, and otherwise "mainstream" consumers. What this does is thrust LOHAS into a liminal space. While the producers in the media and the market might regard these "old labels" as a disadvantage in marketing, they clearly also regard the terms as having enough life left in them to cause problems if one associates too closely with them. Martha Stewart probably thought so and wasted no time putting another semiotic boundary between her newly acquired publication, *Body+Soul*, and the New Age.

Several of the media professionals I interviewed emphasized the challenge they faced in trying to appeal to quasi-alternative–mainstream hybrid audiences that distribute, if you believe the market research, unequally along political and religious axes. These professionals believed themselves "speaking" to conservatives and liberals simultaneously, and we've seen how well that works in the political sphere. Still, they persevere because what choice do they have? And, still, they fail. For example, my informants still receive angry letters and subscription cancellations because of specific articles appearing in their magazines. Paloma's magazine appeals to conservatives and liberals, old and young, religious and spiritual as well as the nonreligious. No matter what angle her editorial takes, she finds readers become angry over perceived political stances taken by the magazine.

"My theory is that our mainstream readers, the people in the middle, they might be interested in the environment, but the word 'organic' is still a big leap for them," she said. "Not so for liberals. For them, [organic] is politics. It's being vegetarian. It's a cause. But for the extreme conservatives, well . . . they come at organic from a different angle, which is basically celebrating self-reliance." Paloma said her "conservative" readers "have a survivalist mentality or they have a suspicion of government interference with nature from a religious point of view." "Carl," an editor at a consumer publication that came to the LOHAS Forums later than other media organizations involved in my interviews, told me that the "breadth and diversity" of his audience's religious values amazed him and that he considered this a "success" of the magazine. But, he said, he was also shocked that "real fundamentalists" even purchased the magazine in the first place.

While the media professionals I spoke with believed that the old language such as "alternative," "New Age," and "mind, body, and spirit" might still serve as an entry-level lexicon to LOHAS culture for some people, they worried not only that the term could set off alarms for those suspicious of spirituality but also that the terms might be thought of as only referencing personal development to those who were looking more for DIY or simple living advice in an economic downturn.

Everyone I spoke with emphasized that their media organization was more interested in a *holistic* model and worldview, one that integrated the individual (the "self"), the social world, and the natural world in a healing ethos. "Sam," the CEO of a national chain of healthy living/LOHAS publications, said, "Healing the natural world, society, and yourself are completely interrelated." He added, "One without the other cannot be done. I don't believe you can heal, do inner work, without engaging in protection and healing of the planet and pursuing healing in the social and political realms, between people and nations."

This is the holistic enterprise of LOHAS. Sustainability and health become articulated through a tripartite of healing self, society, and the natural world, and LOHAS texts point to the work of LOHAS as one of "reawakening" (not creating) a universal sensibility about this. Individuals I interviewed and the texts I analyzed reflected a deep commitment to this notion of holism, and I was told it was necessary for the market to continue to straddle those "old" paradigms of alternative and mainstream to appeal to all people, even if that meant using regnant, if repugnant, glossaries. They were, to a one, keen to point out that LOHAS was about global transformation and the only way to do that was to erase "minor" points of difference, be those between New Age and spiritual, religious and spiritual, alternative and mainstream, nature and culture, or conservative and liberal. The common ground, they said, was sustainability.

The term "sustainability" is the ligature of multiple discourses in the West about personal, social, and planetary health. Sustainability has formed the backbone of "green" politics, launched environmentalist movements, and even informed the practices lumped under New Age holism. The polysemic nature of both concepts can be maddening for scholars but can also be tremendously useful for business because it can point to everything from corporate penny-pinching to agricultural inputs.

For our purposes here, let's start with the broadest definition of sustainability in use. The United States Environmental Protection Agency says that the "most widely quoted definition internationally is the Brundtland definition of the 1987 *Report of the World Commission on Environment and Development*—that sustainability means 'meeting the needs of the present without compromising the ability of future generations to meet their own needs'" (http://www.epa.gov/sustainability/basicinfo.htm). This is, of course, leaving many questions unanswered, for example, exactly whose *generation* are we speaking of here? Are the needs of future generations of the Bemba people of Zambia the same as those of the residents of Dubuque, Iowa?

I'll put forth my own definition. "Sustainability" refers to an amalgamation of methods and practices that replenish and nourish, rather than extract and deplete, the raw materials that compose and support a system. That system can be a human body, an organization, a culture, an organism, or an ecosystem. Think of how to accommodate all of these within the generational framework of the Brundtland definition and you begin to perceive the enormousness of the suggestion.

Sustainability has a benign quality to it—it sounds good to most of us, like saving waterfowl and cleaning up the local stream. But in a June 2, 2009, interview with *MIT Sloan Management Review*, Peter Senge, founder of the Society for Organizational Learning and senior lecturer in behavioral and policy sciences at MIT Sloan School of Management, said the term "sustainability" is actually a negative word that calls to mind what is necessary for survival rather than encouraging the human race to think of quality of life.

"Survival is not the most inspiring vision," he says. "It motivates out of fear, but it only motivates for as long as people feel the issues are pressing on them. Soon as the fear recedes, so does the motivation" (Senge). This was something I heard in my interviews with LOHAS professionals as well.

Because we hear the word so often, it may seem quite familiar and understandable, even though, according to market research released in 2007 by the Hartman Group, most consumers do *not* hold a "deep or extensive knowledge of expert, policy or corporate discourses related to sustainability and sustainable development." According to that same report, a lack of knowledge doesn't prevent consumers from feeling comfortable with the term: 93 percent of consumers "do operate in everyday life with varying degrees of what we have come to think of as 'sustainability consciousness'—a cultural shift [taking] place in terms of consumer awareness, acceptance and practices that relate to sustainability" (Hartman Group).

For such an elusive term, it is interesting that it is so popular. It brings to mind the term "spirituality," and perhaps it's popular for the same reasons: you can pin just about any tail anywhere on this donkey and still be right. A billion-dollar international company that has been actively involved in the LOHAS Forums and sustainability dialogues around the world, Interface Inc., a flooring company, says on its website that "green is just the beginning" of sustainability, meaning that sustainability is a "systems-based perspective" that will guide operations, internal and external relationships, and "the entire web of commerce in which we conduct business" (www.interfaceglobal.com).

In the LOHAS magazine *Evergreen Monthly*, Sean Schmidt and Rebecca Luke, founders of the Sustainable Style Foundation, explained how they define sustainability, saying they "started with the broadest [definition] that's out there—improving the quality of life for everyone." Schmidt adds, "This is like the Holy Grail of social and environmental responsibility, defining this word" (Garland 13). On their website (http://www.sustainablestyle.org), the firm further defines sustainability, saying it is concerned with seven generations (a notion borrowed from Native American culture that mandates any action taken must be done with consideration for seven future generations); living enterprises and economies; family, friends, community; and equality. The site states: "Sustainability is all this and more. Most importantly, it's understanding that each of us has a role in making all of the above a reality."

In LOHAS, judging by an analysis of its texts, sustainability consciousness points to the work that is required to attain a state of health, and that ideal is a balance among your mind, body, and spirit and then an equanimity among your "healed" self and the social and the natural world. This interdependent "holistic" worldview coincides with that represented in the New Age, as well

(Hanegraaff, "New Age"; Heelas, "New Age in Cultural Context"; Roof), but these uses of the term sustainability differ in a substantial way from what sustainability scholars Tábara and Giner describe as a dawning global "sustainability culture." They say: "Sustainability culture refers to a set of new ideological, moral and aesthetic preferences, as well as natural beliefs, which incorporate extended frames of time, space and moral considerations into the configuration of meanings, which make sense of individual social action. This worldview is part of a new and self-conscious historical process which aims to balance and adapt personal and collective needs, desires and lifestyles to the new imperatives of the growing scarcity of natural resources as well as to the difficulties for global ecosystems to assimilate current environmental degradation" (Tábara and Giner 263).

While LOHAS incorporates this interest in the collective, it also embraces a much broader understanding of the concept of "natural resources" than what Tábara and Giner describe. That is, LOHAS discourse is as concerned with *internal* resources as external ones. These internal resources of the "self" include one's physical, emotional, mental, and spiritual health such as fitness, wisdom, peacefulness, clarity, kindness, calm, wisdom, and strength.

I asked Richard what he believed was at the core of the LOHAS concept. He replied "environmental health, social health and economic health." Noting his use of the word "health" rather than "sustainability" I then asked him what he believed "sustainability" meant. He said, "It represents systems that have an ongoing lifecycle and that don't require ultimately more input than they produce." Then how is it different from health, I asked him, or is it? He was thoughtful. It seemed to be a more difficult concept for him to articulate than sustainability. Finally, he said health was about taking care of one's self through the idea of holistic, natural, and sustainable processes that must link up with a mission to make a more healthful, sustainable society. But, he said, "Change begins with the individual."

2. Healing the Self to Heal the World

"Things are only going to change if we change on the inside.
That is social transformation. We change society because
deep within us we know this is right."
—Stephan Rechtschaffen, CEO and Founder, Omega Institute;
presentation at the LOHAS 9 Forum, Los Angeles, California,
April 27, 2005.

How do individuals become change-agents? As publishing executive Richard suggested in the last chapter, "change begins with the individual" in LOHAS, but what sort of individuals are we talking about? Where do they receive their vision for change? What motivates them? What sorts of actions do they take and where?

The LOHAS discourse, particularly that occurring within the consumer-oriented texts, tells us that each individual needs to pursue their "bliss." This idea says that each of us has a unique and distinct path to follow toward ultimate self-fulfillment and happiness, and if yours is making paper airplanes or composting or making a million dollars, you are compelled to do it posthaste. Not only is this foundational to LOHAS, but it is to capitalist economics in general. Where would the "free" market be without individuals and their bliss? Each of us is called to craft an identity, to express ourselves in life. We should be all that we can be, says the advertising jingle, and then spend money being more of it. But the notion that one even has a "self" to develop differently from all the other selves in the cave—that you hold within you a sui generis personality that is but a pupa anchored onto society until developed through your own careful attention and labor—isn't universal or even inherently "human nature." The notion of the moldable, distinctive self is a historically contingent one and the product of sociohistorical constructs of power and domination, where knowledge is created, generated, and dispersed through the collaboration of structures and agents in a society (Foucault).

Through these processes of late modernity, through market capitalism, industrialism, globalization, and rationality, the concept of the self has evolved, thanks to the way in which we have come to view ourselves as authorities with the agency and the legitimate right to act as we so deem appropriate for our chosen identity (within certain bounds of mores and norms). This autonomy, says religion scholar Wade Clark Roof, evolved through the development of a "complex and pluralistic" modern society that "breaks down traditional boundaries and orders" (135).

Late-modern populations know they not only have the capability but also the responsibility to generate meaning from any number of sources, including popular culture. We're no longer having to follow in the elder's footsteps or duplicate their closet or even use their language. We can skip all those traditional sites and modes of authority to look instead to our iPods, our Google, our circle of friends, our jobs, or our subscriptions to *Utne Reader* magazine for information and guidance. We are able to be reflexive, where we as legitimated and legitimizing individuals look back upon the stages of history and personal experience to weigh our choices (Roof).

And where once identity was prescribed by virtue of one's race, gender, religion, social class, language, or citizenship, we can choose just as easily to base our identities on our favorite Harry Potter character if we so choose. We can anchor ourselves on a chosen gender, sexuality, lifestyle, generational association, geography, or culture. But, even though we might not actually see these dynamics, our autonomy is always relative—it continues to be affected by historical, political, economic, and cultural forces.

Our authoritative selves can also choose to be change-agents for the world. In LOHAS there are certain prescriptive steps you have to take to become such a change-agent, and interestingly, that process begins by finding your "true" self, that uber-distinctiveness that marks one person from another. Based on what we have just learned about the construction of identity, this is quite curious. Still, this path to self discovery is so important in LOHAS because it is articulated as the path to *health*. Once you embark on the journey to fulfill your uniqueness you are involved in the "art of life," as the social media site Global Mindshift says (June 23, 2009, http://www.globalmindshift .com). This self-discovery brings you back to a *natural* state of wholeness, where your squawking mind, body, and ultimate spirit, which have been rudely and improperly divided by rational processes handed down from the European Enlightenment, are again reconciled to live in equal partnership or balance.

From New Thought to Quantum Physics:
Self-Healing Spiritualities

Sam, the former CEO of a chain of national LOHAS publications, told me that mind, body, and spirit was "another way to say 'holistic.'" "As an example, let's use the world of healing and wellness," Sam said. "A holistic healing approach must actively work on those three levels in a complementary manner rather than view one or another of those areas as the single key to good health."

The healing of the self, as it's articulated in LOHAS, commences as we journey from a fractured state to one of wholeness, or united mind, body, and spirit. The pot at the end of that rainbow is a certain state of consciousness. While this might sound, and in fact is, closely aligned to what you thought New Age was, there is an even older reference point: LOHAS's healing journey reflects legacies from a plethora of American "popular psychologies aimed at health, wealth and peace of mind through positive thinking" (Meyer 13). Positive psychologies urge individuals to use their minds to control and to heal their bodies. It's a tradition handed down from the New Thought movements of the past century, according to Becker and Maracek, and from "a faith steeped in Greco-Christian dualism" (593).

Throughout the New Thought traditions of the late nineteenth and early twentieth centuries, the New Age, and, most recently, in what I call the "quantum spiritualities" (for example, the DVDs and books *What the Bleep Do We Know!?* and *The Secret*, first released in 2004 and 2006, respectively), individuals have been encouraged to take on self-improving labor within the context of spiritual fulfillment. In each of these traditions the goal is to empower people to take control of their realities by directing their thoughts toward clearly visualized and articulated goals, particularly with a healing perspective in mind.

Pamela Klassen, in her work on the centrality of texts in healing notions of early twentieth-century Protestantism, says healing is "Loosely defined as the restoring of physical or emotional well-being with recourse to medical, symbolic, or religious means, healing is often distinguished from curing as a therapeutic approach with more 'holistic' goals than the cessation of particular physical ailments" (809).

Individuals in the therapeutic New Thought spiritualities were told that they could (and, perhaps more interestingly for the purposes of this investigation, *should*) attain what Alan Anderson states as "health, wealth, and happiness through the control of one's conscious and non-conscious beliefs, attitudes, and expectations by means of deliberately practicing the presence of a wholly benevolent deity" (2). In each of the cases presented here, there is a shared theme: the times caused unnatural stress on social actors and affected health not only of the individual but of society as well.

In the late nineteenth century, for example, profound shifts were occurring in the fabric of American society economically and socially, caused by rapid expansion into the Western part of the United States, innovative technologies, increased urbanization, and industrialization. The new demands and opportunities affected familial relationships, ideas about work or labor, working conditions, and gender roles. Doctors were convinced that these rapid transformations brought about increased "nervousness" in Americans. The diagnosis of "nervous exhaustion" wasn't confined to any one class: it permeated the social strata (Meyer 21).

William James explored these new health concerns and contextualized them in his 1902 book *Varieties of Religious Experience* within emerging spiritual traditions around the turn of the century, including those such as Mind Cure that were grouped under the umbrella term of "New Thought" (Satter), Christian Science, and Theosophy. Each of these movements centered on the power of individuals to find happiness and fulfillment, and William Leach describes them as "wish-oriented, optimistic, sunny, the epitome of cheer and self-confidence and completely lacking in anything resembling a tragic view of life" (225). These new spiritual expressions were, Meyer says, creative and productive responses to the changing, even confusing or frightening, new conditions of the economy.

Physician Phineas Parker Quimby coined the term "New Thought" in the late 1880s. He'd become interested in mesmerism as well as the teachings of Emmanuel Swedenborg and the work of the Transcendentalists (Griffith). Sarah J. Farmer, an early advocate of New Thought, defined it as "simply putting ourselves in new relation to the world about us by changing our thought concerning it. . . . We are not creatures of circumstance; we are creators" (A. Anderson 2, quoting Horatio Dresser). Similarly, mind curists "maintained that people could simply, by an act of will and conviction, cure their own illnesses and create heaven on earth," Robbins says (22). Mind cure enthusiasts were encouraged to find serenity within—to find a healthfulness that could cure the body and the spirit of the unease pervading the United States at the time.

Religious ideas were shifting in late-nineteenth-century United States. American Protestantism was just as concerned with "healing" as were mind curists and other New Thought advocates, but Protestant leaders "faced the tricky negotiation of embracing epistemologies of scientific medicine without surrendering their own theologies of God's omnipotent love, all the while living in an increasingly 'therapeutic culture,'" Klassen says (810). Media, medicine, and religion scholar Claire Hoertz Badaracco argues that "the converged religions of healthy-mindedness" that William James believed formed such a large population "they formed a psychic type to be studied with respect" still exists in America (203).

Within this therapeutic culture of the late nineteenth and early twentieth centuries, ideas circulating within the New Thought movement about self-development differed significantly from those espoused through earlier American Protestantism, which held that conscientious application of labor should be put to the resculpting of physical and economic landscapes as a way to please God rather than focus on the self, per se. Meyer points out that early Protestants wanted to depict humans as *like* God, not *different* from God (as was the case in the Calvinist theories of the essentially corrupt but redeemable nature of humans). They did so through articulations of humankind as "creatures of consciousness and control" rather than filled with "disorderly, emotional, hidden forces," but the mind cure movement "exposed the absurdity of that claim" (Meyer 84). Mind curists pointed to the very nature of the human body for their argument, and it went something like this: whether the mind was conscious of the workings of the body's organs, those organs still went about their functions. And this, claimed the mind curists, proved the existence of both a conscious and a subconscious state of existence. New Thought was providing a new logic that could not only explain morphing religious ideas in Protestantism but also innovations in science that problematized certain canons of American religions.

The point of mind cure, Meyer says, was to dig deeply into the subconscious to direct it into consciousness, specifically, into a consciousness of (or a belief in) a different dimension of being. The subconscious could be retooled and in its new form could offer up a new opportunity to know God. In this way, the subconscious could become a channel allowing for the divine passage into our lives (Meyer 85).

These new spiritualities presented a complicated configuration of God. God had to be everything and everywhere, but he was not be separated from humans' ability to "know" him. If we could not know God, went the reasoning, then human beings were essentially "shut up in cages of our own making," says Meyer (85)—we were doomed to be caught up in the mechanics of the subconscious, tossed like boats upon the waves, with no control of our own destinies. If the subconscious could not be tamed, then humans faced an uncertain and unstable world, and the last thing Americans needed was more insecurity.

If Americans couldn't control the social environment, they could at least know the ultimate power of God. Meyer explains, "being practical, popular psychologies promised power [and] the largest power of all being God's" (13). To make God knowable, mind curists constructed God as "mind." That is, God could be found through the application of thought control. This was mind cure's appeal—the revelation that everyone, with practice, could directly influence the force of the subconscious. Interestingly, Meyer says, it was "no accident" that William James's book began with an analysis of a psychology operating as a theology, which was essentially the case with the new spiritualities he was studying (13).

Around the same time the new spiritualities were appearing, health reformers in the mid-nineteenth century connected spiritual beliefs with the healthfulness of the physical body, advocating for various healing modalities. About Mary Baker Eddy, the founder of Christian Science, for example, Badaracco writes, "Since Christ never used drugs to heal in the Bible, Eddy questioned the morality of their use as well as their efficacy" (51). And New Thought held the premise that "people could simply, by an act of will and conviction, cure their own illnesses and create heaven on earth," Robbins says (22). New ideas were surfacing about the advantages of eating specific diets emphasizing whole, unrefined foods to address illness. Among these early reformers were Rev. Sylvester Graham, a Presbyterian minister who invented the graham cracker in the 1830s, and the Seventh Day Adventists who opened the sanitarium in Battle Creek, Michigan, in 1866, which eventually hired a certain Doctor Kellogg to run the operation. Kellogg and his brother began devising health foods we know now as forms of crispy-flaked cereals, nut butters, and meat analogs.

In her research on modalities of healing among early twentieth-century Protestants, Klassen notes that many church-related newspapers accepted advertisements for foods represented as both physically fortifying and spiritually uplifting: "In accepting these advertisements, with their blend of quasi-scientific proof and personal testimony, these church newspapers at least tacitly sanctioned a view of health that deemed it an affair of science, nation, religion, and the market" (Klassen 823).

The connection of health with spiritual sensibilities remains strong in America, perhaps because, as LaFleur says, "If the human being's body is its own ready-made canvas, it is also its most readily accessible altar or temple" (37). From Kellogg's sanitarium to the Seventh Day Adventists' focus on wholesome clean food, "alternative dietary lifestyles are important forms of alternative healing practices," say Kaptchuk and Eisenberg, and "the themes of 'nature, vegetarianism, and social/spiritual regeneration proved a persuasively attractive and integrative vision for many people" (17). The authors add that often it is not the actual diet or lifestyle itself that is the goal, but rather the symbolism of the diet or lifestyle that can be used "to enhance more esoteric social, political or spiritual goals consistent with a religious-cultural movement" (18).

These same proclivities surfaced in the 1960s through what Baer refers to as a "holistic health" movement, one that links up with "New Age healing." In the *Medical Anthropology Quarterly*, Baer quotes Melton, Clark, and Kelly: "'New Age and Holistic Health movements in theory exist independently, but they are united philosophically by one central concept: that the individual person is responsible for his or her own life and for seeking out the means of transformation needed to achieve a better quality of life'" (qtd. in Baer 235).

Baer grounds the holistic health movement in the "counterculture of the late 1960s" and its "disenchantment with mainstream culture" (234–35) brought on by U.S. involvement in Vietnam, increasing separation from nature, the routinization of labor, mounting environmental crises, and tensions around race and gender. Just as was the case with the emergence of New Thought spiritualities, the holistic health movement and the New Age offered a response to the social upheaval and insecurities of the times. The New Age, in particular, "[sought] to create a 'new planetary culture' that emphasizes inner tranquility, wellness, harmony, unity, self-realization, self-actualization, and the attainment of a higher level of consciousness" (Grossinger, qtd. in Baer 236). While Sutcliffe and Bowman say the "New Age turns out to be merely a particular codeword in a larger field of modern religious experimentation" (10), it imparts an understanding of a "guiding transcendent value," an understanding of the "universe as an interconnected field," says Michael York ("New Age" 364).

The New Age focus on spiritual advancement, Michael York says, sent New Agers "on a quest to find and develop the higher self above the phenomenal self or ego, for 'Spiritual Truth' beyond empirical realities" ("Wanting" 26). These popular psycho-spiritualities were also responding to consumer culture by embracing individualism, even in matters of religion, upholding the individual's right to spiritually shop or "seek" (see Heelas and Woodhead; Roof; Sutcliffe). As part of these processes, the New Age's inclusivity of traditions, faiths, and deities required and accommodated the rise of an increasingly global marketplace of spiritually symbolic resources (see Heelas and Woodhead; Roof; Sutcliffe). This inclusivity and the emphasis on the individual—as an autonomous and legitimate authority of spiritual knowledge—displeased the Vatican so much that in 2003 it issued a report on the threats to Catholicism posed by New Age spiritualities and fads. According to the *New Zealand Herald,* "the report acknowledges 'In Western culture, in particular, the appeal of "alternative" approaches to spirituality is very strong. New forms of psychological affirmation of the individual have become very popular among Catholics'" (Popham).

New Age holism called for a balance among the body, mind, and spirit gained through attention to diet and fitness, but also through spiritual practice including mindfulness. Unification as a theme presented a logical response to the fracturing times of the 1960s but also to the pressures of late capitalism that increasingly reduced the individual as well as society to parts and particularities, emphasizing the rational, for example, or the specialization of labor in the market. In the New Age, Riches says, "The person is indissolubly spiritual, mental, emotional (intuitive), as well as physical. For the *New Age* individual, the means to fulfillment is in the family, in economic affairs, in political life, and in a holistic balance relating to the self" (Riches 670).

These interconnections flow through the positive psycho-spirituality that emerged through the media in the 1990s, one that took New Age interests and married them with the very rationality to which the movement was responding. These quantum spiritualities are most visible through the plethora of films, DVDs, books, documentaries, websites, and salons that have sprung up around quantum physics. Perhaps the two best known of these are the products mentioned earlier, *The Secret* and *What the Bleep Do We Know!?* The marriage of science, positive psychology, and spirituality is a burgeoning field, and *Bleep* and *Secret* have illustrious company, both in terms of sales and author fame, including Deepak Chopra's book *Quantum Healing*, Natalie Reid's *5 Steps to a Quantum Life*, and Sandra Taylor's *Quantum Success*.

What the Bleep, released in 2004, was a sleeper "indie" turned cultural phenomenon, now described as a "movement." *The Secret* (Prime Time Productions, 2005) started life much the same way. Both were released without the fanfare of movie trailers and promotional advertisements, produced outside of the glamour and finances of Hollywood. In the case of *The Secret*, it was a viral marketing success story. Maybe *The Secret* should have been titled "the surprise," because the DVD topped the charts with more than two million copies sold. That popularity spawned the subsequent book, which reached the number one slot on the *New York Times* Best Seller list in March 2007.

Bleep was the fifth highest grossing documentary in the United States by the middle of the decade. The DVD soared to top rankings at Amazon.com, and the film was named the organization's number 1 "DVD surprise of the year" in 2005. Now in international distribution, the DVD and book are available from Canada to the Russian Federation, and have been translated into Croatian, Danish, Spanish, and German. This enormous popularity generated sequels and spin-off products, including additional DVDs and books but also study groups, newsletters, and seminars.

These quantum spiritualities apply quantum (cellular) physics to old American stand-bys: the pursuit of happiness and the idea of success, each once again drenched in the mythology of the individual and his or her unlimited capacity to expand, accumulate, and experience. In the case of the quantum spiritualities, they hearken back to the category of self-help work popularized by L. Ron Hubbard in *Dianetics* and by Maxwell Maltz in *Psycho-Cybernetics*. These works share a conviction that you are what you think—that is, thoughts create your reality.

In *Bleep* and *Secret*, this core truth is represented as the "the law of attraction," which states that whatever thoughts you have will attract more of the same. Scientist and spirituality author Gregg Braden puts it this way: "The world that unfolds around us is simply a mirror of what is happening within us." In Braden's view, this includes natural phenomena such as the climate, which can also be affected by our thoughts and feelings.

But the focus on the intentionality doesn't preclude the idea of a higher source; like the New Thought and New Age movements, the path to that source and, in some cases the source itself, lies within us. In *The Secret* this higher source is a perfectly marketable divine, meaning that, as in the New Age, the higher authority is a concept that accommodates almost any creed by representing the divine as "perfect energy." In fact, according to *The Secret*, energy is another word for God, and the entire matter of locating the divine is more of a semantics problem than anything else, a case of using different words to describe the same thing. *The Secret* states, "in essence, both science and religion describe the same phenomena."

Using quantum physics and neurophysiology, the quantum spiritualities explain how we literally make ourselves, a power once reserved for God. We "work" on ourselves not because our industriousness is pleasing to a God but because it *creates* God. Human beings, then, are hard-wired to be the masters of their destinies, but it requires training of the mind to awaken to this possibility—to cultivate a specific sort of consciousness. *Bleep* declares that all of us are God in the "making" and that the term is actually only a "placeholder name for those parts of the world that are sublime and transcendental" (Arntz, Chasse, and Vincente). "I am one with the great being—how did this get taken out of religion?" asks Ramtha, the channeled being who speaks through the body of J. Z. Knight in *Bleep*. Ramtha's very being is an idea that transcends Christian notions of life and death and Western understanding about space and time in general.

All of this is to say that the reality you experience can be changed to your liking, and this is meant to be a message of hope, even if it is relayed through rather mind-bending tales of chaos and string theories. These spiritual expressions reclaim magic and the religious mysticism found in Mesmerism (and in the New Age), which Protestantism had thoroughly debunked. Of course, the processes in the quantum spiritual products also align strongly with various strains within indigenous and Eastern faith traditions that speak to other ways of being and knowing, including the taming of the mind through meditation and the links between such practices and a notion of wholeness or holistic health.

Contemporary spiritual author and medical doctor Deepak Chopra (also the author of a quantum book) and integrative medicine practitioner Andrew Weil have attempted to bridge the science and philosophies of East and West, to merge spirituality with science as the path to holistic healing. Baer says, "For Chopra, the path to a healthy and fulfilling life is integrally intertwined with prayer and the broader quest for spirituality," adding that for Chopra "God is another name for infinite intelligence" (240). According to product marketing materials, this is a state we create individually and collectively as part of the process of becoming healthy.

LOHAS in the Positive Thinking Tradition

LOHAS maps the nature of existence and our knowledge of it through the concept of holistic health—where labor on the self is the primary tool to attain that state and is done with the understanding that such work is performed to attain and align with the sacred. The healthy self in LOHAS is a unified and balanced mind, body, and spirit. Like the positive psychologies and psycho-spiritualities we have just traversed, LOHAS starts with the focus on that "ready-made canvas"—the individual body.

Just as Protestants of early America understood that they were on an "errand in the wilderness" (Miller)—sent by God to cultivate the wild lands of America as a metaphor for sculpting themselves into a more God-worthy form—LOHAS audiences or consumers are encouraged to embark on their own inner errand, to heal divisions within.

An article in *Body+Soul* states, "In today's world, holistic is about interdependent parts that make up the whole" (Stark 98). The article continues, saying, "When they all work as one, undissected, you can live a balanced life. These interdependent parts include your physical well being, your mental and spiritual states, and how you interact with the environment." The reuniting of our physicality with our emotions, our intuition, our souls, and our intellect is what integrative medical doctor Judith Orloff, interviewed on *Oasis TV*, calls a "a democracy of healing, wherein every aspect of our being is granted a vote in the search for total health."

Everyone has, it seems, "total health" at birth, but thanks to the effects of late modernity and late capitalism, most of us end up "in shards," says Gabrielle Roth, a New York–based theater director, dance teacher, and recording artist, in *Body+Soul* (70). The idea that we are by nature holistic is a direct reparation of the Cartesian splitting of mind from matter, and LOHAS explicitly acknowledges this Western development, treating this unnatural and unfortunate side effect of the Enlightenment as the historical moment that led us to a ruinous over-reliance on science, rationalization, physical labor, and materiality. The following excerpt from *Spirituality & Health* speaks to this: "We'd love to talk about how Descartes, Gnosticism, and the narrow materialism of the Enlightenment era drove a wedge between body and spirit, a schism that's led to the modern sense of Balkanization and meaninglessness. . . . It was well explained by T. George Harris in the preview issue of *Spirituality & Health* magazine. He said we're now breaking through a matching pair of contradictions that have outlived their value" (*Spirituality & Health*).

Considering how much the discourse strives for a nondual understanding of holistic nature, it is surprising to see such a dual take on the subject of the mind in LOHAS texts. On the one hand, the mind is regarded as the essential and primary tool for reformation of the world—through science, creativity, and awareness or consciousness. On the other hand, we are warned of the threats of rationalization and are encouraged to develop other muscles, the irrational, if you will.

In the past, society associated the irrational with the female, and various physical complaints and emotional feelings such as "hysteria" were cited as evidence. This had the effect of rendering women unsuitable for the type of intellectual work required for the new stratagems of industrialization. *Spirituality & Health* says, "Reason and mind, associated with masculinity, are considered trustworthy, while emotion and body, associated with the feminine, are seen as dangerous" (Greenspan 38). The article goes on to say that this "patriarchal favoritism" not only caused an emphasis on "emotional control" at the expense of "emotional flow," but that it prevented us from experiencing the learning that comes with "painful emotions" that serve as "sources of vitality, understanding, and transformation" (38).

Emotions in LOHAS lifestyle media are the "messengers of authenticity" (Neimark 54); creativity becomes the mark of the unique self; and by listening to the heart, one can access the "wild and powerful" parts of the self (53).

In the New Age and in LOHAS, the texts celebrate other ways of knowing, those irrational sweet spots of intuition, divination, and even physical orgasm. Intuition and emotions are held up as ideal ways in which to mediate the intellect and to achieve our human potential. In *Yoga Journal,* author and meditation teacher Sally Kempton writes, "With the 20/20 vision of hindsight, I could recall dozens of occasions when I 'knew' something and ignored it, because some social consideration, desire, doubt or fear spoke louder than my own inner wisdom. But I've also discovered that the more I'm able to listen to that inner knowing, the deeper my sense of personal authenticity becomes" ("Guided" 87). Even "science has confirmed that the body has more than one brain, just as shamans and poets have always said," says Zuniga in *Spirituality & Health* (26). Scientific rationality is treated as one of the competing paradigms in LOHAS, or what John Ehrenberg refers to as a set of convictions (90).

These other ways of knowing are not just means toward an end, they are considered in LOHAS culture to be essential to good health, which is why the discourse attempts to bridge the long-standing conflict between the rational and the irrational. For example, Judith Orloff says, "it is our birthright, both as health-care givers and health-care recipients, to reclaim our intuition, restore it to full standing in the medical realm and thereby carry medicine into the future." When we "embrace multiple ways of knowing and being in the world," we not only "honor the fullness of our lived experience," but we ground it in a "broad and inclusive approach to science" (Schlitz, "Child" 12).

In the *Evergreen Monthly* magazine, Winninghoff explains the historical distinction as one of fast versus slow thinking. "Fast Thinking, which is linear and logical, is what we do under time pressure," Winninghoff says, "but it is Slow Thinking, which we do in the shower or walking the beach that results in insight and creative epiphanies." The latter is "alive," "unpredictable," and "free." With this, Winninghoff then validates the irrational by linking it up with sacred American mythologies: slow thinking is "a key element required for independent thinking—the true recipe for a true land of the free" (62).

To develop this dual approach to thinking, the LOHAS lifestyle media have ample suggestions for products and practices. In *Spirituality & Health,* for example, the author finds "laptop journaling every morning a way to get the analyzing over with, so I can experience the rest of the moments of the day Just as They Are, not Just As I Think Them To Be" (Cunningham). Lassoing the mind enables one to experience some sort of objective reality that stands outside of thinking, which is contradictory to much of the intention-setting discourse in the quantum spiritualities. But certainly it is a clear nod to the downside of the hyperactivity and speed of modern times that impairs holism.

An article in *Conscious Choice* magazine illustrates this: "As strange as it may seem, I'm addicted to my fast-paced way of living. At the same time, my hustle-bustle lifestyle is driving me absolutely insane. Again my teacher weighed in, saying that meditation would not only give me peace of mind but it would help me confront my fear of change as well" (Paris 33).

We are urged to quiet the mind that wants to behave like a chattering monkey, jumping from stimulus to stimulus in the consumer-centric economy with nary a thought for anything but immediate self gratification. Dance therapist Gabrielle Roth says that the goal of our self-labor "comes down to the eternal battle between ego and soul" (70). She says that the ego wants to "define us, limit us, diminish us," and that its "loud, reactive voices try to overwhelm our intuition—the language of our souls, that spark of divine wisdom we're all born with." To Roth, the labor to quiet this ego is really a struggle to "reclaim our integrity" and that, she says, "is the mission of our spiritual lives" (70).

In *Body+Soul*, a writer explains how his true self finally breaks through the obfuscating layers of modernity in a bid to be heard: "Finally one afternoon during your commute home, you hear yourself. You say you need to nurture your soul." The writer explains the "symptoms" of the ignored spirit: "A dull sense of separation from my own heart. Uncertainty about what I loved. A feeling that even my family didn't really know me. Doubt that a career path was the only thing worth striving for" (Clores 76).

Quieting the mind allows us to access these other sites of our selves, such as the body, which is to be treated as "someone, not something," states Neimark, in *Spirituality & Health*. "It has its own desires and wisdom and can sense danger" (55). Through the body, we can access a wisdom that rises from emotions, creativity, and the heart. Stewart Hoover (*Religion*) refers to expressive acts of the body as the "repressed modes," because of the manner in which these were subjugated in Protestantism. These acts not only deliver sensual pleasure but also tap into wells of creativity in ways that, it seems, the mind cannot.

Still, Margo pointed out to me that even in the LOHAS and healthy living industries, there is a tendency for people to forget to tune into their bodies. Margo said she had a "contrarian point of view" with regard to healthy living because "so many people are so stressed out because they think they aren't living the kind of healthy lives they should, according to the latest popular view." She said people needed to become more self-referential, to listen to their own bodies, and their own purpose.

"All of us have our own natural, individual ways of tuning in to this internal wisdom—whether we feel it in the gut, in the heart or as some other form of inner sensation," says yoga teacher Sally Kempton in *Yoga Journal* ("Guided" 87). Gabrielle Roth says in *Body+Soul,* "It's the fastest, cleanest, most joyful way to break out of your ego chains, liberate your intuition and become deeply rooted in the mysterious working of your inner world" (69).

No matter what mode and method we use to lure forth our inner world, the process of self-development in LOHAS serves in the way Arne Naess, progenitor of the philosophy of Deep Ecology, refers to as "self-realization," a spiritual process of inner searching and examination of the meaning, purpose, and responsibility of life (qtd. in Sessions 7). Naess saw this as central to the ecological sensibility. LOHAS finds it the key path to consciousness of a truly sustainable world.

In *Spirituality & Health,* Parker Palmer, the best selling spiritual author and the recipient of ten honorary doctorates, states: "True self will come to our rescue, if we let it. The divided life is pathological, so it always gives rise to symptoms—and if we acknowledge the symptoms, we may be able to treat the disease. In this phase, we reach for integration by reordering our onstage lives around our backstage values and beliefs . . . This is the yearning to be 'centered,' a word that is, I would guess, one of the most frequently encountered in the spiritual literature of recent decades" (42).

If we each hold a truer self buried somewhere within us, it seems we must each have been born with unique life maps but lost our way under the corrupting influences of modern life. This mirrors the contention put forth in the quantum spiritualities. But an assumption that we each have a pure self also means that the idea of self is essentialized: there is an inherent "nature" of yourself: something resides within you, whether you are aware of it, that was there from birth and lies beyond affect from the external world. "We inherit a set of predispositions that make our brains eager to embrace a higher power," says an article in *Body+Soul* (Hamer 110). Tucked into this is the same sort of transcendentalism found in the Kantian treatment of *noumena,* the mysterious beingness that cannot be proven or disproved to exist. Woodhead says this essence of beingness may "refer to the belief/awareness that there is some reality more real, more valuable, more important and more extensive than that revealed by science, and to the practices by which people hope to get in touch with this reality" (177).

By getting in touch with our true, primordial self, we tap into an innate wisdom or "inner knowing" (Louden 70). In *Spirituality & Health,* Schlitz says that the ancients understood the presence of wisdom or "inner guidance" that exists in children ("60-Second" 12). Parker Palmer echoes this, declaring that this inner something is the soul, and it is perfect at birth but immediately comes under attack from exterior and interior "deforming" forces caused by "social cancers" such as racism and social injustice and personal demons such as "jealousy, resentment, self-doubt, and fear" (40).

Schlitz says the soul was called "the Daimon, or divine" by Socrates and that "William James used the term 'noetic' to denote insight unplumbed by the discursive intellect—a kind of direct knowing" ("Child" 12). But Parker Palmer makes a point that follows the logic in *What the Bleep* and *The Secret* when he says that whatever we call *it* simply doesn't matter. Despite philosophical debates "about what to call this core of our humanity," Palmer himself is "no stickler for precision." He recites various usages, including Thomas Merton's "true self," Buddhism's understanding of "original nature or big self," the Quakers' "inner teacher or the inner light," and the humanists' "identity and integrity." But through all this, Palmer says, "in popular parlance, people often call it soul" (40).

The soul, then, is something unique to the individual, but one linked to a shared consciousness. Palmer says this commonality provides the "objective, ontological reality of selfhood that keeps us from reducing ourselves, or each other, to biological mechanisms, psychological projections, sociological constructs or raw material to be manufactured into whatever society needs—diminishments of our humanity that constantly threaten the quality of our lives" (40).

This part of the LOHAS discourse follows a middle path between Hegel's claim that existence is that which can be rationalized and a priori claims to truth and validity. This is an interesting juxtaposition to Western philosophical traditions of rationalism and humanism. LOHAS attempts to overcome the received dichotomy of science and spirituality captured in this quote from Emile Durkheim: "In all the history of human thought, there exists no other example of two categories of things so profoundly differentiated or so radically opposed to one another" (in Hoover and Venturelli 254).

With a nod to quantum physics and the quantum spiritualities, LOHAS texts explain that when one taps into the true self, one can exert the power of intention, beaming it upon specific goals in order to generate biochemical and psychological changes. It proves, says Schull in *Whole Life Times*, that we have the power to "interrupt the old programming" and to become as "gods"—creating our own realities (24). This mirrors the intense type of self-transformation elemental to religious life.

LOHAS is filled with testimonials and biographies about how people discover their true selves. These individuals have undertaken personal development strategies in order to heighten their consciousness. While some of these people are well-known personalities such as Ram Dass, Andrew Cohen, Caroline Myss, Andrew Weil, Ken Wilbur and Deepak Chopra, many more are workers, parents, activists, and consumers, but their message is the same: with work, any self can transform into a happier, healthier person.

The motivation to transform and to convert varies. Some individuals are inspired by mentors, some are motivated by supernatural experiences, and still others are drawn in by hobbies and personal interests.

Andy Lipkis, founder of TreePeople in Los Angeles, for example, became an environmental activist in summer camp at age fifteen by planting a meadow in the remains of an old parking lot. He went on to "challenge the California Department of Forestry to hand over its surplus stock—8,000 seedlings—and the California Conservation Project was born" (see http://www.treepeople .org). Today, TreePeople is one of the largest environmental groups in California with 15,000 members planting and maintaining more than two million trees, according to the website. Lipkis says that his own mission is to "inspire people to take personal responsibility and participate in making Southern California a sustainable urban environment" (Gili 21).

A frequent speaker at LOHAS Forums, Ray Anderson, founder of the international carpet and textile firm Interface Inc., said the motivation to transform his company along more environmental lines was an "epiphany" that came after his sixtieth birthday, which left him thinking about what sort of "legacy" his "creation" would leave on the planet: "It was like a spear in the chest and gave me all the vision I needed for what our company could be" (qtd. in Nachman-Hunt, "Ray Anderson's" 17). Anderson once said, "By our civilization's definition, I'm a captain of industry—in the eyes of many a kind of modern day hero" (qtd. in Shalmy 27). Interviewed in the documentary *The Corporation,* Anderson admitted that people who run businesses the way he had in the past would someday be put in jail. One of the film's producers, Mark Achbar, said he found Anderson's admission "stunning" (Shalmy 26–27).

Not all transformations and conversions manifest with Anderson's clarity. Often, there's a trial of sorts, a deliberation, isolation—voluntary or forced— and judgment. And some, despite desiring change, may not be able to dial in their vision or path. In this case, the texts warn against impersonation, betrayal of identity, and avoiding "conflict, challenge and change," as *Spirituality & Health* says (P. Palmer).

The texts speak to keeping faith with one's inner voice, remaining patient and true to the dream. *Spirituality & Health* states, "The thread of trust is not knowing everything" (Helwig). The faithful will be provided the resources needed in much the same message we have heard in the world's religions, where parishioners and practitioners journey through layers and levels of learning through the study of scripture, participation in physical practices, and the acceptance of certain dogmas and rules about how to live.

Leadership trainer Margaret Wheatley encourages people to not despair during difficult times because "[w]hen life has kind of dissolved around you, you're at your most humble and that state of humility is really a state of sur-rendering" (Rosanoff 75–76). According to a *Yoga Journal* article, "By bring-ing radical acceptance to our inner experience, we recognize and transform our own limiting stories and emotional reactions" (Brach 122). Evoking the quantum spiritualities, a *Body+Soul* article says that by focusing one's aware-ness on the whole self, all sorts of opportunities can arise. "When you ask what is possible, you move into the future and you engage creativity, vision, desire, all of those things," says Wheatley (qtd. in Rosanoff 75–76).

The awareness that you bring to that vision is proportionate to the de-gree of improvement or happiness you receive, meaning that "setting your intentions" is vital in order to birth your dreams, the same process we have seen in the positive thinking psycho-spiritualities. Inspirations are the inner beacons; they motion us onward to our path. "Don't just mull over them, daydream about how the world or we might change, and then allow them to evaporate," says Helwig. Instead, "weave them into reality as part of [the] spiritual journey."

As Greenspan writes in *Spirituality & Health,* intention is the means by which the heart, mind, and spirit are engaged and focused and the vehicle by which one can even "use [their] pain to set the intelligence of the dark emotions in gear. . . . What does your story of suffering ask of you? What is your best intention for using it for healing and transformation?" (40). This is a start-where-you-are process in LOHAS. Finding your True Self doesn't mean spending countless hours on the meditation mat. There are hundreds of ways in which to balance, or heal, the mind, body, and spirit, no matter what condition yours might be in. Even doing backbends in yoga becomes a way in which to "cultivate the deeper kind of flexibility it takes to face our limitations with acceptance and self-love" (Dowdle 8). The key, then, is to build on your strengths. "Who are you really" asks Spayde in the *Utne Reader,* in a section that explores how "Americans find their true callings" (Spayde 61). By doing so, one connects with one's soul and finds one's higher purpose, says Susan Davis, founder and president of Capital Missions Company in Elkhorn, Wisconsin (qtd. in Middendorf, "For a Higher" 50).

In LOHAS, transformation and conversion are not so much about eradicat-ing parts of the self as they are about reinventing and integrating. At LOHAS Forum 2009, for example, Anthony Zolezzi, founder of Pet Promise and Bubba Gump Shrimp Company, said his latest reinvention is plastics. His new company, called GreenOps, "will be a consumer revolution through plastic," he said. "It's a miracle product when used properly." Leading the opening presentation titled "Re-inventing Ourselves," Zolezzi said, "It's a different world; . . . there are no more resources, so reinvention means something very different now." Reinvention, he said, means making the planet a better place and putting heart and soul into the process.

Bringing our "selves" into wholeness in LOHAS, as part of what Baer has called the holistic health movement, is necessary for genuine health. Janesse Bruce, editor-in-chief of *Body+Soul*, once said the "holistic culture" that includes "natural eating, balanced fitness, a more natural, integrative approach to health, healthy homes, and spiritual practices" gave shape to today's healthy lifestyle. To attain this lifestyle, we've seen how LOHASians are encouraged to follow their "inner knowing" in order to, in the words of *Body+Soul*, "find ourselves naturally reconnecting back to wholeheartedness" (Louden 70), but there is another reason why we are to do this, another important part of the LOHAS construction of "health." By "doing what gives us the most joy," says Louden in *Body+Soul*, we "most effectively offer our gifts to the world" (70). The result, said Cynthia Sheets, CEO of Wisdom Media, is a "paradigm shift that is expressing itself in every area of life" (qtd. in Garcia, "Personal Development" 21).

"Penny" has been an editor in the LOHAS space for eighteen years. I asked her if health and sustainability were related. "They totally are," came her fervent answer. But does one lead from the other, I asked? She didn't hesitate: "To be healthy means you can then be mindful about sustainability." I asked her what she thought made a healthy person. She laughed and responded, "Balancing the mind, body, and spirit!" By this point in the interview, we had encountered that phrase several times. This time I asked her to explain specifically what those three things had to do with being healthy. She said she used the phrase "mind, body, spirit" so often in our interview because "it takes those three things in balance to be sustainable; I really feel that strongly. And that's why, for me, it turns into spiritual living because I need to be healthy to help society and I need all three dimensions to do that. That's your body."

An article in *Experience Life* magazine goes further by claiming sustainability should not be a concept linked solely to "the environment and natural resources," but rather "sustainability principles are equally relevant to other parts of our lives, including our health, happiness and collective well-being" (Gerasimo 40). This is the broader idea of holistic health whereby the healed individual comes to realize his or her interconnectedness with the world, with other people, with environments, and with organisms and forms.

At LOHAS Forum 2009, for example, the central ballroom was nearly filled in anticipation of a presentation by consultant and psychologist John

Marshall Roberts, who was there to speak about the evolution of thinking. Armed with an impressive slide show, Roberts explained that thought had matured through a process of seven stages to reach the currently emerging level eight, or holistic thinking. Roberts flashed a slide on the big screen bearing a quote from Albert Einstein, whom Roberts called "a famous level seven [systems] thinker" and a man who naturally understood holistic thinking. The quote read: "A human being is a part of the whole, called by us, 'Universe,' a part limited in time and space. He experiences himself, his thoughts and feelings as something separated from the rest—a kind of optical delusion of his consciousness."

It is a delicate balancing act in LOHAS between promoting personal development—the touchstone of many lifestyle market organizations—and framing it as a socially minded act and thus avoiding the charges of overt navel-gazing and narcissism, two missiles commonly leveled at the New Age and at the quantum spiritualities. In the LOHAS texts, as part of the transformation and conversion tales, individuals carefully explain that their creative and personal development expressions are not simply done for self-gratification. Consider, for example, the case of Terry Helwig, a human development specialist who created the Thread Project, an international art exhibit that represents a "fabric of humanity" by using strands and bits of cloth from ordinary people around the world (http://www.threadproject.com). Helwig explains why she initiated the project, saying, "My heart wanted to create a cloth of humanity, cloths that celebrate our diversity and symbolize our unity, cloths that can be repositories of stories and goodwill." Self-development should add value to the world, in other words.

At LOHAS Forum 2009, spirituality author Andrew Cohen spoke to the nature of the relationship between self-development and social responsibility. In his seminar, Cohen said, "Narcissism is a cultural epidemic and it is a cultural problem. The new Enlightenment is helping us to find a new way to live to overcome narcissism. Your body and mind are the vehicles for consciousness." To Cohen, the new Enlightenment is the recognition that we need to transcend our own cognition—our narcissism that we are the center of our experiences. "When I speak of Enlightenment," he said, "I speak of the Eastern meaning of Enlightenment, an awareness . . . a transcendence, but not a transcendence of the life process." Cohen explained in his hourlong presentation that human beings and the notion of God are one in the greater cosmic intelligence. This intelligence produced us and we produce it in return. This, he said, is "evolutionary intelligence."

Cohen's insistence on the interdependent nature of this Enlightenment—one that holds the collective welfare foremost—provides another way to think about the quantum spiritualities. The media lambasted both *What the Bleep* and *The Secret*, for example, for promoting egregious self-satisfaction and materialism, saying that by grounding the God-force within the individual, the focus is on how individuals act within their culture rather than how the culture acts on individuals. That, went the criticism, elided the structures of power that oppressed individuals and made the world seem as if all people were perfectly at liberty to do whatever they like or could imagine, an insinuation that many critics found deeply troubling.

In a 2005 lecture in Boulder, Colorado, *Bleep* filmmaker William Arntz seemed to be trying to overcome these critiques by saying he hoped that *Bleep* would spark a paradigm shift similar to what occurred in the 1960s and the way in which Rock and Roll ignited new perspectives, acts, and ways of being. By using the Law of Attraction as explained in *Bleep*, Arntz explained, one could use intention-setting positively so that "as a planetary species, we will become one exalted, vibrating organism." The work of setting our intentions to change our own lives serves as the starter for healing the social and the natural world.

When asked in an interview with *The LOHAS Journal* how she defined personal development, Marilyn McGuire, president of the Networking Alternatives for Publishers, Retailers & Artists Inc. (NAPRA), responded that it was a matter of both "inner development" and "external development of the person." McGuire differentiated these processes, explaining that inner development meant understanding that the body, mind, and spirit, were "essential components of the whole person." She said inner development has a more spiritual focus and moves the practitioner toward greater development in the areas of awareness, self-realization, and enlightenment (qtd. in Garcia, "Personal Development" 20).

All of this seems to say that individuals should use the healed or true self as a barometer of truth. At LOHAS Forum 2005 in Los Angeles, for example, Nina Utne, then publisher of *Utne Reader*, said in her presentation: "The heart is the real locus of the tipping point." She was referring to the book by Malcolm Gladwell, *The Tipping Point*, in which the author explains how social change occurs through the attainment of critical mass. "Consumers make change, and it's as simple as listening to our hearts and making small choices," Utne said.

3. A Vision of Health

Self, Society, and the Natural World

Sam, CEO of a chain of national LOHAS-related magazines, considered my question: did social and environmental change figure into the ideals of the health?

"Healing the natural world, society, and yourself are completely interrelated," he told me. "I don't believe you can heal yourself and do inner work without engaging in protection and healing of the planet and pursuing healing in the social and political realm, between people and nations." He added, "I reject that you can reach an inner level of Nirvana somehow when you are sitting in a country that is at war or even sitting on a planet that is moving toward ecological crisis. You must be involved in those three levels."

Likewise, Margo, the publisher of a national consumer publication, told me that bridging the idea of personal health to social and environmental health was not a choice: "You can't really have one without the other," she says. Too, Richard said his board of directors had asked him to integrate new concepts of sustainability into the company's key consumer publication: "Because [the magazine] has been primarily focused on health in a narrower definition of it, relating to physical health, and I hope to expand that concept to include mental, spiritual, environmental, social justice, and economic health." I asked him if these areas were interconnected, and he replied they did indeed "all work together."

The Ideology of Health

On the surface of things, the notion of health doesn't seem to be such a complicated concept. We know when we feel healthy as opposed to feeling sick, for example. You miss work due to influenza and you are paid, hopefully, from your sick-leave account; the days you miss are deducted from the total days you are allotted. But let's say, for the sake of argument, that you miss work because you enjoy gambling and you think betting on the ponies will be a better way to spend your time than sitting in your work cubicle. Gambling addiction is also considered a sickness in American culture, but your honesty with your boss about this condition nonetheless gets you fired. You have just been ideologically compromised, thanks to a host of disciplining effects of sociohistoric influences.

The twentieth-century philosopher Michel Foucault made a similar argument about how some ideas about health and normalcy in culture trump others. He theorized that *norms* about health—those ideas taken at face value and reiterated in a million polite conversations every day among people as a "given"—should be seen for what they are: expressions of power. Why should it be that the flu is a sickness inflicted upon us and one we tolerate, while gambling is a sickness we choose and that society does not tolerate, for example?

Foucault was very interested in how society defined abnormality as deviant behavior. He might respond to our question above by saying that certain narratives, ideals and concepts operate in societies as types of conceptual land-grabs, as claim stakes pounded into the cultural turf. Whoever gets there first or who has the most muscle lays the claim that holds. These *truth claims* aren't inherently real or better, any more than claim stakes are real, objective boundaries in nature. We know claim stakes and survey markers are human-made, legitimated by laws that have the power to bespeak symbolic boundaries into being.

These legitimated constructions rise from various struggles in the culture over the right to establish knowledge and "facts." These struggles might occur over the course of time and take place among a heterogeneous ensemble of discourses, institutions, architectural forms, regulatory decisions, laws, administrative measures, scientific statements, and philosophical, moral, and philanthropic propositions (Rabinow 1984). History shows us that claims about what is true and what is not, change. Some truth claims fade, only to reemerge; others are constructed in their ebb and flow. It's all part of the contest over meaning, over the claim of what constitutes knowledge or truth. If you need convincing of this, just think about the past popularity of bloodletting. It fell out of favor with the evolution of medical knowledge, but in its heyday, you would have been considered mad to argue with the doctor, and doing so could have multiplied your problems by landing you in another questionable medical institution, the mental asylum.

The question is how do we come to hold some ideas to be truer than others? Karl Marx used the term "ideology" to refer to the manner in which various power holders in society could distort and shroud structuring processes underlying social life. Decades later, sociologists were not so interested in this overt sense of "power" as they were in the techniques used to delude the masses, and they started to study instead the manner in which ideas *function* in the social world. This was done with the understanding that meaning making is a complex process that engages multiple dimensions of life that make us all complicit and resistant at the same time. It wasn't something sold to an unsuspecting public, people who were somehow less able to see the real conditions of their lives than the controlling power elites. These scientists were more concerned with how meaning was generated rather than whether ideas were true or untrue, in other words (Eagleton, *Ideology*).

John Thompson said, "meaning is mobilized in the social world and serves thereby to bolster up individuals and groups who occupy positions of power" (*Ideology* 56). That is, power isn't only relegated to those sites we traditionally think of as "powerful"—the military or religion, for example. Rather, everyone is vying for power all the time as part of his or her daily life. As a result, discourses develop. Certain configurations of meaning become useful to some as a way to convince others, and the meaning continues to be circulated in ways that become familiar to a population, to the point that people begin to assume that it represents the truth, taking assertions at face value or without expressing much resistance.

As a discourse, LOHAS, too, competes with other narratives of health and sustainability. There are discourses that maintain conditions of power, and there are discourses that resist the status quo, called "contestatory" discourse by John Thompson, who describes these as "challenging, disrupting interventions" that serve as incipient forms of critiques of other, existing ideologies (*Ideology* 68). But, LOHAS is both: it sustains an ideology about the free market and about American liberalism in general, but it also contests the form and direction of these.

The way in which we represent or convey meaning is called "signification," and the media and the marketplace are central in signifying processes—pivotal to the creation, contextualization, and distribution of truth claims. A "mediazation of culture" has occurred (Thompson, *Media*) whereby we have seen an unprecedented array and availability of symbolic forms circulated in the world through global and globalizing media. Individuals use these symbolic forms to make sense of the world and even to shape the world to some degree. Innovations in media technology, consolidation of media organizations, and the expansion of media around the world means that media have come to insert into and even replace other, traditional means of social interaction. It also means that mediated narratives have become fundamental to the way in which we organize our experiences, and perhaps even define our experiences (see Cronon, *Uncommon*; Hoover, *Religion*; Thompson, *Media*).

LOHAS media and market have generated and circulated an idea of healthfulness, as we've seen. And, as is the case with most discourses, it isn't completely new. Like a pueblo, it is built over and over again on the foundations of predecessors. It creates new bricks out of ancient clay. In the case of LOHAS, we've also seen that the substance of its making can be traced to the therapeutic narratives about self-help that emerged from American Protestantism. And these narratives were largely dependent on mediated processes, particularly on print culture including marketing materials and tracts (Klassen 810).

Pamela Klassen points out that the rise of "medicalized Christianity [in] early-twentieth-century mainstream Protestantism," in particular, "was underwritten by a particular 'text-based cosmology'—an ordering of the world that imparted a therapeutic and even salvific role to texts in the process of healing" (811). Defining cosmology as an "understanding of the world inextricable from language," Klassen argues that this Protestant understanding needed media to not only establish the relationship among one's "body, mind, spirit, science, and divinity," but also to "mediate" those relations (811).

Looking at alternative health practices later in the century, Ted Kaptchuk and David Eisenberg (the lead researcher on the groundbreaking 1990 and 1997 studies revealing that 33.8 percent of the U.S. adult population or 60 million people used at least one form of alternative medical therapy) show the significant role that media played in the circulation and construction of ideas about health-foods both in the events leading to the development of healthy foods and in the health food industry's worldview that food was connected to a worldwide transformation. According to Kandel and Pelto (qtd. in Kaptchuk and Eisenberg 19), "A loose network of Charismatic travelling lecturers, commercial stores and restaurants, residential programmes and retreats, alternative health care providers, exercise teachers and media—not to mention various books, journals, advertisements, and classes—maintain and inform a vague cohesiveness and allow for different layers of commitment and participation in health foods."

This isn't much different from the way in which media and the market played out in the later healing narrative, the New Age. In fact, says New Age scholar Wouter Hanegraaff, the New Age is no "longer the symbolic system of an existing religion, but a large number of symbolic systems of various provenance, bits and pieces of which are constantly being recycled by the popular media" ("New Age" 304–5). As a meshing (and rethreshing) of multiple "symbolic systems," the New Age relies on the media and the market that have not only collected and circulated various world faith traditions and belief systems for consumption, but have also been doing the threshing or mixing (303). Too, media and market serve as the sites of practice (for example, in websites and chat rooms or retail shops) (see Hoover, *Religion*; Hoover and Clark, "Controversy"; and Hoover and Venturelli).

The "quantum spiritualities" could be just as easily and accurately termed the "quantum media," taking form as they do through books, DVDs, websites, television, salons, films, and podcasts. This is similar to what media scholar Arjun Appadurai described as "mediascape," or the distribution and dissemination of information by media in a way that gives shape to an image of the world but which is also dependent upon political, cultural, and social determining forces such as ownership, language, censorship, and audience characteristics. The "mediascape" of LOHAS brims with claims about the nature of the world we face, claims that eventually bind people together to become a community or a discourse community of social actors (Clark "The Turn"). In this sense, LOHAS media and market organizations are "mobilizing attention . . . by deciding what constitutes an [issue] and what constitutes a desirable outcome," as Blackmore and Thorpe say (590). This is captured in a "lifestyle of health and sustainability" and in an understanding of what a natural state of health should be.

As we saw in chapter 1, the essentializing of the true self as an uncorrupted essence tells us something about what LOHAS discourse understands to be a "natural" state of being. In the case of the individual, the true self is a healthful composition of the balanced mind, body, and spirit. And while we are told that we can achieve health through our own intentions and focus, LOHAS texts also articulate our health as a matter of partnership (one forced by a recognized interdependence) with the health of the social and natural worlds. An article in *Body+Soul* states, "In today's world, *holistic* [my emphasis] is about interdependent parts that make up the whole," parts that include your "physical well being, your mental and spiritual states, and how you interact with the environment," and these must work "undissected" (Stark 98). Our natural form of existence is this very juncture of self, society, and natural world, three spheres in a balanced orbit.

This idea of nonseparatism between self and other is ingrained in the LOHAS discourse and surfaces in myriad ways. For example, in the *Natural Solutions* magazine (formerly *Alternative Medicine*) article titled "Love Thy Neighbor, Heal Thyself," the author reports scientific evidence for the health benefits accrued through "other-directed love" (Reder). People who are kind to others live longer, develop healthier immune systems, and are happier, according to the article. Sam said much the same thing. To him, the word "sustainability" means "living in harmony with the natural world." He told me this was an "organizing principle" for not only his personal values but also for the "editorial mission and social mission" of his magazines. Here, Sam paused before saying, "my spiritual practice is expressed in my work." He explained to me that his company was a "complete product of the spiritual commitment I have and for me that definition is any service I bring to the rest of humanity, to the natural world, all creatures that inhabit it." This, Sam said, was his "dharma," the path he believed he was following.

"Sustainability means the recognition of relationships," Charlotte, the editor-in chief of a national consumer lifestyle magazine, said during our interview. She used as an example the practice of yoga, a word she said means "unite." "With yoga, the endgame is union with everything," Charlotte said. "Ultimately, what you attain is no separation between yourself and everything that exists," she explained, adding that the whole point of uniting the body, mind and spirit through yoga practice, was to "go out and unify with all other things: Be the change you want to see in the world."

Clearly, recognizing ourselves as interdependent with other people allows us, as Terry Eagleton has said, to build a fellowship with others based on the commonality of survival and our reliance on the finite earth (*After Theory*). Pulling the natural world into this, into what religion scholar Sally McFague calls an "organic" worldview, makes room for "difference and unity" to coexist, informed by the idea that there is an "interdependence of all parts" (28).

Writing about the ways in which health and wellness are reliant upon the "integrated effects of mind, body and spirit," Pesek, Helton, and Nair make a case applicable to LOHAS, in the way in which LOHAS represents a "reawakening of traditional healing and stewardship worldview ideals internationally" (115). They note the emerging and rising interest in what they call "mind-body-spirit philosophies" and the "impact of spirituality on one's ability to heal," but they argue that these factors do not operate alone and are set "within a backdrop of a fourth component not given nearly enough attention, that of our environment" (Pesek, Helton and Nair 115).

Following Sally McFague's argument, if we acknowledge that all life springs from the same seed, it not only centers ecology in human activity, but by doing so also forces us to focus on our human *praxis*, our concrete daily activities and how those affect the environment, other people and future generations.

Why we should consider the effects on unborn generations is made vividly apparent in this illustration of time-space intimacy: environmentalists say that the water we drink today may once have served as Cleopatra's bath, driving home the reality that we are all drinking water filtered through millions of other kidneys, jugs, and taps. Ynestra King says it is only logical to think of the environment and our connection to it in this way because without a healthy environment we face "a paradox of liberation." That is, there is "no point in liberating people if the planet cannot sustain their liberated lives, or in saving the planet by disregarding the preciousness of human existence not only to ourselves but to the rest of the world," she says (114, 121).

In great part, this dawning recognition that we live in a state of "complex connectivity," to borrow a quote from scholar John Tomlinson, is a symptom of globalization, which produces "the rapidly developing and ever-densening network of interconnections and interdependences that characterize modern social life" (2). The resulting flows of people, products, currency, and ideologies through the borders of nations and cultures have restructured societies, identities, and organizations. We are keenly aware that boundaries do not hold. In LOHAS, these forces are not explicitly used in the storyline. Rather, we are told, as *Yoga Journal* put it, that through the "yoga of relationship" we "discover our connectedness and realize the loving awareness that is our deepest nature" (Brach 122).

In any case, by constructing human nature as a state of one-ness with other *natures*, it cannot be master of those natures in return. This may be a reassuring narrative in a world beset by upheavals in the social structure. The notion of interconnectivity shifts the notion of the individual from missionary—a person sent forth to do God's bidding—to one of collaborator. The articulation of "nature"—be it human nature or Mother Nature—serves as the axis mundi in LOHAS, meaning it operates as the engine of a "belief system, a ritual form, and a guide for everyday living that expresses relationship to the ordinary and to the extraordinary, as a culture construes them" says Catherine Albanese (*Nature* 7).

This is a useful construction of nature for LOHAS, a discourse focused on our ability to implement global changes. In fact, Marxist political theorist Frederic Jameson once called the idea of nature "a subversive concept with a genuinely revolutionary function," and said that "only the analysis of the concrete historical and cultural conjuncture can tell us whether, in the postnatural world of late capitalism, the categories of nature may not have acquired such a critical charge again" (qtd. in Wolfe 1991, 66). The idea of "nature" is exactly this pivot in LOHAS. Not only can the term point to the core essence of a person or thing (Cronon, *Uncommon*)—or the true self—but also to the situating of the individual within a tripartite holistic worldview. As such it becomes sacrosanct, an inviolate philosophy, and when we live within the holistic model, we achieve authenticity—another LOHAS keyword.

German cultural critic Walter Benjamin used the concept of *authenticity* to describe the essence of a person, object, or practice, which he regarded as a combination of history, authority, and the aura of originality. The word was also employed by both the philosophers Martin Heidegger and Herbert Marcuse to describe the manner in which humans achieve authentic being through the expression of *praxis*, or productive labor on one's self, and committing decisive action in the world.

These understandings of authenticity are particularly useful to its construction in LOHAS. First, Benjamin's notion of "originality" upholds the consumer culture's need for the uniqueness of the personhood; "praxis" ensures the continuity of the LOHAS products; while the notion of "authority" serves to empower the individual. A glance at the way in which the sociologist Paul Ray, who coined the term "Cultural Creatives" (CCs), uses the word "authenticity" shows similar refrains. He writes: "CCs are seriously concerned with self-actualization, spirituality and self-expression. They like the foreign and exotic and enjoy new ideas. They're socially concerned, advocating ecological sustainability, women's issues, peace, social justice and planetary awareness. These aren't separate concerns; when marketing to a CC, you'll do much better appealing to the whole package of principles. CCs are the ones who invented *authenticity* [my emphasis]" (Ray 36).

Healing the Division between Nature and Human

While admitting that she did not have "an apocalyptic bone in her body," Paloma, CEO of national consumer magazine, told me that if people did not learn to live in balance, the planet would carry on, but perhaps not with the human species on board. "If we as a species are going to survive, thinking holistically and integrating our minds, bodies, and spirits is key."

In the LOHAS discourse, once we perform that integration, we come to an innate understanding of our one-ness with the natural world, a site we have been artificially divided from in late modernity. We are inextricably and reciprocally linked to the "other," both human and nonhuman (Bartkowski and Swearingen 313). Where the European Enlightenment resulted in a construction of earth as homogenous, mechanical, and insensate and thus exploitable and passive (Kinsley), LOHAS texts instead endow it with an intelligent power.

I was speaking with "Sasha," a woman in her late fifties who had spent the greater part of the past thirty years involved in the natural and organic products industry as a marketer, entrepreneur, and communications specialist. We were talking about the separation of modern people from the natural world. "A lot of the malaise that we see in the world, in this country, is directly related to our lack of connection with nature," she said. "Look at the cities, places where there are electric wires and cement and nothing but artificiality; people are disconnected and lost and unhealthy."

The separation of humans from the natural world rises through various social structures and narratives, from religion to science. In the 1960s, UCLA historian Lynn White wrote enduring essays on the way in which Christianity shaped and informed the desecration of the environment; Rachel Carson's book *Silent Spring* called out the scientific community for its ignorance of ecological principles and questioned the human right to master nature; in 1986 Marxist philosopher Murray Bookchin wrote that "will and reason are not sui generis" (46).

While LOHAS is not explicitly an "environmental" movement, it is an environmentalist discourse. It argues against the Cartesian duality between mind and matter that reframed the Western relationship with the natural world. LOHAS, that melting pot of industries, keeps to a theme: that the separation of human from nature was unnatural and now threatens to deliver varying but equally apocalyptic disasters on individuals and societies.

Andrew Weil, a pioneer and best-selling author in the field of alternative or integrative medicine (also called complementary and alternative medicine), has argued for years that the separation of the human body from that of the natural world—exacerbated two hundred years ago when the study of medicine was delinked from botany and reframed within the study of chemistry—has had "enormous consequences for our society because, fundamentally, healing is a natural process." He says that in order to truly "understand healing and how to make people better, you must understand the ways of nature" (86). The message in late modernity is that nature is essentially the adversary of human beings, Weil says, speaking "as a doctor who often has to deal with the casualties of pharmaceutical science" (86).

The division has hurt us in social ways, too, leading to "atomization," says Jan Roberts, vice-chair of the Tampa, Florida–based Foundation for Ethics and Meaning. To Roberts, interconnectedness forms an alloy of four basic areas: "Respect and Care for the Community of Life; Ecological Integrity; Social and Economic Justice; and Democracy, Nonviolence and Peace" (Garcia, "International" 5). These areas, she explains, stem from the Earth Charter, "a widely recognized, global consensus statement on ethics and values for a sustainable future that has been formally endorsed by over 2,400 organizations, including global institutions such as UNESCO and the World Conservation Union" (http://www.earthcharter.org). The Earth Charter, Roberts says, reflects the current "paradigm shift" away from the self-interest of modernity to "unity, wholeness and community." She explains, "There is a new emphasis on the interconnectedness of humanity through the environment, economics, social interactions, culture, and ethical and spiritual aspirations" (Garcia, "International" 5).

To Sam, the Earth Charter represents a "long overdue" vision that can be integrated into a "greater set of activities." Echoing Roberts's sentiment of a paradigm shift, he said, "It is long overdue that companies come together, for example, and make a covenant with nations to set standards that will support the reversal of the ongoing damage being done to the planet." Sam believes the ability of the planet to support life is in jeopardy, but that a worldwide "commitment to action" was underway to reverse that.

But the discourse in LOHAS regarding our relationship with the natural world also engages another narrative that goes beyond the logic of treating the earth as the source of our physical survival, as a resource for human life. It spiritualizes the planet as well.

The idea that humans are distinct from the natural world was handed down through the Age of Reason, supported through the philosophical traditions of culturalism and humanism, and not without good reason (Eagleton, *After Theory* 162). As part of the Enlightenment's elevation of human authority on earth, the earth was, in a sense, demoted: it was soulless, passive, mechanistic, and inert (see Capra; Kinsley). It existed to serve our needs. If humans were equated with nonhuman matter, on what basis could we argue that humans are not to be used as "resources" to be mined, used, and disposed of (see Eagleton, *After Theory*)?

Throughout the twentieth and twenty-first centuries, however, various environmental and ecological efforts struggled against this monolithic positioning of nature. Social critics such as Henry David Thoreau, conservationists such as John Muir, organic agriculture proponents, and the ecocentrists (founders of the movement known as Deep Ecology) each raised their concerns about dangers inherent in a conceptual division from nature. These concerns included potential threats to human health caused by environmental degradation, the threats to our quality of life by the loss of wild spaces, and the social and economic problems created when family farms were replaced by factories. But new arguments were also raised, such as that which stated that nature had a right to exist for its own sake—its right to life, as it were.

This latter argument posed a new "anthropocentric challenge." New environmentalists such as Rachel Carson questioned the right of human supremacy over the natural world and the environmentalism that had emerged after World War II in reaction to the pollution caused by the war effort's industrialization (Cronon, *Uncommon*). This was "survival environmental-ism," says George Sessions, editor of *Deep Ecology for the 21st Century*. It was too "narrowly focused on the issue of human survival," having split off from the earlier, more ecocentric approaches of Muir and Lynn White, the author of *Ecology and Religion*. Both of their approaches took a "wider ecological perspective that involves a concern for the ecological integrity of the Earth and the well-being of other species, along with humans" (Sessions xi).

In the ecocentrist version "the quality of life for both humans and non-humans is more important than mere survival" (Sessions xi). Ecocentrism argued that nature and its systems hold an "intrinsic value" and "the well-being and flourishing of human and nonhuman life on Earth have value in themselves," said Arne Naess, founder of the Deep Ecology movement. According to Naess "These values are independent of the usefulness of the non-human world for human purposes" (Naess 68).

The environment was reimagined as a moral universe, similar to religion but operating as a secular religion, Cronon says (*Uncommon*). For example, Lynn White wrote, "The remedy to ecological crises must be religious as well"; later, Roger Gottleib said in his book on religious environmentalism, *A Greener Faith*, "The environmental crisis challenges us not just to save our skins, but to discern anew what we are doing with our lives" (6).

Not all have found the ecocentrist approach viable, including former Vice President Al Gore, and these critics charge Deep Ecology, in particular, with being misanthropic (Sessions xiii). Murray Bookchin charged the movement with a "crude biologism" that ignores the social crises that he says are the roots of the deepening ecological crisis. Arguing for an evolutionary "nature" of human beings that understands progress as moving through experiences, including environmental ones, toward an "ethical [human] nature," Book-chin believed humans would add to the integrity of the natural world with their own developments of "freedom, reason and ethics" (224). This would, he argued, "raise evolution to a level of self-reflexivity that has always been latent in the emergence of the natural world" (224). To Bookchin, it was only rational that humans would envision and actualize the greatness of their potential by enacting a deep empathy for the natural world. This would then initiate a reversal of environmental damage while simultaneously instituting a rational society, which Bookchin infinitely preferred over spirituality as a path to forging a new relationship with the environment. Spirituality was less reliable and more individualistically oriented than rationality and, to Bookchin, an ecological society is a rational society.

Poised among these narratives, LOHAS attempts to stitch together parts of the arguments from survival environmentalism, conservation, Bookchin's social ecology, Deep Ecology, and even nature religions and ecospirituality. Caught between extremes, LOHAS discourse is forced to ride a conceptual fulcrum: on the one hand, too transcendental of a treatment of the earth could scare away potential stakeholders, notably advertisers, business partners, speakers, and politicians. On the other hand, treating the natural world with too much relativism could essentially derail the LOHAS project by displeasing the core consumer base of Cultural Creatives, who view the natural world with reverence and respect (Ray; Ray and Anderson).

Although plenty of sustainability and environmentalism proponents would argue that capitalism is fundamentally antithetical to a sustainable world, LOHAS discourse nevertheless focuses on what Ynestra King calls the "ethical possibles of the future," while working within the confines of capitalism (116). LOHAS reinforces laissez faire idealism that says the free market is ultimately innovative and inspiring, but the discourse also criticizes the same, calling for a transformation of the system based on a model called "conscious capitalism." According to the Conscious Business Alliance, conscious businesses "respond to a deeper purpose" than profit, which implies that something exists that is of value that, quite literally, money cannot buy (http://consciouscapitalism.com).

Conscious capitalism treats the environment as a resource, but one with intelligence and power. The roles of master and mastered are exchangeable between human and the natural world; thus, achieving the right balance within that exchange dynamic is the precondition to sustainability. An article in *The LOHAS Journal* about a factory being built near two national parks in Kenya presents the project as a win-win for environment, culture, and capitalism. The article states that the new factory "represents a partnership between industry and conservation that strives to protect wildlife by providing work for locals whose subsistence needs would otherwise drive them to hunt animals and destroy habitat" (Garcia, "Eco-Manufacturing" 6).

This, of course, ignores the fact that the local indigenous cultures had managed to not destroy the environment and the wildlife over the course of thousands of years by practicing subsistence living. It also ignores how global capitalism bears down on these cultures in other ways besides environmental ones, forcing them to give up traditional ways of living for salaried work in factories, that the *partnership* is actually a sort of coercion because of the hegemony of capitalism. And, because of this, one wonders if the local population might have far preferred there was no factory at all and what they really think about having their environment turned into a national park.

In spite of the blind spots running through the discourse, LOHAS Forum 2009 keynote speaker Hunter Lovins impressed upon the audience that time for the environment was running out. "Don't ask what is possible, ask what is necessary," she told the crowd. Quoting physicist Jim Hansen, she said, "If the U.S. fails to act next year, then it may become impractical to prevent disastrous climate changes that spiral dynamically out of humanity's control."

But how to act is what baffles. Consider the following excerpt from a LOHAS publication: "The emergence of global environmentalism has been one of the most dynamic and influential social movements of our time. If there's hope for this planet, we have to act now. But acting now doesn't necessarily mean spray-painting baby seals or taking up residence in a redwood tree. It's also a quieter kind of activism, one that involves making mindful choices in our day-to-day lives that are ecologically and socially sound, like recycling, eco-volunteering, or driving a hybrid" (Stark 97). In this excerpt, LOHAS preserves traditionally mainstream ideas regarding certain kinds of activism as "radical." After reassuring us that these extreme acts are not necessary, the discourse focuses on "small things you can do now" to save the planet. The texts assure us that even baby steps become giant steps forward and that our individual efforts eventually coalesce into a forcible mass movement for change. The means through which we can bring about change are infinitesimal. We can install solar panels on our roofs, eat locally produced organic food, remodel our homes with eco-building materials, invest in socially responsible mutual funds, make our next vacation one of volun-tourism, and we can take the bus to work.

Barbara Harris, then editorial director of Weider publications, said at the LOHAS 9 Forum in 2005 that "every day is Earth Day." Firing up her Power-Point, Harris flashed onto the screen quotes from the Buddhist teacher Thich Nhat Hahn about mindfulness, explaining how doing one "good and positive thing" can create change in the world, even if it is as simple as not topping off the gasoline in the tank of the family car. In fact Weider's magazine, *Natural Health* (now owned by American Media) runs a monthly column titled "Make One Change" that provides directions to making small steps toward sustainable living.

The environment is our partner, and partnership is a familiar concept to Western consumers and producers because it incorporates the basic concepts of compromise, respect, restraint, and sharing. Through this partnership we are assured that we stand to reap even greater rewards than we did through the older, exploitive relationships with the earth. As an example, Bill Shireman, CEO of Global Futures Foundation and the Future 500, says in *The LOHAS Journal* "the most valuable resource in the rain forest is not the trees we can extract but the lessons we can learn. . . . We can use less and have more, consume less and be more [and] the path to guide us is all around us, in nature" (50).

Environmentalism in LOHAS, clearly, is no retro-dialogue along the lines of *Backwoodsman* magazine, skinning prey and building huts from willows. It isn't about to rake up visions of sacrifice or minimalism. Being environmentally minded in LOHAS is ultimately framed as "life-enhancing," offering up "exciting" business strategies, improved health, and a heightened sense of peace. "For those of us seeking a more satisfying and sustainable way of life, nature's lessons about what works and—what doesn't—can help point the way," says *Experience Life* magazine (Gerasimo 40). The graceful leaps of deer become lessons on how to adjust to obstacles and challenges; the salmon's push upstream becomes an opportunity to "follow a deep instinct or calling that often involves struggle and sacrifice" (N. Utne 69). The website for a book advertised in LOHAS media titled *Open Spaces, Sacred Places* (TKF Foundation), by Tom Stoner and Carolyn Rapp, states nature can also "heal and unify in our increasingly frenetic twenty-first—century world" (http://www.openspacessacredplaces.org).

Ontologically, LOHAS texts underscore the need to recognize not only the throb of life within the natural world, but also the fact that it incorporates the pulse of our own existence. With our own lives not only reliant upon the natural world, but also engaged with it in a coevolutionary process, we find a new ethics in our relationship with nature. Quoting Aldo Leopold, an *Utne Reader* article says, "One can be ethical 'only in relation to something we can see, feel understand, love or otherwise have faith in'" (Dodge 65).

This sort of affinity reforms our relationship with nature. No longer insensate, nature now has power and intelligence; we see that we can access nature differently, beyond a mere physical interaction. In the *Utne Reader*, the author incorporates quotes from Alexander Pope—"Let Nature never be forgot" and "Consult the genius of the place in all" (Hamilton 50). The author evokes both a Puritan metaphor of reverence and cultivation—giving and receiving and also as nature as source of wisdom. John Marshall Roberts, at the LOHAS Forum 2009, said, "Inspiration is our direct link to nature's intelligence—it's what happens when we directly experience nature's creative power on a psychological level." Placed on more equal footing, nature and human learn to serve the other, in the way in which Bookchin described in his theory of social ecology. This mutually beneficial situation is exemplified in the *Utne Reader* article about the joys of horticulture and agriculture. The author is comparing the "wild" spaces of the natural world with those that have been cultivated. "I don't mean to belittle the devotion that comes with loving a wild place. Without the fruits of that love, our country would be spiritually handicapped (not to mention paved from one end to the other). But I do mean to say that people know a place differently when they depend on it for a livelihood. In needing something from the land, you learn how much it will share, when to take that, and what to give in return. Rather than view the land as a delicate giant, you respect it as a partner full of power and energy. It is a relationship of reverence and gratitude, but also one of exchange" (Hamilton 50).

In an interview with me, Paloma said she viewed the earth as the most visible manifestation of the "Goddess," because it was the ultimate source of all human needs, from food to pleasure. She explained, however, that this belief was not about deifying nature but rather about understanding that everything one does is ultimately connected with the planet. In much the same way, the wilderness of America—its untamed rushing rivers, Great Plains, soaring cliffs and geographical expanse—came to reflect the greatness of God. Thus, the greater the natural world, the more honorable was the human who occupied it. By allowing that God gives humanity reason to be able to run the world in a moral way, the wilderness becomes the place that God designates for his chosen people to do battle (Jacobson 50). The scale and splendor of the New World was a useful form to symbolize the essence of American-ness: courageous, free, and independent. Catherine Albanese describes a "republican nature," whereby the natural world "provided the theological frame on which to hang a civil religion" (*Nature* 121). The nation's greatness was predicated for the forefathers in the magnificence of its landscapes, but if the grandeur of the wilderness signified the approval of the American experiment on behalf of the Supreme Being, it also represented an enormous responsibility.

For America's early European settlers, the transformation of nature served as the powerful metaphor and symbol for the transformation of the human being into a more perfect vessel of God's love. The cultivation of America's wild landscapes again brings to mind Miller's phrase "an errand into the wilderness," an errand commissioned by a holy force that had provided a paradise in the rough (Miller). Evoking that, best-selling novelist Barbara Kingsolver spoke about her family's one-year commitment to grow their own food and eat locally in the *Utne Reader*. Kingsolver, having recently completed a new book about her experiences called *Animal, Vegetable, Miracle: A Year of Food Life*, writes, "Modern American culture is fairly empty of any suggestion that one's relationship to the land, to consumption and food, is a religious matter. But it's true; the decision to attend to the health of one's habitat and food chain is a spiritual choice. It's also a political choice, a scientific one, a personal and a convivial one. It's not a choice between living in the country or the town; it is about understanding that every one of us, at the level of our cells and respiration, lives in the country and is thus obliged to be mindful of the distance between ourselves and our sustenance" (Kingsolver 56).

In *Body+Soul,* psychotherapist Will Johnson spiritualizes nature, saying, "[M]ountains do the work of churches: They fill him with a sense of peace and oneness that makes him feel at home in the universe" (qtd. in Lefkowitz 93). Johnson uses his trek up Mount Kailas as a tool to understand the inter-relationship between the nature of the mountain and his own. Like Paloma, he stops short of deifying nature instead viewing it through the lens of equal partnership. "It has nothing to do with conquering the mountain," Johnson says. "It is rather, about surrendering oneself completely to the forces and presence of the mountain, about dissolving the egoic fiction and being con-quered and liberated by the mountain in the process" (qtd. in Lefkowitz 93). That is, we may assign meaning to the natural world, but we can never know its true nature (Laclau and Mouffe).

Steve Apfelbaum, an expert in ecosystem restoration, says that what he has learned is that it doesn't "pay to be a control freak" when it comes to the natural world (qtd. in Leaf 22). "What I've learned in ecological systems training is that it's not about control," he says. "It's about interdependen-cies and inter relationships and whenever an organism attempts to control a system—like a human being attempting to control an ecosystem—there is a series of unpredictable changes, catastrophic events that show the human being that control isn't the way to interact" (qtd. in Leaf 22).

This is not just a matter of "common sense," of learning to respect the limitations of the environment, it is also a matter of ethics, which Terry Eagleton describes as "excelling at being human" (*After Theory* 142).

4. Apologies, Redemption, and Repair

"Leading thought is usually countercultural. We are making change, but transformation takes time in the evolutionary cycle."
—Peter Totorici, president of Mindshare Entertainment, LOHAS 9 Forum, April 27, 2005.

Ray Anderson, founder of the international carpet and textile firm Interface Inc. faced the room of business people at LOHAS Forum 2009 in Boulder, Colorado, and told them that "the first industrial revolution" was mistaken. A frequent speaker at LOHAS Forums and other sustainability events, his message never wavers: capitalism is both the cause of sorrows and the bearer of hope.

Like other industrialists in the LOHAS space, Anderson's presentations are one part confession and one part ablution—attempting to both remonstrate and rehabilitate capitalism while supporting democratic liberalism. It's a narrative that manages to avoid both what Patrick Brantlinger calls the negative classicist view—where modern life is doomed to fail when it reaches the zenith of corruption (associated with the Roman empire)—and the positive classicist view, which perceives modern life as a failure and idealizes the past. Instead, Anderson encourages his audiences to find a middle way, to move on to "another and better industrial revolution," one that will allow us to "get it right this time" (Shalmy 26–28).

Dan Montgomery, host of the Internet talk radio show *Sustainable Leadership*, cites author and organizational management scholar Peter Senge, saying that "For the last 250 years, we have been living in the 'industrial age bubble,' based on a 'take, make, waste' worldview" (D. Montgomery; this article originally appeared on the LOHAS.com website). That particular "party" is over for Westerners, says Jurriaan Kemp, editor-in-chief of *Ode* magazine. While past investment bubbles have produced important opportunities and economic growth, he says, the latest bubble resulting in the economic crisis of 2008 seems to have produced only debt. "Americans borrowed $1 trillion more than they earned over the past 10 years," Kemp says in his editorial (8). It was, he says, a "consumption bubble."

Dan Montgomery argues that we need a new perspective on capitalism and industrialization, to understand that these forces do not operate by some sort of "natural law," but are instead only the results of "received knowledge, the inheritance of centuries of cultural, political, and philosophical tradition." This interesting challenge to the ideal of a self-regulating and free-willed economy nods instead to the idea that we construct our reality, which not only underscores the message in the quantum spiritualities but also brings to mind Berger's and Luckmann's well-known theory about the "social construction of reality"—a way of "knowing" the world that is generated through intersubjective communication, or the repetition of messages and beliefs in ways that eventually attain legitimacy.

That repeated narrative in LOHAS says ordinary people can bend systems and institutions through their acts in the marketplace. LOHASians are people who are "conscious" of needed change, enlightened in ways that enable them to see beyond the veil of illusion about capitalism and its associated tropes. Through the LOHAS discourse, individuals discover how to be creative, freely acting *selves* who can deconstruct competing narratives about reality (Horkheimer). What's important in the LOHAS discourse is enabling or encouraging social actors to stay actively imaginative about the possibilities of the future, about what *could* be, and to avoid fetishizing the so-called "facts" (Marcuse).

Richard, a journalist with twenty-plus years in the LOHAS media and currently working in upper management for a LOHAS-aligned consumer magazine, reflected on LOHAS as an idea ripe for the times. "All points in history are the result of what has gone beforehand, and we are at a place in the development as human beings that [LOHAS] is starting to come to the fore and be considered as part of the discussion," he said.

Margo expressed this same thing, saying, "The planet is at a tipping point." This popular LOHAS metaphor was put to use in Denver, when Mayor John Hickenlooper recommended that the audience at a business conference, the 2009 Sustainable Opportunities Summit, read *The Tipping Point* by Malcolm Gladwell. He did so because, he said, the planet "was there," poised at that cathartic point in history. Society could, he said, continue the status quo of industrialization or embrace the tenets and ideals represented by the new sustainability, or "green economy." Hickenlooper solemnly told the audience that this meant contemporary populations had a "Faustian choice" to make: "Do we condemn significant portions of future generations to a poorer quality of life, or do we create an energy that is completely different than what we have now?" he asked.

In our interview, Penny agreed with this sentiment saying, "We are in total breakdown mode and we need to see how we are going to get out of that." Like Margo, who told me "the foregone conclusion is that this system is going to break down because growth like this is not sustainable," Penny was adamant that positive change was underway, even if the vision was not yet perfectly clear. Despite the blurriness of the path, the discourse of LOHAS provides a platform for my informants from which they can, as Frederic Jameson put it, view the cultural evolution of capitalism as both catastrophe and as progress. Those I spoke with believed we were on the road to progress, even more so since President Obama's election in 2008. This is captured in an editorial by Dan Montgomery: "Since the 1960's, there has been an increasing counter-cultural rejection of this worldview [the industrial age], and a declaration of the value of healthy food and lifestyles, social justice and environmental sustainability. New generations of LOHAS entrepreneurs have emerged—people who express those values with distinctly capitalist solutions for improving quality of life" (D. Montgomery).

The worldview, as *Newsweek* senior editor Jerry Adler says, is sustainability. Adler writes, "All over America, a post-Katrina future is taking shape under the banner of 'sustainability.'" LOHAS companies couldn't agree more: sustainability is a "new narrative," says BBMG, a branding and marketing company and LOHAS Forum presence, in its 2009 *Conscious Consumer Market Report*. According to that report, sustainability consciousness "is shaping our collective experience and changing how we think, how we work and how we live" (BBMG).

Paloma told me that sustainability meant just that—the world would be sustained. She declared, "There will not be an *end* to the world, but an *end* of a way of *being* in the world." But her view reflects not so much a departure from modernity, as Paul Ray and Sherry Ruth Anderson have suggested is the case with the Cultural Creatives, as it does an *extension* of those processes (52). That is, LOHAS discourse isn't rejecting late modernity—it embraces the potential that late modernity has to offer. LOHAS is the corrective to the system, showing the way toward improvement, to how we can build upon modern technologies and processes to be the same, yet different.

Repairing the "Consequences of Modernity"

"Getting it right" in the next "revolution," as the carpet manufacturer Ray Anderson put it, depends on how well we can address a plethora of social and environmental ills. If you thought the environmental movement was broad, wait until you take a look at LOHAS. It addresses a dizzying menu of

problems: poverty, global warming, hunger, animal cruelty, chemical agriculture, corporate greed, ageism, racism, sexism, disease, urban blight, rural
exodus, sweatshops, rainforests, endangered species, corrupt politicians, lack
of health care, genetically modified organisms, and broken families. And, this
only scratches the surface. The belief articulated in the LOHAS discourse is
that "there is a war going on against nature and people," as ecofeminist and
biophysicist Vandana Shiva declared at the 2009 Natural Products Expo trade
show and exhibit in Anaheim, California. The audience that packed the ballroom in the convention center gave her a lengthy standing ovation in response.

Sociologist Anthony Giddens has another term for this menu of problems.
He refers to the "consequences of modernity" as the effects of globalizing
institutions, ecological disaster, disembedded social networks and traditions, nuclear war, totalitarian power, and the breakdown of mechanisms
of economic growth (*Consequences*). Shaped by the effects of capitalism,
industrialism, and rationality, late modernity, says Giddens, has affected
the world in three important ways: a.) the separation of time and space such
as is caused by globalization; b.) the disembedding of local social systems
and where "self" and "society" are increasingly becoming interrelated in a
global milieu for the first time in human history (*Modernity* 34); and c.) the
reflexive ordering and reordering of social relations whereby new networks
across new spaces reshape old conceptions of affinities and identities into
new interconnected webs of multiculturalism, transnationalism, and plurality
(*Modernity* 16–17). Late modernity has generated modes of social life and
organization that are "more radicalized and universalized than ever before,"
Giddens says (*Consequences* 3).

The LOHAS movement is in agreement, it seems. Benedictine nun and
author Joan Chittister minced no words about these effects in her article
in *Spirituality & Health*. She called the processes of industrialization "the
new faceless evil of our time," specifically blaming "corporate laboratories
that engag[e] us all in the service of death by making seeds, making toxins,
making spy satellites, making bunker blasters, making financial decisions
that impoverish the rest of the world, silently, secretly, smilingly, smugly"
(Chittister 47–48).

The LOHAS market research organization BBMG opens its report opens
with a staccato refrain of concerns about American culture in 2009: "Fore-
closure signs. Tent cities. Banking industry turmoil. Stock market struggles.
Consumer confidence reaching record lows." As *Utne Reader* editor Dave
Schimke says, "Even if you're barely paying attention, it's near impossible to
duck headlines about arid aquifers, blood-soaked oil fields, stranded polar
bears, politics as always, and corporate opportunism" (4).

"We are losing capacity of the planet to support life," warned Hunter Lovins, coauthor of *Natural Capitalism* with Paul Hawken and Amory Lovins, at the 2009 LOHAS Forum. "Observed reality is outrunning scientific models," she said, noting that it was already too late to reverse much of the damage (Hawken, Lovins, and Lovins). LOHAS Forums had anchored the notion of sustainability to the assumption that we can fix anything, and Lovins's presentation marked a change of attitude. Not everything is salvageable, she said.

The shift is not surprising really, considering the convergence of bad news in 2009 from Iraq to the tanking of the economy. In this "insecure world," as the website of the retail giant Gaiam, Inc., owner of the LOHAS Forums, put it, things no doubt do feel "distinctly out of control" in new ways for certain populations (Giddens, *Consequences*). Many Westerners are just now encountering the sort massive ruptures in their "security" and "control" that other populations have suffered for millennia. This isn't lost on LOHAS audiences. In 2009 one of the keynote speakers at LOHAS Forum was the prolific author and anthropologist Wade Davis, who spoke about the imminent loss of traditional knowledge as well as the cultural and ecological systems of indigenous populations. Davis implored the audience, "How can we find a way for all to benefit from modernity without losing their indigenousity?" It was not just a matter of compassion, Davis said, adding, "We need these people and their knowledge."

There's always been an emphasis on the need for diversity and difference in LOHAS. It's a marker characteristic of the Cultural Creatives, according to Paul Ray and Sherry Ruth Anderson. Cultural Creatives are people who have come to understand the history, trajectories, and links between subjects, actions, people, and institutions globally, and hence they crave new types of relationships among all people and reveal a deep concern with social injustices (Ray and Anderson 11–13). They're environmentally aware and politically savvy. They understand the deeper implications of interconnection across time, our debt to future generations as well as our ties to other places, spaces, people, and organisms. What's more, they're ready to do something about it.

But that awareness brings to the LOHAS discourse guilt tinged with the hope of restitution. The texts urge reflection on our complicity with planetary suffering; they call out greedy corporations, unsuspecting (and uncaring) consumers, xenophobes, the military complex, industrialists, missionaries, and national leaders, to name a few. "The profits of the system are reaped on Wall Street and leave us all innocent, all intentionless, and all guilty at the same time," Chittister says (47–48).

Richard voiced similar concerns about our group guilt when we spoke. He said, "we [in the West] consume the majority of the energy without the majority of the population. We are wasteful. We are not mindful. We polluted the waterways, the land and the air." This sort of head-hanging is common in the discourse. As one example, in his interview with *The LOHAS Journal,* William McDonough—the architect and designer who was once cited by *Time* magazine as a "hero for the planet"—admonished the LOHAS community, saying "If you are perpetuating the existing system (being-less-bad), you can't say it's not part of your intention to destroy the world" (Nachman-Hunt, "Less Bad" 64).

But perhaps no one so directly confronted the LOHAS movement as Hunter Lovins. When she marched to the LOHAS stage in 2009 amid a standing ovation, she didn't waste much time getting to her point, nor did she seem concerned about sparing the feelings of the conference organizers. "Is LOHAS short for lifestyles of health and sustainability or lifestyles of hedonism and self-righteousness?" The audience laughed and Lovins kept going. Referring to the luxurious Boulder, Colorado, hotel in which the conference was being held, Lovins pointed out, "The St. Julien is a lovely hotel, but 50 percent of people live on $2 a day—what are we doing about them?" It is, after all, the ultimate question that shadows LOHAS at every turn.

No wonder then that a sort of mea culpa effect has surfaced in the LOHAS culture. The texts and podiums serve as open-air confessionals. Industrialists publicly confess to their past wrongdoings with such directness that you can't help but feel a surge of affection for them as they bear witness to capitalism's rehabilitation to a sustainable model. Speaking in 2004 to a group of civic and business leaders at North Carolina State University, for example, Ray Anderson started his presentation with this kicker: "Do I know you well enough to call you fellow plunderers?" he asked (Shalmy 27). "There is not an industrial company on Earth, not an institution of any kind, not mine, not yours, not anyone's that is sustainable," he said. Going further, William McDonough in his interview with *The LOHAS Journal,* fingered other occupations, even his own of architecture. "If you look at the tragedies that are occurring because of modern life and the making of things, you have to ask yourself, if you're a designer, is this what you intend?" he asked (Nachman-Hunt, "Less Bad" 64). It is jaw-dropping stuff, especially when you consider how much money these people made in their fields, but this sort of apology might be the best kind of public relations.

In *The LOHAS Journal,* Pax World Growth Fund Portfolio Manager Paul Gulden says, "One of the great things about the American system is its capacity for self-cleansing" (15). "We tend to put our problems on the front page. Companies are cleaning up their acts because the public is crying out for it."

This "can-do" attitude in LOHAS falls right in with an "obligatory" American cheerfulness, as Carlisle and Hanlon have written. At any rate, it is certainly part of the cultural script of LOHAS. As motivational speaker Marianne Williamson said on a segment on Oasis TV (Oasistv.com): "I'm telling you it was true 200 years ago and it is true today, when Americans get a buzz, watch out, the world does change."

The buzz in LOHAS is rehabilitation. Healed industrialists apologize for their past sins of unsustainability before concluding with the uplifting moral of the story, or the "sustainability imperative," as Hunter Lovins called it at LOHAS Forum 2009. Like any good parable, the tales of prior wrongdoing are used to educate followers and to encourage them to innovate, to change, and to commit to a specified moral code, in this case one that puts sustainability at the top of concerns. These admissions make for a good story, too. They capture the spirit of LOHAS and America, which says everyone is capable of doing something, no matter the scale. Small acts add up to big-picture change.

At LOHAS Forum 2009, themed "Reinventing Ourselves," Anthony Zolezzi—founder of the Bubba Gump Shrimp Co restaurants, Pet Promise natural pet foods, and other high-profile companies—said to the audience "I used to reinvent myself so I could get a bigger house, etc." But he said, that sort of reinvention was no longer tolerable. "Now, you better be reinventing because you want to make the planet a better place—work your reinvention around your heart and soul." He asked for members of the audience to share their own "stories of reinvention" and the tone of the seminar was suddenly reminiscent of a 12-step group meeting. One man came before the group to speak. "I was a Coca-Cola executive by the age of 32," he said. "As a global vice president, it was everything I thought I wanted." He shook his head and declared, "I was miserable, unfulfilled, and hitting rock bottom." He said he spent seven years trying to reinvent himself within the company until finally he realized it wouldn't work. "Now I am a consultant," he said, explaining that his goal was to discover how to "inspire leaders to see [sustainability] is a pragmatic solution." The attendees applauded loudly for him.

Plenty of industrialists are entering the LOHAS fold, people who have a less comprehensive (and entertaining) reinvention story. Some of these executives hail from corporations that even ten years ago would have been unthinkable to see at a LOHAS Forum or a Natural Products Expo. They've arrived on the shores of LOHAS, driven by a change of corporate heart. It doesn't hurt that there are also some alluring sales figures connected to the sustainability market. According to BBMG's *Conscious Consumer* report, three in four consumers agree (77 percent) that they can make a positive difference by purchasing products from socially and environmentally responsible companies (7). The Natural Marketing Institute reported that in 2009, health and wellness industry sales reached $112 billion, showing a 9 percent growth rate despite the global economic nosedive. These are the kinds of statistics to make a marketer's heart flutter.

At the 2009 LOHAS Forum, April Crow, Global Sustainability Packaging Manager for Coca-Cola Co.—not a firm renown for producing healthy or sustainable products—shared a stage with Candace Taylor from Wal-Mart Corporate. Crow was there to talk about Coke's commitment to recycling and resource reduction. But as a personal aside, she said "people ask me why would I want to work at a company like Coke, and I say its an opportunity to make a difference; when we do make a change [to sustainability], it has a tremendous impact." She bravely continued to tell the tale of Coke's attempts to lessen its carbon footprint.

It may be the very fuzziness of sustainability that creates such an amiable environment for industry. Individuals are invited to tell their tales of trial and error with sustainability and let the audience decide for themselves. This collective narrative building has, however, resulted in an odd allergy to critique, which one would think rather necessary to judge anything sustainable or not. Margo explained that while some things were "just wrong" there is a rigidity in construction of "right and wrong" and that "needs to evolve," she said. She reflected for a moment before adding, "What keeps me doing what I'm doing is the number of people who tell us that they've changed their lives and how they see the world and have gone on to change the world around them."

Likewise, Paloma told me sustainability was all about focusing on what people were doing to improve. "[Sustainability] is not optimistic or pessimistic," she said. Like Margo, she was strongly averse to the use of dichotomies, even that of right versus wrong, because such dualisms served to "mobilize the sense of division and fragmentation in the world." As long as acts of sustainability atonement are made clear, it isn't difficult to be welcomed into the LOHAS fold. You'll find, especially, a warm understanding generated on shared experience of failures.

As an example, when candy manufacturer Cadbury Chocolate decided to reintroduce palm oil into its milk chocolates, the international environmental community squawked, saying the move threatened the habitat and survival of the orangutan. It didn't take long for the company to reconsider and to issue an apology. According to the *New Zealand Herald*, Cadbury New Zealand's managing director Matthew Oldham explained that the decision to bring back the palm-oil recipe was a direct response to consumer feedback. He said: "At the time, we genuinely believed we were making the right decision, for the right reasons. But we got it wrong. Now we're putting things right as soon as we possibly can, and hope Kiwis will forgive us" (NZHerald.co.nz).

Say you are sorry and move on. Trial and error is part of the path to what Deepak Chopra—the author of numerous books on spirituality, health, and wellness—calls a "wisdom-based business." He says in the newsletter *Natural Business* that companies should "restore the eco-system—heal the ecosystem, make it a sustainable culture and civilization" and "eliminate poverty" (Lampe, "Chopra" 8). He adds, "There is no reason why there should be poverty in the world. It is nothing but the impoverishment of soul and spirit." As Chopra implies, wisdom in LOHAS has little to do with the amount of wealth one accumulates, but has everything to do with *how* one becomes wealthy.

Kartar Singh Khalsa, founder of the Golden Temple and Peace Cereal grocery brands, fleshed this thought out at a LOHAS Forum 2005 seminar. "Prosperity is a matter of personal balance," he said, adding that sustainability means "thinking of others and generations of the future." This "consciousness" is similar to that of parenthood, and all of us, producers and consumers alike, must bring "the consciousness of parenthood to all of life," Singh Khalsa said. Similarly, Paloma viewed sustainability as an evolution of human existence and businesses were scattered about on that continuum. Think of it, she said, as being given a wake-up call by the universe and the opportunity for us to change our ways, to engage our minds, bodies, and spirits in the reversal and halt of destruction and suffering.

You'd be hard pressed to find a LOHAS text that didn't carry some nugget of this tale—the road traveled toward consciousness of sustainability, a consciousness that Margo told me "comes from a knowledge that we are all connected." Sustainability, she said, "needs to be the core principle of all we do." But after atonement and redemption comes repair, and in that regard, the LOHAS discourse has little time for weak rhetoric. It's time for "guts," declares France Moore Lappé, the author of the renowned *Diet for a Small Planet* (21). "I keep asking myself, how did we get into this mess?" she asks, saying that what the future needs is for us to master "the act of positive courage." At LOHAS Forum 2009, Lovins said the current times call for "extraordinary courage by extraordinary people."

Americans are expressing "yearnings of hope and possibility" that are fueled by "a new administration" and "a new direction," says the BBMG *Conscious Consumer* report. Despite the grim headlines of war, environmental disasters, and economic failures, LOHAS keeps a stiff upper lip: it's no time to let grief and worry get the better of us. Michael Lerner, president of Commonweal, an environmental research institute, captures this sensibility in *Utne Reader*, saying, "We can serve the cause of life on earth better if we move through our anxiety, and if we find an underlying place within our-selves that acknowledges the reality of the tragedy we are facing and, at the same time, commits to doing whatever each of us can do to move beyond this tragedy" (qtd. in Schimke 4).

As the Monty Python song goes, "Always look on the bright side of life," and this is key to understanding LOHAS's roots in positive thinking. In LOHAS, positive thinking translates into "having passion," and this is so crucial that old-timers in the natural products and healthy living industries have mentored new entrants into the field because they feared passion was lacking. Richard, for example, told me he attended a leadership conference in Texas where he joined some of the most successful business people in the natural and organic products industry, many of whom had sold their businesses, retired, and other-wise moved on from their original ventures. These "greybacks" had organized the Texas conference with the intent of passing on their legacy—values that had so impassioned them to use their businesses to manifest change in the world—to the upcoming "newbies" in the field.

When I asked Richard about the content and source of these values, he replied that they had been formed for the mentoring crowd during the 1960s, as part of those social movements of feminism, civil rights and anti-war protests. "People were questioning the status quo as it pertained to people's roles in society," he said. He didn't think these values were necessarily new or revolutionary forces even back then but did believe they gained a "critical mass" during the 1960s and were a "boomer-based phenomenon."

These values or ideals, Richard said then, would enable the United States to lead the world in the redress of social and environmental problems. Years later, when I interviewed him again it was eight months after the swearing in of Barack Obama. He was even more optimistic that finally the LOHASian progressive view, that it's time to roll up our sleeves and get to work on find-ing solutions, was back at the fore of the political agenda.

There was after Obama's election an outpouring of what seemed almost surprise from those in the environmental and healthy living industries—surprise that their dreams of change had come back from the gulag where the Bush administration had exiled them, thin and pale but still alive. Writ-ing in *Newsweek,* Jerry Adler quoted Marty Hoffert, emeritus professor of physics at New York University: "If the United States became a world leader in developing green technology and made it available to other countries, it could make a big difference." The article goes on to state, "For $100 billion a year, which is at least what we're spending on Iraq, it could be done" (42).

Everywhere you looked in those heady days, LOHAS values gleamed like the fever in a consumptive's eyes. At the Denver-based Sustainable Opportunities Summit conference in 2009, Hickenlooper told the audience it was time to think "long-term." "This future is real and is something we can embrace on a universal level," he said about sustainability and the green economy. He encouraged those in the audience to be willing to "accept some risk" and to innovate. As did Barack Obama in his campaign speeches, Hickenlooper invoked Abraham Lincoln, the sixteenth president of the United States, saying that like Lincoln, we need to retain our passion for change and betterment. "Take it and find fresh perspectives," said Hickenlooper. "Keep talking because you are the foot soldiers delivering that passion to the future."

But even before Obama was sworn in, LOHAS kept its passion for change and betterment pumping, even during regimes unfriendly to its causes. During those times LOHASians regarded themselves as foot soldiers, a sort of illuminati charged with carrying the sacred scrolls of sustainability into the future. Innovation was always the LOHAS call to arms. At the 2005 LOHAS Forum, conference producer Andy Marks of MATTER Entertainment told the audience we were there to get to the "heart" of health and sustainability through conscious commerce and to talk about how "business, media and entertainment could be leveraged to educate consumers that making purchasing decisions based on their personal values and beliefs can transform the world."

LOHASians treated sustainability with a revolutionary's fervor. *Body+Soul* quoted Charles Reich, author of the 1970 book, *The Greening of America,* saying, "There is a revolution coming" and pointed out that Reich didn't envision revolution as a violent act but he did predict it would spread with amazing rapidity. "Its ultimate creation will be new and enduring wholeness and beauty—a renewed relationship of man to himself, to other men, to society, to nature, and to the land," he said (qtd. in Stark 97). Certainly this captures both Penny's and Paloma's visions of sustainability—as a revolution in understanding and awareness, but one that is a "continuation" of processes much alive in the world. This kinder, gentler revolution is tempered with a hefty dose of "blind optimism" as Dave Schimke, editor of *Utne Reader* put it. He said that "it's about abandoning the doom and gloom in hot pursuit of innovation" (4).

We have no choice in the matter according to general thrust of LOHAS texts. The planet "cannot support the level of growth we live at," Margo told me, and, with an end-of-the-world scenario out of the question, the question becomes "what will we model our new system on?" Penny's sentiments were much the same, but she was not as positive as others about capitalism. Finding that new model, she said, represented "a Catch-22—how do you solve the problem with the tools that made it?"

Reworking Desire

If we're going to keep capitalism as the engine for change, then it's the driver of the car and not the car itself that needs to change. Benedictine nun Jean Chittister says in *Spirituality & Health* that the effort will require every individual to take on the mantle of doing good in a world of evil, "to act without guile and greed" (49). Essentially, her call, which is a running theme in LOHAS, is that it is the core of our selves that has gone rotten, thanks to the abundance, or illusion of it, bestowed by market capitalism. "Whether you read the Stoics and Epicureans of Greece, the Tao Te Ching, the teachings of the Buddha, Indian texts like the Yoga Sutra and the Bhagavad-Gita, or St. Paul's kick-ass letter to the Corinthians, you'll discover that the bottom line practice for contentment is to give up wanting what you don't already have and learn how to accept what you cannot change," says an article in *Yoga Journal* (Kempton, "Real Joy" 104).

You may be scratching your head wondering how industrialists can continue to be such if the Cultural Creatives, their core LOHAS base, are being advised to give it all up. But living a simple life in LOHAS doesn't mean that those market organizations are advising you to live without. In fact, simple, sustainable living is framed as the road to having *more*. It's about having *more* joy and better things, even if there shouldn't be heaps of those better things. LOHASians are encouraged to recognize their power to "save the planet and have fun, too," because, after all, "the environmental crisis can improve our lives" (Spayde 58).

Sustainability shouldn't be negative. An article in the *Utne Reader* criticizes much environmental coverage in the press for attempting to exact only "guilt and worry" from audiences rather than to empower people. "Environmentalists and futurists like Murray Bookchin, Stephanie Mills, and Jeremy Rifkin suggested that the planet's peril is also an opportunity to remake society by finding rewarding work, avoiding the thoughtless worship of the new and doing daily tasks in the simplest ways," the article states (Spayde 58).

Living more simply might mean eating lower on the food chain or spending less time at one's job and more time with one's family. Doing "nothing" becomes an honorable, even spiritual choice in LOHAS discourse. "The abiding and self-congratulatory myth regarding Americans and relaxation is that we've got too much on our plates to partake," claims an article in *Yoga Journal*, which goes on to state, "But as a culture, clearly we have underdeveloped ideas about nothingness" (Colin 77).

But "nothingness" can imply very different things to people. For example, in LOHAS discourse "doing nothing" might be interpreted as "free time," as time away from salaried labor during which one might choose to "work on oneself," meditating in order to reunite the mind, body, and spirit. But "doing nothing" can also relay the angst that accompanies the struggle to find a job. That is, to people out of work, doing nothing certainly may not point to anything positive, much less evoke a choice about whether to spend their "restful" times painting, bathing, dancing to salsa music, cleaning the closets, or "taking a nap between fresh sheets" (Louden 70).

The LOHAS texts don't directly tussle with class issues very often, with the exception of the more news-oriented media such as *Ode*. The lifestyle-oriented LOHAS media and market organizations are clearly after "middle-class" Westerners who have gotten soft around the middle, both metaphorically and physically, thanks in great part to the misguidance of the classic American Dream. Any phenomenon such as LOHAS that is built on market capitalism and on promulgation of the 1960s social movements is going to have to eventually chew on the bone of class issues and the attainment (or not) of the American Dream.

Considered a "key building block of the U.S. social fabric," as Kopczuk, Saez, and Song put it, the phrase "American Dream" captures a nation's founding ideology that any person can become whatever they so wish, unfettered by class distinctions and restraints. It reemerged in popular parlance after the Great Depression and has remained with us since (Perrucci and Wysong). The elements of the "dream" include: a good education, wealth, happiness, home ownership, a fulfilling job, and passing on even greater opportunities to one's children than experienced by previous generations (45). "The Dream resonated as a mythic cultural ideal, and, at least for a time, as an attainable reality," Perrucci and Wysong say (46).

In *Utne Reader*, Jeremy Rifkin, president of the Foundation on Economic Trends, in Washington, D.C., says the American Dream of "economic growth, personal wealth, and independence" is not sufficient for modern-day life. "The European Dream," he says, "focuses more on sustainable development, quality of life, and interdependence" (76). The American Dream becomes the American nightmare when it manifests as overstimulation, overconsumption, obsession with the new or the young, alienation, isolation, poor health, and pollution. This is why, say LOHAS texts, so many of us who presumably reached the pot of gold at the end of the American rainbow are not all that happy, often for reasons deeply spiritual in nature. While the pursuit of materialism and financial success is upheld in LOHAS, the texts do warn that the old tropes have not worked at the scale once promised.

"People want more depth, more truth, more profound subject matter, more healing and more enrichment, and they want less hype," says Cynthia

Sheets, CEO of Wisdom Media in *The LOHAS Journal* (Garcia, "Personal Development" 21). Paul Ray says the Cultural Creatives are disillusioned with contemporary Western culture's idealized notion of "success" in the form of material gains because too often that construction arises within narrow ideas about what one should accomplish, in what order, and at what time in life. The Cultural Creatives question these received narratives, finding them "not so much a life path as a career path" (Ray and Anderson 48). This sentiment is expressed in an advertisement in *The LOHAS Journal*:

> 'Rethinking The American Dream,' a video that is now available online, helps viewers think about their current lifestyles, and presents individual choices that can improve the natural environment and personal quality of life. Produced by the Oregon State Extension Service, this 20-minute video focuses on what Americans report is most important in life: health, fulfilling work, education, connection with family, friends, community and the natural world, and spirituality. It points out how merely consuming 'stuff' and increasing material wealth can get in the way of achieving these important goals. (Fall 2002, 16).

Revamping the *Dream* in LOHAS doesn't mean dumping its mythic contents—improving quality of life is what LOHAS is essentially all about, after all—but it does mean adjusting the processes through which those contents are achieved. The Center for the New American Dream, for example, is "dedicated to helping support and nurture an American dream that upholds the spirit of the traditional dream—but with a new emphasis on sustainability and a celebration of nonmaterial values. We envision a society that values not just 'more' but more of what matters" (http://www. newdream.org)." The center claims the culture's focus on consumption has actually derailed the American Dream, which was about well-being, but has, as a result, devastated the very things we thought we were after in the first place.

The unsustainability of the current consumption–production model, according to the center, has jeopardized our health and happiness through the destruction of environments and that of other people's lives who are forced to make the cheap goods consumed on the global commodity market. Where work was once thought to bring joy through service to one's family and community, it has become a "treadmill," says the center's website. We have less security, less time and fewer of the real joys we once envisioned as our right.

5. LOHAS, Social Reform, and Good Capitalism

"Every single pressing social and global issue of our time is a business opportunity."
—Peter Drucker.

Joan Baez, singer and activist, stood before the 2005 LOHAS Forum 9 audience. "We are a greed society and the rich are going to have to give to the poor," she said. "I believe you are all here to address this. This is community." With that, she deftly wove together the assortment of nonprofit workers, doctors, consultants, industrial powerhouses, yoga teachers, movie stars, recording artists, politicians, and publishers, interpreting them as a collective of people who shared deep convictions about the nature of capitalism as a contradictory system of "power and conflict, of poverty and inequality, of environmental degradation" (B. Fine 213).

Getting rich isn't the endgame any longer, at least it's not explicitly laid out in those terms in LOHAS. It isn't that wealth is snubbed—there are plenty of wealthy entrepreneurs in LOHAS culture—but it needs to be a *slower* wealth, one that takes into consideration environmental and social impacts in its creation and distribution. LOHAS Forum director Ted Ning, for example, wrote on his blog, "Bling is out" ("Can't Buy"). "Flaunting wealth now is to be out of touch with current circumstances and seen as arrogant," he said. "There has been a shift in attitudes across the board from companies to individuals on spending. There is more of a focus on quality rather than quantity."

LOHASians, say LOHAS media and market organizations, want to link up with the traditional rituals of life around community, sustenance, and family. LOHAS clearly wants us to rethink what wealth has stood for in American culture. The *Utne Reader* ran an article with the alluring title "Reimagining the American Dream: What the Good Life Really Means and Why We Can Still Grab It." In it, author Nan Mooney writes that we have to believe that "identity equals more than money" (39). "Are we content enough, free enough, secure enough that we'd really prefer to just sit tight," she asks, referring to the troubled financial waters coursing through the world. "Look around and ask yourself: what sort of society do I really want to live in? What sort of society do I want to pass on to coming generations? The choice is there" (41).

That choice, says novelist Barbara Kingsolver, also writing in *Utne Reader,* is a "tangled path between money and morality." She says money does not represent "a new question by any means" (56), but that American culture is "confused" about the difference between "prosperity and success—so much so that avarice is frequently confused with a work ethic" (56). Kingsolver says she resists the "tyranny" of the marketplace and does so because it undermines her values and goals; market activities do not make her feel whole. In essence, she's echoing philosopher Michel de Certeau who advised that we resist that market-based tyranny by awakening to materiality's power to impose itself upon our will via the products we purchase.

Success and the LOHASian

Throughout the past 150 years, Americans have been extolled to "improve, advance, and actualize" (Richard Weiss qtd. in Starker 2002, 170). We've been suckled on various success storylines—from the mental, moral, spiritual, and physical rigors handed down from the Puritans and articulated through the Protestant work ethic. The myth continued on through the "reconstruction of U.S. capitalism around the turn of the century, facilitated by new political leadership," says media scholar Janice Peck (109). This was the time when success became deeply "privatized and commodified" (Traube 279).

Influenced variously by markers of religion, politics, class, race, age, and gender, we've refashioned through the generations the specifics about what does and doesn't constitute a successful life. As nineteenth-century America underwent urbanization and industrialization, for example, ideas about personal achievement shifted correspondingly. During the homesteading of America, husband and wife shared in the required physical labor to tame and cultivate frontiers and farmlands. As these populations migrated to cities, however, women's "work" and men's "work" began to separate physically and culturally. Although plenty of women and men in the cities were working in factories, the idealization of "womanly" success assigned her to the domestic sphere, as homemaker, wife, and mother, while her husband was off to seek his fortune in the public workplace.

Men who attained financial "freedom" in the late nineteenth and early twentieth centuries were understood to hold highly prized individual attributes, including pluckiness, fortitude, competitive spirit, and cunning.

"What more and more impressed the public was the aggressive competitiveness of the robber baron, as well as the material wealth these men enjoyed," Traube says (277). He had managed to lasso the increasingly competitive and complex economy, one undergoing the structural changes brought on by regulation, taxation, and other institutional changes.

As the middle-class and white-collar sector of the American economy expanded, and as incorporation and organization replaced entrepreneurship, so did the ideas about what constituted success move from an emphasis on the motivation, hard work, and intelligence of the subject to the outward appearance of that subject and on his or her personality (Traube 278). Education and appearance replaced cunning, perseverance, and physical labor. The cult of the personality, according to Traube, aligned with the emergence of a consumer culture and eroded the emphasis on innovation and individual talents that contributed to the shaping of American capitalism and culture.

Received understandings of success in LOHAS reflect this lineage with its links to the mind cure traditions and their emphasis on the "transformational power of thought" as the path to both spiritual and material success (Becker and Maracek 592). The mind cure movements, say Becker and Maracek, continue to find popular expression in what is known as *positive psychology*, which manifests in both popular culture and in the discipline of psychology. Like earlier movements, positive psychology, they say, makes "individual flourishing the primary object of study and intervention." Positive psychology upholds "a time-honored, quintessentially American way of dealing with collective uncertainty and demoralization" by turning "our energies ever more forcefully to the quest for private success and the American Dream," say Becker and Marecek (600). They describe the way in which positive psychology produces "rosy promises" for people in the wake of September 11 by assuring them of their own power to produce happiness and success.

LOHASians are articulated as plucky, positive, and able to generate full-on global change. In the LOHAS publication *Whole Life Times*, an article says that setting intentions can manifest change biochemically as well as psychologically, proving that we have the power to "interrupt the old programming" and to become as "gods"—creating our own realities (Schull 24). At LOHAS Forum 2009, the daughter of Deepak Chopra, Mallika Chopra, spoke on a panel about corporate social responsibility. Mallika Chopra is the founder of Intent.com, a website devoted to helping users achieve their "focus." She said to the audience, "I am responsible for what I see—everything that happens to me I have asked for."

There is plenty of space and time devoted in LOHAS culture to positive thinking and to the market for personal development. With the self-improvement market estimated at $9.6 billion in 2005, and projected to grow to more than $11 billion in 2010, according to MarketData Enterprises, Inc. (www .marketdataenterprises.com), there is more than enough help available to repair the dysfunctional self in need of therapeutic management in its quest for success (Peck). But, in typical LOHAS fashion, as it juggles and reconciles contradictions between capitalism and sustainability, LOHAS media take the ads but also are happy to engage with critiques of positive thinking.

Some of those broader critiques of the ideas of success, which are put forth in the quantum spiritualities and their foundation—the Law of Attraction—say that the belief in intention-setting as a way to dramatically transform the conditions of one's life erroneously redirects the gaze from structurally determining factors of success—including racism and ageism, social mores about beauty, or unequal employment policies, for example—and thus constructs success as only an intellectual problem while evangelizing an idea of all-powerful individual agency. This lacuna in the quantum spiritualities agitates critics, including a pioneer of the New Age movement, William Bloom, who condemns the "lack of morality and compassion" threading through "half-baked ideas about how energies, karma and the laws of attraction work." Bloom writes: "This often reaches a peak of disturbing smugness when a new age 'philosopher' faced with cruel suffering says authoritatively: 'People create their own reality' or 'Their soul chose it—it's their karma' or 'Everything is perfect in God's Plan—you just need to perceive it differently.' People who say such things seem to have no idea how smug and nasty they sound. Nor of the hurt they cause."

In the LOHAS publication *Conscious Choice* magazine, in an article titled "Beware of New Age Bullies," Julie Ingram writes about the difficulties that might be faced by those who question the positive-thinking traditions, who then find themselves in direct opposition to axioms held by their communities or traditions and, as a result, are isolated or reprimanded.

But as it stands, the Law of Attraction and the individualism narrative of success actually present a tautology when considered within the whole of LOHAS discourse. This occurs because within the Law of Attraction itself, there is no logic by which one can actually critique the ability of the system to bring about real transformation in one's life, because by posing the question, one is simply manifesting negativity and wrong group-think. This disembowels the project of politics, forcing us to spend our time attempting to make sense of the unseen world within us rather than committing to acts in the political, economic, and social spheres. Those who adhere to the Law of Attraction might argue this, saying that one can only change one's self and by doing so, one manifests an example for the world, or even changes that world by visualizing betterment.

LOHAS attempts to marry the notions of "happiness, material success, and good health," (Becker and Marecek 592), with the idea of an expanded consciousness, and that is where LOHAS diverges from the individualistic narratives of the positive psychologies. By contextualizing an individual's flourishing as dependent on broad-scale social change, LOHAS moves away from an emphasis on "limited person-centered" process and toward one on "just and equitable social arrangements" (598). That is, LOHAS makes clear that personal bliss depends on the good of the collective, and it celebrates specific types of values, ideas, and practices, marking some as good and some as wrong.

We can see this sort of collective imagining in this excerpt from the *Yoga Journal*: "We are told that if we are seeking happiness, we should look beyond our own point of view," says *Yoga Journal* (Isaacs 21). In that same vein, "Fran," an editor and a former owner of a LOHAS-related publication, told me humans have a moral duty to look beyond their self-absorption to recognize the needs of the greater world.

This is real success, true happiness, she said.

This balancing of personal bliss and global social good makes an odd marriage in LOHAS. While narcissism is in many ways reinforced in LOHAS, it tries to be an enlightened narcissism. That is, people should act sustainably even though LOHAS texts openly acknowledge that they often don't. Fran told me that she believed the reason for that is because a certain laziness is reinforced within the greater American culture. She was not happy about the apathy, discouragement, and disbelief that she believed prevented individuals and organizations from committing to sustainability. She said, "I think it is laziness or business that keeps people from acting in a sustainable manner for the greater good." She paused and reflected before saying "either that or there is just too much chatter and input." Fran said she imagined that many people experienced a "sense of helplessness, as in 'I'm not going to make a difference by recycling my little plastic bag, so why bother?'"

Paul Katzeff of Thanksgiving Coffee said he has little sympathy for people who don't make an effort by, for example, demanding fair trade, organic, shade-grown coffee. He does not "buy" the argument that some people might be rushed for time and unable to locate a coffeehouse that doesn't offer fair trade products. "When you go into a place with no fair-trade coffee, just say to yourself, 'I'm outta here,'" he says. "And tell the café manager why [you are leaving] on your way out. If you need a cup of coffee so bad you sacrifice your usual standards, you are totally lost" (qtd. in Condor 21).

"Iris," a twenty-year veteran editor and writer in the LOHAS industries, was more circumspect about why people might not do all they could for sustainability. While she said that certainly everyone *could* do more and that "we all have responsibility" to do so, "we live in a kind of me, me, me society." She was opposed to the type of narcissism inherent in capitalism where success was seen as a battle among contestants for limited resources. She had more sympathy than Fran did for the sorts of structural constraints on people that might keep them from committing 100 percent to sustainability behavior, understanding that failure was sometimes impossible to avoid. She said, "If you're unhealthy, psychologically, spiritually, or physically, you might not have whole lot of extra time to spend on helping others." She said she thought about her own busy life and wondered if people like her were just too busy. "It takes so much work just to keep your own life together, that you don't have time to worry about coffee farmers in Guatemala, you know?" she mused. "People are like . . . 'That's their problem, I'm sorry about it, but you know, I really have to worry about my own job and about feeding my own kids and, or my own high cholesterol or whatever.'"

And, this is exactly why LOHAS sustainability is based on the individual—constructing sustainability as a process of spiritual evolution toward consciousness enables LOHAS discourse to focus on the seedbed, the individual, where consciousness of sustainability first takes root. Ken Dychtwald, founder of Age Wave, a consulting firm in San Francisco, says "Do I think that the average boomer gets up every day and worries about the rain forest? No." "But," he says, "do they worry about whether there is asbestos in their kid's school ceiling, or whether there is toxic waste affecting their drinking water?" (Nachman-Hunt, "The Hunt" 30). The answer is yes. It is an enlightened self-interest. Sustainability values à la LOHAS can be seeded by contextualizing them within an individual LOHASian's everyday life.

LOHAS texts pound home the need for us to "recalibrate the measure of happiness," in order to imbue sustainability consciousness with urgency, as the kernel of happiness and success (C. Montgomery 48). "Most of us don't need to worry about freezing or starving to death," says the *Utne Reader*, referring to the quest for the ever-larger home that has been a staple of the notion of success and upward mobility. In fact, the "status anxiety" we might experience from giving up these things could be countered through the benefits we receive from socializing, from trust-building interactions, and from teamwork, according to a study by Stanford biologist Robert Sapolsky (C. Montgomery 49).

This is exactly what U.S. Senator David Boren, interviewed in *Utne Reader*, said is the focus of the younger generation of Americans. These people "want to be better stewards," he says. "Part of their American Dream involves a country that's more environmentally healthy, more pristine, and maybe most importantly, they really want to recreate community," Boren says (qtd. in Schimke 43).

Good Capitalism, Bad Capitalism

At LOHAS Forum 9, a member of the audience stood up to ask a panel of speakers a very pointed question: didn't they think that capitalism and profit were at loggerheads with the notion of sustainability? The panel members glanced at each other until Tony Krantz, CEO of Flame TV said, decisively, "no." "That LOHAS culture is incompatible with capitalism? Let's give that vestige of doubt up," he said. The panelists vigorously shook their heads and the silenced speaker sat down. It's a shame the question did not incite a more inspired discussion because it is, after all, the most important question one can put to LOHAS.

"At this moment," Sam told me, "enlightened capitalism and cooperation are two of the most powerful ways to cause a level of change in the way people live on this planet to avoid what could be catastrophe, in historical terms, in a short period of time in the future."

Sam told me that while he had sympathy for the "argument" that capitalism was not compatible with social change, we had to live in the "real world." But, he said, "I think if you have a system built on capitalism that does not include economic democracy, then even if you are talking about organic and sustainability issues, you are still going to have a recipe for failure of the human experiment."

Hunter Lovins, Amory Lovins, and Paul Hawken wrote a seminal book, *Natural Capitalism*, in which they say, "Capitalism, as practiced, is a financially profitable, nonsustainable aberration in human development." "Industrial capitalism," they write, does not "conform to its own accounting principles." "It liquidates its capital and calls it income" while at the same time neglecting to "assign any value to the largest stocks of capital it employs—the natural resources and living systems, as well as the social and cultural systems that are the basis of human capital," they say (Hawken, Lovins, and Lovins 5). Instead, "natural capital," refers to the "natural resources and ecosystem services that make possible all economic activity, indeed all life" (see http://www.natcap.org/sitepages/pid5.php).

These ideas rest on the inclusion of a different set of values from those underpinning neoliberalism. Natural capitalism is presented as a pragmatic and effective fix to the current economic system by forcing capitalism to tell the *truth* about its costs, and according to renowned environmentalist Lester Brown, "Socialism collapsed because it did not allow prices to tell the economic truth," and capitalism may collapse for the very same reason (Lampe, "Brown Calls" 19).

The Lovinses and Hawken put it this way: the values of conventional capitalism since the industrial revolution have been based foremost on the level of output production, which has diminished the importance of natural resources as capital. In the early stages of industrialization, this might have made sense because natural resources seemed inexhaustible. Today, we live in a "new pattern of scarcity," the authors say: "[I]t is people who have become an abundant resource, while *nature* is becoming disturbingly scarce" (Hawken, Lovins and Lovins 8). The industrial view of the economic process has been as a "disembodied, circular flow of value between production and consumption," says economist Herman Daly, but this "is like trying to understand an animal only in terms of its circulatory system, without taking into account the fact it also has a digestive tract that ties it firmly to its environment at both ends" (qtd. in Hawken, Lovins, and Lovins 7). The result is an unsustainable capitalistic economy that gobbles up the source of its existence and maintenance while simultaneously polluting those disappearing resources via the waste stage of the economy.

The sustainability espoused by LOHAS falls in line with these general theories: the economy needs to move from "the lifeless abstractions of neoclassical economics and accountancy" to face up to "the biological realities of nature" (Hawken, Lovins, and Lovins 9). The good capitalism of the future, says market research firm BBMG on LOHAS.com, will comprise companies that adhere to sustainability, and these "sustainable brands" will not be "ends unto themselves, but empowering platforms that allow us to meet the full spectrum of our needs, make a difference in the world around us and realize our truest selves and best society." Speaking at LOHAS Forum 2009, the former president of the Sierra Club, Adam Werbach, now CEO at Saatchi & Saatchi S and sustainability advisor to Wal-Mart, said business has acted as if it survived outside of social and ecological obligations. This, he said, this has been the root cause of business failure and of the economic crisis. In the future, he said, the only businesses that will survive are those that recognize that they are part of these greater systems.

But natural capitalism is still capitalism, and that means there's nothing wrong with profit but that the conditions of its generation and distribution have to be revised. In her presentation at LOHAS Forum 2009, Hunter Lovins underscored this, saying, "Wal-Mart is driving change in the green marketplace; believe me, they aren't doing it out of the goodness of their hearts." It's the profitability of the sustainability sector attracting newcomers. At the Sustainable Opportunities Summit held in Denver Colorado in 2009, I was seated at a table with a man who had never been involved in sustainability. He told me he was only there because "sustainability had become unavoidable" especially now that it was buoyed by Obama stimulus dollars. Whether attracted to the sustainability sector by the stimulus dollars, personal experience with a sustainability crisis such as the Gulf oil spill, or consumer demand for sustainable goods, the new voices in sustainability have brought new perspectives on business that might help expand the market overall.

At LOHAS Forum 2009, Hunter Lovins told the audience that the *outliers* of society have led us forward by establishing new modes of being or thinking, and they have been financially rewarded for doing so. To illustrate her point, she popped up a slide showing a long-haired, bearded, and distinctly young group of people posing for the camera. The photo showed the founders of Microsoft in 1978. Amid laughter from the audience, she asked, "Would you have invested in them?" Her point was that if LOHASians wished to succeed, they had to be risk-takers and innovators, and she referred to the 2007 best seller *The Black Swan: The Impact of the Highly Improbable*, by Nassim Nicholas Taleb, in which he describes how unpredictable events can have tremendous impact in a culture.

These predictable characteristics of business—profit, innovation, marketing, and so forth—need to be wedded to passion, which will require for many newcomers a change of heart. The Lovinses and Hawken say it is wonderful to witness the "growing numbers of business owners and managers who are changing their enterprises to become more environmentally responsible because of deeply rooted beliefs and values" (see http://www.natcap.org/sitepages/pid45.php).

Richard and I were discussing values. He said that despite the fact that sustainable and healthy products are gaining in the greater marketplace, he was concerned that there was a lack of passion among new entrepreneurs in the LOHAS space. I asked him what he meant by passion and he replied, "a base of morality, ethics, and spirituality"—this was what gave the "work" meaning. But if sales were rising, I asked, why was that important? He said the profit motive alone was not enough to keep sustainability aloft in sales. While he admitted that there was a "mercenary" side of corporate life, whether "selling advertising or producing a return on investment for stakeholders," ultimately LOHAS companies, like his, should have a "mandate to create healthier lifestyles" for their consumers. "There is a higher vision at work to try and create change," he said. "It's more than selling boxes."

Paloma told me that "cause marketing" is helping people understand the new value-centered capitalism. The bigger companies are applying sophisticated marketing to explain their social values, she said. Certainly Whole

Foods Market has successfully used this type of cause-marketing to advertise the company as a socially responsible business. But, as Whole Foods CEO John Mackey made clear in an interview with *The LOHAS Journal*, this is not done because it's lucrative, it's what business *should* be doing in the first place. In fact, Mackey decried the way business had contributed to society in the past. "Business has done a terrible job of portraying itself as invaluable," he said. "And it never will be accepted by society as long as business says it has no responsibility except for maximizing profits," Mackey said (qtd. in Lampe, "Business as an Eco" 60).

Margo voiced much of the same concern. She said she disapproved of "corporate personhood," whereby corporations "share the same rights as people." This is just an illusion, a fallacy, she said. Margo felt society had privileged corporations in ways that allowed them precedence over other human rights. "Add to that the pressure of quarterly improvement, reports, and bottom lines, and we designed a system that emphasizes all the worst," she said. "We have lots of assumptions about how it [capitalism] should look," Margo told me, but she added that while she identified herself as a "capitalist," she wasn't even sure what that meant any longer. Times were changing and so was business. Her own international publishing company was "morphing into a nonprofit and continuing as a for-profit." "There is a quality of nimbleness and ingenuity in capitalism that I value," Margo said. "I don't think we have developed it to its full potential—I haven't given up on it."

John Mackey says business has work to do to overcome "greed" and "selfishness" and to stop "despoiling the environment" (qtd. in Lampe, "Business as an Eco" 60). "Business is always painted as the bad guys," he said. "They're never the heroes." The late Anita Roddick, founder of the international retail chain the Body Shop, said business has no choice but to change that image because they are in a position to serve as the global catalysts for social change. "[Multinational corporations] are now more powerful than most governments and wealthier than most countries," she said. Not only that, Roddick said, but also these businesses "are more creative than any other institution and absolutely more powerful" (qtd. in Middendorf, "Business" 31). Because of this, "They must have a moral center," and Roddick explained that this included focusing as much on social justice and human rights as it did on making a profit because companies' acts "ripple-affect millions" (31). As the new social leaders, Roddick said businesses are responsible for protecting society, not just extracting from it, and this meant they had to do "everything governments aren't prepared to do" including making themselves "clean up their mess." Businesses should protect indigenous cultures and encourage governments to heal the sick, educate children, care for worker rights, and more, she stated (31).

In the same vein, Sam told me that for a social movement to be effective, "it must integrate inner and outer engagement issues into an effective whole." He said, "Personal growth and the spiritual path are linked to and inform the act of engagement in broader society in what we call political activism and service." This means no one is exempt simply because of his or her line of work—business leaders must link these parts of their life world together to manifest social change. To that, when I asked Richard about the relationship between his corporation's values and his management values, he said they were inseparable.

He told me the CEO of one of the largest companies in the natural foods industry was "notorious" for his temper, lack of information, and cynical attitude about many of the deeper principles of sustainability—namely, to treat employees well, to be a good community neighbor, to reduce the company's carbon footprint, and to commit to corporate social responsibility. Richard said the person's way of doing business took the soul out of companies. What was that "soul," I asked? Richard replied that it reflected the motivations of the original founders of the companies and their attitudes toward the environment, their employees' welfare, and other "values."

It's called "walking the talk," Richard said.

The term refers to aligning one's acts with one's words. Brad Warkens, the former president of Conscious Media (which owned both the LOHAS Forum and *The LOHAS Journal*), discussed how he "walked the talk," saying personal values guided not just his own work, but also the mission of Conscious Media. "For me personally, I draw the line at those [business] relationships that I cannot defend to my children and my peers," he said.

Sam told me there were plenty of examples to illustrate what happened when one's personal and social values were *not* aligned. Just think about some activist organizations that are specifically positioned as "socially transforming," he explained. Many of the individuals running these operations do so in a way that only reflects their own "rigid, myopic views" rather than the broader social good, Sam said. Not only did Sam feel that these activists are "leading lives utterly out of balance," but because of it, they are not truly sustainable. "The work they do is not sustainable from a personal standpoint," Sam said. "They are not joyful, loving, or positive personally," and, as a result, he told me, "the organizations that they create reflect that lack of balance."

If you don't walk your talk, you'd better be prepared to be called out for it. It's a serious charge in LOHAS culture because it doesn't only point to hypocrisy, it connotes a betrayal of *authenticity*. As an example, consider the 2009 uproar over the editorial written by Mackey that appeared in the *Wall Street Journal* denouncing the Obama administration's health care plan.

A vocal Libertarian, Mackey wrote that "we should be moving toward less government control and more individual empowerment." He said much illness was self-inflicted through poor lifestyle habits such as smoking, diet, and lack of exercise, and he led the article with a quote from Margaret Thatcher: "The problem with Socialism is that eventually you run out of other people's money" (Mackey, "Whole Foods").

As word spread about Mackey's piece, a call went out on Facebook and other social media for a boycott of Whole Foods Market. Consumers were furious. His comments, they said, were anathema and downright disrespectful to the Whole Foods liberal consumer base. They complained that Mackey's views represented health care as a commodity, one that, under his terms, would only be available to those who could afford it, people such as himself. They said his editorial reflected an ignorance of the structural constraints on populations that left them unable to afford the high price of health care in America. He had, it seemed, revealed himself as just another capitalist whose personal values were completely out of alignment with those of health and sustainability, the core values of his own company.

In a report on the events, ABC News interviewed a Whole Foods shopper who vowed she would never again shop at the stores because, "I think a CEO should take care that if he speaks about politics, that his beliefs at least reflect [that of] the majority of his clients" (Friedman). In response to the international outrage, Mackey posted an entry on his blog at Wholefoodsmarket. com: "I was asked to write an Op/Ed piece and I gave my personal opinions" and "while I am in favor of health care reform, Whole Foods Market as a company has no official position on the issue." He argued that the headline on the *Wall Street Journal* op-ed piece was not of his choosing; it implied that the views in the article also represented the corporate stance of Whole Foods Market on national health care when that was not the case.

Mackey had, it seems, violated his "authenticity"; he wasn't *walking the talk*. LOHAS consumers don't want to be "sold" a product—they want a holistic package, according to Paul Ray and Sherry Ruth Anderson. That means the product they buy needs to stand for more than its immediate utility. It needs to be a reflection of the company's values regarding the environment, health, and social justice.

Related to this is another issue known as "green-washing." Brad Warkens said in *The LOHAS Journal* that he did not intend to allow his company's "media properties [to] be used to blatantly green-wash products or companies." Green-washing is a take on the idiom "white-washing" whereby certain facts are hidden from view if thought to be less than helpful to the goals of the company. It refers to companies that attempt to use the ideals of environmentalism and sustainability to sell their products and services but actually have a shallow commitment to environmental or sustainable values. According to *Greenwashing Index,* "It's green-washing when a company or organization spends more time and money claiming to be 'green' through advertising and marketing than actually implementing business practices that minimize environmental impact." The site goes on to give examples such as a hotel chain that advertises itself as green because it allows patrons to reuse linens but does nothing to reduce its carbon footprint "where it counts" such as "on its grounds, with its appliances, in its kitchens and with its vehicle fleet" (http://www.greenwashingindex.com).

Paul Katzeff of Thanksgiving Coffee once complained that Starbucks was guilty of green-washing because that firm claimed to be a socially responsible company based on the fact that the company carried some fair trade coffee. (Fair trade coffee refers to coffee beans grown organically or naturally, without toxic agri-chemicals, and are purchased in ways that ensure farmers a livable, fair wage for their product.) "[Thanksgiving Coffee] revenues are about $4 million," and "Starbucks does billions," Katzeff said in 2004 (qtd. in Condor 20). "Does it seem right they only do five to ten times more fair-trade coffee than our company?" Katzeff argued. He said it was not and that it amounted to a "form of green washing because Starbucks makes most of its billions in annual global sales on non–fair trade coffee" (20).

"If you're lying about what your product can deliver, you're lying," says Ken Dychtwald, CEO of Age Wave (qtd. in Nachman-Hunt, "The Hunt" 26). George Zimmer, CEO and founder of the men's clothing chain Men's Wearhouse, told *The LOHAS Journal,* "As human beings we have the ability to sense whether or not there's congruence, if you will, between what somebody is saying and what somebody feels inside. That's what authenticity means" (Fleming, "True Values" 42). As the infamous Kermit the Frog once said, it isn't easy being green.

But to be fair, how can companies avoid charges of inauthenticity and green-washing when the concept of sustainability is so broadly and poorly defined? BBMG's 2009 *Conscious Consumer Report* measured consumer reactions to a number of product attributes. After price and quality, the highest rankings were good for your health, made in the United States, energy efficiency, convenience, hormone- and pesticide-free, fair-labor practices (safety, nondiscrimination, and fair wages), raised humanely, minimal or recyclable packaging, biodegradable, not tested on animals, locally grown or made, made from all natural ingredients, not genetically modified (GMO-free), made from recycled materials, manufactured by socially or environmentally responsible company, cause marketing, USDA organic, carbon neutral, and independent certification. That's *a lot* of measures.

Despite the breadth of meanings attached to sustainability that would, it seems, allow for endless loopholes with regard to what sustainability is or is not, the market seems to know green-washing when it sees it. When Bill Coors of Coors Brewing Company, based in Golden, Colorado, was featured in an early edition of *The LOHAS Journal*, for example, readers responded with surprise and disappointment, even anger, saying that Coors was a bad choice because his company did not reflect a strong sustainability commitment. Coors has been taken to task because of the Coors family's funding of right-wing foundations and the company's staunch anti–labor union sentiment (Dangle). Nonetheless, Frank Lampe, editor-in-chief of *The LOHAS Journal,* defended the story saying that it reflected the overall mission of the *Journal* because it described how a company was trying to become more sustainable, particularly through the vision of the company "elder." The story relayed how Coors vowed to improve the company's environmental impact after being shown two photographs, one of a Coors beer can lodged in the delicate mountain tundra and another of the same spot taken ten years later— the beer can was gone but the landscape still bore the depression made by the can's impact. "It was a very adept illustration of how fragile some of this country's ecosystems are," Coors said (Nachman-Hunt, "Bill Coors" 29).

Richard, who had worked at several LOHAS-related media organizations, was wary of companies that wanted media exposure for their sustainability efforts. In order to thwart potential green-washers, his current publication would only accept advertising from companies that spoke directly and solely about the specific branch, product, or practice of the company that was sustainable. "Think about public utilities companies," he said. "We would not be interested in having them advertise the fact that they broadly support green initiatives in their company, but we'd be interested in the fact that they derived a certain percentage of their power from wind power. The latter is a demonstrable commitment to sustainability."

Media and market organizations that want to succeed in the LOHAS marketplace should know that the target consumers are hypersensitive about green-washing. Brad Warkins of Conscious Media said that "the reality of our LOHAS world is that consumers are our foundation" (Warkins 23). "Consumer sentiment has reached a tipping point and there is a significant portion of the buying public making purchasing decisions based on ingredients, impact, manufacturing practices and company ethics," and, he said. "[T]hose buying decisions impact how people drive, eat, watch and invest" (23). And, with "three out of four consumers believing they can make a positive difference by purchasing products from socially or environmentally responsible companies," LOHAS media can afford to be more selective in the advertisers they choose to accept (BBMG). Paul Hawken, Hunter Lovins, and Amory Lovins say there is little need to "approach business as a supplicant, asking corporations to change and make a better world by respecting the limits of the environment." Rather, they say, "Companies that ignore the message of natural capitalism do so at their peril" (see http://www.natcap.org/sitepages/pid45.php).

When *The LOHAS Journal* ran a story on Patagonia, the outdoor outfitter and clothing company, it was meant to illustrate how personal ethics could be successfully combined with the workplace and still allow the company to turn a healthy profit and, in fact, even enhance the company's profitability potential. The article bluntly stated, "Patagonia Inc. is out to make money." And, that was just the teaser. The article went on to state "the outdoor gear and apparel maker also is out to save the planet. In fact, Patagonia plans to save the planet by making money" (Fleming, "Patagonia's" 18).

According to the article, Patagonia founder Yvon Chouinard told a business consultant he would not sell the company because he felt a responsibility to help the planet by making money and supporting charitable causes (Fleming, "Patagonia's" 19). The consultant considered him gravely for a moment before replying with an expletive. He pointed out that if Chouinard would sell Patagonia, the proceeds would provide an enormous pool of donations exceeding what Chouinard was presently giving. Chouinard was stunned: "It was as if the Zen master had hit us over the head with a stick," he said. "[I]nstead of finding sudden enlightenment, we were shocked and confused." It set him back several months, which he spent "soul-searching" before realizing "that once again we had fallen into the trap of thinking about the result and not the process" (19).

Chouinard realized that while selling Patagonia might have increased the flow of dollars to the chosen charities in the short term, it also would have also short-circuited his long-term view of sustainability by leaving the company in the hands of new management—possibly people who might not embrace Chouinard's sustainability principles, which guided his company.

This same problem faced another pioneer in the natural products industry, Steve Demos, the founder of White Wave, maker of tofu and of Silk soy beverages. Demos's company kept to three main goals: to change people's diets, to build a billion-dollar brand, and to change the way business was done in the United States (Lampe, "The Deal" 32). But when Demos decided to sell the company to Dean Foods, he found that Dean didn't share these goals and that was when the trouble started. White Wave sued Dean Foods, charging that the latter had acted in a "clandestine nature not in keeping with White Wave's desire to conduct business in a sustainable manner" (32).

After the case was eventually settled and the "deal with Dean" was consummated, sealed, and delivered in the form of $189 million, Demos vowed that all who had supported the company (not just those who had invested money) would benefit from the proceeds of the sale. For every year of employ, work-ers received $15,000. Demos channeled more than $17 million to managers, board members, and tenured employees with three or more years of service (Lampe, "The Deal" 35). His actions were hailed (and still are) in LOHAS culture as the act of a true visionary of sustainability because he had used the most expansive definition of that term, including not just environmental and nutritional health but worker rights as well.

"Doing the right thing," says Andy Acho, Ford Motor Company's director of environmental outreach and strategy, means keeping the company true to its principles, and hoping that "that people will see the accomplishments" (qtd. in Lampe, "One Man's" 56). This, Sam said, is what he had in mind when he started his national chain of publications. Sam wanted his media organiza-tion to focus on social transformation through educating people about the need for awareness, the need to live sustainably, and the need to be active in the process. Similarly, at LOHAS 2009 Adam Werbach urged the audience members to engage their employees fully in the sustainability vision of the company. "They are building a better world by coming to work," he said, pointing out that the integration of worker welfare into a company's focus is as vital to overall sustainability as environmental efforts such as lessening the company's carbon footprint.

"It's actions that matter, not motions," said Ford Motor's Andy Acho. In his interview with *The LOHAS Journal*, Acho emphasized that a "great" company was no longer one that simply provided quality products and services; it also had to "strive to make the world a better place" (qtd. in Lampe, "One Man's" 56). In an *Ode* magazine article on spiritual capitalism, Susan West Kurz, the owner of Dr. Haushka Skin Care products, explains how the firm sources the shea butter it needs. The butter, which is used in the company's high-end cosmetic line, is purchased from women's cooperative farms in the African nation of Burkina Faso, one of the world's poorest countries. While noting that "A business has to have a profit to be sustaining," Kurz said it's "what you do with the profit is the key" (qtd. in Hawn, "Gospel"). Kurz and her husband invested Haushka profits in the Burkina Faso farms, teaching the women biodynamic farming techniques so that they could produce raw shea butter for Kurz's company. "For the residents of Burkina Faso, the spiritual is material," states the article. Today, the farms produce more than what the company needs, and the extra is sold on the competitive market. "A bigger market for biodynamic cosmetics benefits everyone—the people of Burkina Faso, [Dr. Haushka], and its competitors," Kurz says (qtd. in Hawn, "Gospel").

Sustainability can "translate into profitability," says Ray Anderson of Inter-face Textile, Inc. (qtd. in Nachman-Hunt, "Ray Anderson's" 17). In his book, *Mid-Course Correction*, Anderson wrote, "In the strictest business sense, in the hardest-headed business sense, we have found [sustainability] to be incredibly good business" (20). He explains how adhering to sustainability principles created more than five hundred public speeches for him during six years, saying, "That in itself has lifted the image of [Interface] and created a perception in the marketplace" (qtd. in Nachman-Hunt, "Ray Anderson's" 20). Anderson, Demos, and Chouinard integrated personal values "like self-actualization, authenticity and a healthy lifestyle" with business interests to bring about a "humanization" of corporate culture carries many rewards, including profit (Fleming, "True Values" 41).

And that integration, Sam told me, isn't always easy to do. Sam said he believed there was a bias in Western culture that segregated the spheres of personal growth (self-actualization) and social welfare. Overall, personal enrichment (especially in the form of wealth gained through business) and spirituality, "to varying degrees, have been antagonistic to each other in Western culture," Sam said.

Spirituality author Parker Palmer writes in a LOHAS publication that the combination of these forces and practices are no longer a choice but an urgency. The current crises of the world, he said, stem not from a "failure of ethics," as much as "a failure of human wholeness" (P. Palmer 41). MIT professor Vaclav Simil, interviewed in the *Utne Reader* about energy use, says, "shaping the future energy use in the affluent world is primarily a moral issue, not a technical or economic matter" (qtd. in Creedon 88). In fact, Simil said, this was the case with many of the world's crises: the tools with which to solve global problems were there, but the larger issue was that tools are useless without "a new open-mindedness" and the "right attitude" (88). That attitude allows us to "deepen our respect for each other and for the living planet that supports us" (88).

Through this type of holistic thinking, business is transformed from a "career path" to a "destiny path" (Middendorf, "For a Higher" 50). This "work ethic" has carried through LOHAS as it has throughout American culture in general. In *The Protestant Ethic and the Spirit of Capitalism*, Max Weber brought attention to how Protestantism changed ideas about work as a *calling*, a way in which to use one's special God-given talents to serve spiritual or religious values. Developing those talents required devotion to self-development, and being paid for labor on the self was reconciled to a more noble purpose by framing that work as a way in which to make manifest more of God's intended abundance on earth. These puritan ethics rationalized money as a virtuous endeavor, reflective of the devotion of the spiritual practitioner in the workplace (Weber).

Employees and entrepreneurs, service providers, and CEOs alike become interpellated as servants of humanity in LOHAS. For example, Susan Davis, president of Capital Missions Company, an investment company in Wisconsin, defined herself in *The LOHAS Journal* as a "servant-leader" and said "living for an altruistic purpose within the business world can bring recognition and financial success, but the deep gratification of service takes your life to its highest level and brings unimaginable joy" (qtd. in Middendorf, "For a Higher" 50). By earning our livings without "violat[ing] our basic values," we remember that our work is meant to serve people, not just a bottom line, says Parker Palmer in *Spirituality & Health* (40). A speaker at LOHAS Forum 2005 put it differently: "Don't be a Democrat in life and a Republican in business."

Patricia Aburdene, coauthor with John Naisbitt of the best seller *Megatrends 2000* (1990) and who keynoted the LOHAS Forum 2006, authored her own version of a megatrend, *Megatrends 2010: Conscious Capitalism*. Quoted in the *Christian Science Monitor*, Aburdene says: "The focus on spirituality has become so pervasive that it stands as today's greatest megatrend. Its impact on personal lives is spreading into institutions. And spirituality in business is converging with other socioeconomic trends to foster a moral transformation in capitalism" (Lampman 2005).

Many companies in the LOHAS marketplace are explicitly spiritual in their product materials, such as *Yoga Journal*, Golden Temple, and Dr. Bronner's 100 percent Environmentally Friendly Magic Soaps. Founded by the late Dr. Emanuel Bronner, Dr. Bronner's Magic Soaps can be found in stores around the world. Bronner was born to a successful soap-making family in Germany and immigrated to America in the 1920s after his desire to modernize the family's business along with his Zionist views caused conflict with members of his immediate family. His parents would later die in the Holocaust concentration camps. In his new country, Bronner resolved to do what he could to promote tolerance, and as a soap maker that commitment manifested on his product's labels, which are crowded blocks of nearly imperceptibly tiny inspirational messages based on his philosophy of the All-One or the universal divine force. These thirty thousand words of "truth" relay his conviction that all people and all gods (and goddesses) are one, interconnected in their diversity much like an ecosystem. Bronner espoused what would later become articulated in conscious capitalism, where the goal of one's life should be to "create constructive capitalism where the corporation shares the profits with its workers and the earth" (Shalmy 28).

In LOHAS discourse, the individual initiates constructive capitalism by applying spiritual insights and motivations to work, no matter what that work might be. For example, *Spirituality & Health* ran an article about hair stylist and entrepreneur David Wagner, who described how he reinvented his job, turning it into a conduit for spiritual work. While shampooing and styling the hair of one regular client, Wagner started joking with the woman. He thought no more of it until a few days after the appointment, when he received a startling communiqué from her. She wrote him saying "his kindness and the fun they shared that day had given her hope enough to check herself into a hospital instead of taking her own life as she had planned." This inspired Wagner to start Daymakers, his new business speaking at beauty shows around the country sharing his philosophies about making work meaningful, what he calls creating "inner wealth"—"giving others joy (which brings joy) . . . and practicing the most basic spiritual aphorism: do unto others" (qtd. in L. Palmer 22).

Carl, editor-in-chief of a national consumer publication in the LOHAS space, told me that his publication focused on this type of conjoining of the inner and outer realms of experience, calling it an "activist magazine in a lot of ways," because it inspired people to "do" things in different ways, including infusing their jobs with spiritual purpose. Fran, the editor and former owner of a LOHAS publication, told me she believed "it is spiritual to be sustainable." When I asked her why she would consider sustainability to be a spiritual issue, she replied that sustainability meant "seeing the continuity of life" and that in itself was spiritual in nature. "When they built the pyramids they knew that—that life would go on past one's own self," she said.

While my informants mostly praised spirituality as a bridge between liberal individualism and social solidarity, there are solid critiques in the sustainability scholarship that argue spirituality only serves to mystify the "facts" of social and environmental problems (Porritt 2002). Porritt has argued that any "whiff of New Age mysticism," in particular, is regarded by many in sustainability activism as potentially damaging to the "scientific credibility" of environmental and social justice efforts.

The fear that the application of spirituality would obfuscate rather than empower change lies at the root of an interesting critique of the 1960s European Green Party. Carl Boggs commended the party's "post-industrial" approach to the "pervasive crisis of industrialism in the West" through a vision of an "ecologically balanced, non-hierarchical society," but he questioned why the party included what he felt was a peculiar and unnecessary emphasis on spirituality. He pointed out that Green leaders emphasized "inner values and commitments—for example, the intimate connection with human community and nature—that suggested that the crisis of industrialism is ultimately rooted in a pervasive moral and spiritual breakdown" (881). But why was it necessary? he asked. Why weren't human and environmental crises such as fascism, pollution, and starvation enough in themselves to call people to engage in social change without the addition of love and spirituality?

Boggs was convinced "[p]reoccupation with the mystical experience can only force popular struggles back upon themselves, toward the embrace of an inner consciousness and individualism, with its arbitrary points of reference, which inevitably undercuts the process of collective mobilization" (882). The Greens responded that love is "the "emotional power that drives people to collective action"; that love is the act where "spiritual and physical are united and not reduced to performance or to consumer goods. This form of spiritualism leads people toward the experience of their real being, toward eroticism, toward a yearning for wholeness" (881). The Greens' response to Boggs reflected a very different interpretation of spirituality from Boggs's rather reductive treatment—as mystical, as something clouding the collective goal in such a way as to provoke a destructive individualism.

This argument between Boggs and the Greens is of interest because it is one that hasn't gone away. Those who defend spirituality's utility in sustainability efforts say spiritualization can provide another way of "knowing" or *perceptions* about the understanding and practices of sustainability. Like the Greens, Porritt says that despite the "arrogant secularism" of those in sustainability movements, it is spiritual sources that can address the two most "pressing sustainability challenges"—controlling the "seduction of consumerism and developing a reverential ethos for natural systems." Sustainability scholars Tábara and Giner offer that sustainability may be on its way to becoming the fourth moral and cultural pillar necessary for maintaining the social fabric of modernity for the next generations to come (280).

These arguments favoring the pragmatic application of spirituality echo research findings of William James in his study of practitioners of mind cure and New Thought in America, practices that form the bedrock of LOHAS. James found that practitioners of those therapeutic traditions reported living happier, more fulfilling lives—but their spiritual practices only operated successfully (in any pragmatic sense) when practitioners believed they had received them with the "'the force of a revelation' which requires novelty to spark faith, enthusiasm and example," (qtd. in Duclow 49). Focusing on the individual as the first step in creating global sustainability, LOHAS discourse aims to make its audience members conscious of the urgent need to live a sustainable lifestyle, and this revelation comes through the use of spiritualized appeals. Spirituality as revelation, then, provides the bridging logic in LOHAS between consumerism and sustainability.

To understand how LOHAS achieves this, it's helpful to understand the pragmatic relationship Americans have with "spirituality." Since the American

Revolution, the religious sphere has been fertile ground for the creative, ideological, and counter-hegemonic thinking of U.S. citizens. Nathan O. Hatch has described how the democratization of Christianity from the American Revolution through 1845 occurred through the proliferation of new religious movements such as mind cure and new thought. These were propelled by a swelling belief on the part of ordinary people that they were just as capable as educated elites of being thinking, free, and authoritative bodies empowered to resculpt the social spheres of life through dissension, debate, and distribution of information and ideas. "They dreamed that a new age of religious and social harmony would naturally spring up out of their efforts to overthrow coercive and authoritarian structures," Hatch says (10–11).

Toward that end, "the very structures of society were undergoing a democratic winnowing," Hatch says (6). During that time, there was a rising sense of egalitarianism rooted in popular culture as a way to shift sharply away from the European legacy of hierarchical authority, the privilege of birthright, and the exclusion of workers from positions and expressions of power. So completely outside anything these early Americans had experienced up until then, they turned to religious teachings to help them work through the revolutionary times they understood themselves to be a part of. As "a diverse array of evangelical firebrands went about the task of movement-building in the generation after the Revolution" their inspirational rhetoric blended spiritual learning with "the new democratic vocabularies" that were sweeping through the American popular cultures (7).

Former Czech president Vaclav Havel has argued that social change *can only* occur in tandem with changes in the "sphere of the spirit, in the sphere of human conscience, in the actual attitude of man towards the world and his understanding of himself and his place in the overall order of existence." I put this idea to Frank Lampe, asking him if he saw spiritual work as the natural precursor for social transformation. He replied, "I think that people who pursue that path see value in it to societies and want to manifest it on a bigger scale than just personal life." He added, "Once you arrive at some level of health or awareness of these concepts surrounding mind, body, and spirit, I think you can make a conscious effort to influence the world around you."

Religion scholars Catherine Albanese, Linda Woodhead, and Ursula King have referred respectively to "New Spirituality," a "turn to life," and a "Postmodern Spirituality," where the worked-upon self becomes the tool for social transformation based on "a strong social ethic" (Albanese, "Fisher Kings" 138). "This ethic might be called an activist form of mystical endeavor, for it supports transformational work in society as an outgrowth and manifestation of transformation of the self. . . . Those who embrace the new spirituality have thereby stayed in touch with the social, political, and economic texture of their times," Albanese says (138).

LOHAS texts take an expansive view on spirituality in terms of its contents, as Thomas Moore, author of such spiritual books as *Care of the Soul*, intimates. He says in his article in *Spirituality & Health* that perhaps we have "too limited a notion of the spiritual." He argues that without spirituality, people spiral into chaos and that spirituality needn't be "mysticized" at all. Instead, Moore says, spirituality is a pragmatic and natural act, one that enables individuals to move toward a collective understanding. Everything we do, political or otherwise, is spiritual in nature, he says, and we ignore this at our peril. "Money, traffic, business, building construction—all of these are spiritual activities to the polycentric spiritual person," he says, and when "any aspect of life is deprived of its spiritual depth, it becomes demonic and destructive" (T. Moore, "Spiritual"). Spirituality's disentanglement from formal religion allows participants and organizations to articulate deep values without being constrained by any one path (see Schlehofer, Omoto, and Adelman).

This pragmatic spirituality is essentialized in LOHAS as "natural" or inherent to each human. It is the path through which to experience life fully, including obtaining a sustainability consciousness. The use of healthy and sustainable products and practices assist consumers and producers in their (re)discovery of the spiritual dimension of their everyday lives. As an example of this, the introduction to a segment on *Oasis Television* about interfaith minister Marianne Williamson reads, "Marianne shows how we can apply our years of personal growth, meditation, affirmations and universal love—not merely for a better life, or a better job, or better relationships—but for a better planet." That is, through our shopping, playing, work, family life, and more, we simultaneously participate in a deep and meaningful spiritual practice under the rubric of "fair trade," "organic," "natural," "socially responsible," "green or eco," "integrative," "holistic," "sustainable," or "healthy." Each of these bespeaks a path toward both self-fulfillment and social and environmental improvement.

6. Mindful Consumption

In this chapter, we continue to examine the ways in which the "producers" of LOHAS overcome conceptual hurdles between sustainability and capitalism and between market dynamics and spirituality by fortifying and refuting various mythic components of the American Dream. The resulting set of spiritual and intellectual "values" infuses the work of LOHAS producers and their personal values and identities as well. Let's look more closely at the LOHAS response to the received, conflicted narrative about consumer culture's incompatibility with sustainability.

Even though "LOHAS" is mostly a trade term, we have to keep in mind that everything LOHAS producers make, sell, and promote is ultimately done with an idealized "LOHAS" consumer in mind—that is, business isn't done for its own sake. Consumption is production's dance partner; consumers and producers dialectically create and direct the actions of each other through the interchange of messages and texts.

Obviously, producers market products and services based on real or perceived benefits (ease pain, improve sleep, deodorize, or add pizzazz to the wardrobe, for example). In this way products and services serve as "valued symbols" (Csikszentmihalyi 23). This means that objects have an aura or a value that stretches beyond their actual usefulness. Products and services can be turned into self-identifiers; they make "individuals" out of people by marking their unique preferences in ways that set them apart from others. And, in the case of LOHAS, it's hoped that these products and practices will serve as the "external props" that keep the sustainable self firmly in focus (23). This is metonymic work, articulating some actions and objects (a hybrid car, for example) as stand-ins, symbols, or representations of other beliefs, such as "consciousness," "wisdom," and "sustainability."

In the mediated and commodified articulation of sustainability-as-lifestyle, accoutrements of the consumer culture—the "stuff" you eat, sleep on, wear, and invest in—become your statement of consciousness to the world and to yourself, as the following excerpt from a LOHAS consumer magazine illustrates: "For Roxanne and Michael Klein, living well means living in balance with the earth. From the food they eat to the materials they used to construct their home, the Kleins have a lifestyle that reflects their philosophy of honoring nature" (Monte 78).

How did the Kleins learn to arrange their lives in a way that reflects their principles? How did they decide to adopt a philosophy of honoring nature at all? Pierre Bourdieu's notion of "cultural intermediaries" provides a way for us to think about these questions (*Distinction* 359). Bourdieu's intermediaries include media, which, in our case here, visibly and publicly generate meanings about sustainability and health as "LOHASian," reconciling those terms with specific consumer goods. As part of this, these texts need to be able to neutralize certain potentially harmful narratives about consumption that have circulated in the culture, especially when contextualized with environmental or social activism. In general, these LOHAS-unfriendly dialogues say that consumerism is narcotizing and narcissistic, imperialistic and oppressive. LOHAS's most important job is to reposition consumption in the popular imaginations of the target audience in such a way that it can be understood as a service to sustainability, as a "ritualized expression of collective consciousness, the moral act and the hoped-for transcendence of hegemonic economic and political systems," as Belk, Wallendorf, and Sherry say (59).

Amy Domini, founder of Domini Social Investments and an acknowledged pioneer of the socially responsible investing movement, said in an early issue of *The LOHAS Journal* that "consumption has been the greatest social-change force on the planet—it hasn't necessarily been a positive one, but it has driven the world we live in" (Lampe, "Eight Questions" 34). This ambivalence about consumption dogs the LOHAS discourse, and no wonder. The 1960s social movements that informed so much of LOHAS and the early entrepreneurial market of natural and organic products generated deep and troubling questions about how profit, money, and power, played a role in social ills, including the acceleration of the Vietnam war, racism, and Western imperialism.

These movements revived Marxist concerns about the exchange of labor for money and the erosion of the fulfilling nature of productive activity, viewed as essential and vital to human sustenance, serving as a creative and satisfying act (*Capital*). Marx warned about the fetishization of the commodity form, whereby goods became laden with meanings far beyond their utilitarian nature. This resulted in shifting the nature of social relations and obscuring the actual terms of production, including the quantity and condition of the raw materials and labor resources used in the process. Various critiques of consumerism surfaced throughout the twentieth century including those that treated it as a result of the sheer "manipulation of individuals' wills," say Moisander and Pesonen (177). Critics charged that consumer culture and its relentless advertising created an obsession with the *new* and posed "luxuries as necessities" (Robbins 16).

As World War II came to a close, scholars Max Horkheimer and Theodor Adorno focused on the expansion of the "culture industries" of media, accusing these of producing a mass culture that squeezed out individual thought and innovation and substituted genuine experience for the facsimile of it, creating airy diversions from serious social issues. The culture industries manufactured desires that supported the goals of capitalism but had little or nothing to do with the aims of civic engagement, they said. Adorno and Horkheimer, along with other critical theorists of the time, feared entertainment and goods distracted consumers through the promise of an easier life, tricking people into believing that through consumption, they were expressing freedom of choice and improving their quality of life when, in truth, their wants and desires were actually being carefully crafted and nurtured by market organizations for the purposes of company profit only.

Later in the century, Pierre Bourdieu proposed that ideals and lifestyles were manufactured and conveyed through culture and materiality by constructing relationships between goods and practices and notions of "good taste" and "distinction." By linking the culture industries, social networks, and products and practices to class interests and the dynamics of power, Bourdieu showed how symbolic forms engender and reinforce material inequalities and disparities.

Classical social theorist Emile Durkheim said the economy, if left unchecked, would lead to the "destruction of the moral basis of social order" (Zukin and Maguire 174). French theorist Jean Baudrillard followed up with this argument, saying that consumption had become the new driving force of social relations, and, as a result, had become the means of ideology, of power and control over the masses (Baudrillard 80; Payne 50). Bourdieu, too, rejected the claims being made by market organizations and social institutions that consumers were experiencing a new sort of freedom, thanks to the plentiful choices in the marketplace. He argued that "consumption was not so much an option as it was a duty of the consumer-citizen," say Zukin and Maguire (183).

Contemporary critiques have carried on in the same vein, charging consumer culture with veiling deep-rooted anxieties and unhappiness by stimulating endless desire for more things at any cost. Critics argue that capitalism is incapable of serving reform movements because of its innate need for profit maximization, which breeds deception as well as inequalities and injustices that trickle through the strata of societies. Laborers become locked into the structure of capitalism without the means to resist its hegemony, and this argument has intensified under the terms of global trade.

Environmentalists point out that the rise of consumer culture throughout the twentieth century plundered natural resources in order to serve amped-up production. They say consumerism equals a *throwaway* society, one that ignores the implications of a product's lifecycle, and that consumerism serves to justify the notion that new is better because it represents innovation, quality of life, and economic health. The result is increased air, land, and soil pollution. Even "green consumerism" has been castigated, called out as an ineffective answer to environmental and social issues because it doesn't go far enough to educate consumers about how to minimize their impact on the planet, nor does it adequately destabilize the centrality of consumerism overall. As a result, according to these critiques, consumers can't envision the other roles and sites of power they could potentially occupy that would better support environmental efforts than would the purchase of eco goods.

Writing about the role of consumerism in the transition to a sustainable society, sustainability scholar Michael Cahill echoes Durkheim. He says consumer society undermines collective life because of its tendency toward the private and the personal. Consumers are unable to understand the web of their influence with and impact on the earth or other people. And, Cahill accuses media as largely responsible for these developments because of their promotion of privatized lifestyles during the course of the past thirty years (630).

Amid this hefty criticism, however, stand those who say these concerns are based on a very facile treatment of consumer culture. Lawrence Moore, for example, reminds us that "consumption once served a reformist perspective" in America. Writing in the early twentieth century, social critic and novelist Edward Bellamy believed consumption could be "the promise of deliverance from routinized toil and social anarchy," because it would finally enable the masses to enjoy the fruits of their factory and industrialized labor (Fox and Lears ix). While novelist Emile Zola vilified the opening of shops as "snares of desire" that trapped and numbed individuals, mostly women, Zukin and Maguire point out that these same boutiques also provided new opportunities for women to leave the domicile unescorted and to form new relationships and to glean new perspectives about the world.

In America, goods served to cohere collective activism. Early Americans wore homespun against the skin to serve as both a symbol of a citizen's loyalty to the cause of American Independence and as reflection of appreciation of the greatness of the wilderness, regarded as part of God's divine plan (Albanese *Nature*). Even the temperance movement—which encouraged individuals to pursue new spiritual directions—included efforts to reform "capitalism so that wealth and moral choices acted as mutual reinforcements," Lawrence Moore says (208–9). These resistive uses of consumer culture have faded from view in light of "attacks on the consumptive mentality of Americans [that] have become cottage industry of recent social criticism" (208).

Examining the cause of this, Zukin and Maguire found that scholars conducted many of the studies on consumerism during the 1970s and early 1980s, a "period when developed economies were moving from a production base to one of consumption," and when, as a result, "consumption was becoming a more visible factor in both the creative destruction of the landscape . . . and the conscious reshaping of the self" (Zukin and Maguire 176). To put this into perspective, consider that money spent on advertising leapt to $437 billion globally in 1998, "a figure that rivals the $778 billion spent on weapons" (Robbins 16–17).

It is little wonder these researchers regarded consumption so suspiciously. The new economy brought with it changes that shook American society to its core. Throughout the twentieth century, social institutions shifted to accommodate the new emphasis on consumption: for example, higher education created business courses and the federal government developed the Federal Commerce Department, which aimed to "break down all barriers between consumers and commodities" (Robbins 16–17). The most basic of everyday practices, from sleeping to eating, were reshaped to accommodate the new culture of consumption. But as commodities replaced other traditional markers of success and of identity, new forms of class-consciousness appeared.

Robbins attributes the rise of consumerism to four major developments: "a revolution in marketing and advertising, a restructuring of major societal institutions, a revolution in spiritual and intellectual values, and a reconfiguration of space and class" (16). As for spiritual and intellectual values, these had moved away from the early American emphasis on "frugality and self-denial" and toward values "that sanctioned periodic leisure, compulsive spending, and individual fulfillment," Robbins says (16).

The assumptions about consumerism and commodities arrived at through those 1970s and 1980s studies were often based on reductive and simplistic models that assigned *types* of consumers to *types* of products (Zukin and Maguire, 175). The notion that consumers are manipulated by more powerful and all-knowing market organizations operates too much like the early "hypodermic effect" theories about media, which asserted that media were capable of "injecting" receivers with meanings, rendering them the dupes of propaganda and corporate pleasure.

Later empirical studies of both media and consumerism made a "cultural turn," meaning scholars began to factor in "culture" in their investigations, paying attention to the manner in which goods are culturally embedded. This opened room to consider materiality on a micro scale—where individuals use various resources, including media, to project meanings onto goods different from those that might be intended by the manufacturers. This meant that scholars rethought how goods could become the tableau of the "subjective experience of people and the small details of everyday resistance," as Colleen McDannell says (12).

Subsequent studies on consumption following in this vein resurrect earlier thinking about consumption as a practice productive of civic identity and action. For example, Latin American anthropologist and cultural critic Nestor Garcia Canclini argues for consumerism as a viable channel into civic engagement, saying that the marketplace promotes people's analytic or critical factors by encouraging them to consider what they need and what sorts of attributes different products offer (see Zukin and Maguire 187). "The mediated discourse of consumer culture provides a symbolic language—increasingly, a global language—for men and women, teens and children, to think about their needs," Zukin and Maguire say (187).

Along with the perspectival shift in consumerism studies came a clearer understanding of the complexity of the processes involved in meaning making. Researchers posited that material goods could be as productive of symbolic meanings as any other realm of life. Goods could represent certain needs and experiences in social life, the meanings of which were further facilitated by media and market. Discourses and representations about social life stand as dialectical constructions occurring "through the interplay" among consumers, media, and market (Varman and Belk 230). "Representations involve elements like the words used to describe products, the stories told about them, the images produced, the emotions associated with them, the way they are classified, and the values that are placed on them," say Varman and Belk (230).

In the case of eco-goods, "green" commodities may serve to anchor and to renew the sense of stewardship regnant within Protestantism by making visible and real the consumer's commitment to environmentalism. The discourse about "environmental ethics" might facilitate different types of identity, specifically more collective-oriented subjectivity, "through the rejection of the kind of individuality that has been imposed on citizens as 'consumers,'" say Moisander and Pesonen (331).

Peter Jackson's question, posed in the beginning of this book, bears repeating here. He asks if there is a way to understand consumerism as capable of promoting collective conscience and moral social order as a lifestyle without either overemphasizing "consumer sovereignty" or engaging in a negative critique of "consumer-as-dupes" (210). It is possible only if we consider capitalism and consumerism as flexible phenomena and only if we acknowledge the sites of power operative within these. To this, Langley and Mellor have argued for analysts to consider a "middle way" approach to the economy that opens up "spaces" that can "enable transformative action despite the contemporary advance of global markets in terms of extent and intensity" (49). This is a relevant argument in defense of LOHAS.

For this to occur, the "market" must be conceptually disentangled from "economy." This makes obvious the enormous variation of exchange behavior already existent in the economy such as bartering and buying locally. These "domestic-local" practices, Langley and Mellor say, represent "everyday forms of resistance" because they support local economies and workers (59, 62). These types of practices can reveal the real costs of production because the cycle occurs within view of the consumer, either directly or through the local press, and this firsthand view generates a deeper understanding of what it takes to grow, harvest, process, and distribute crops and goods. Additionally, locally based processes reduce the environmental costs incurred by long-distance distribution of goods while also minimizing the adverse market pressures on growers from middlemen, transportation costs, commodity market prices, and more (see Marx *Capital* and *Grundrisse*).

The LOHAS "Middle Way"

There's lively contestation over the idea of money, profit, and consumption in LOHAS culture and discourse. On the one hand, LOHAS reweaves ideas from the 1960s counterculture about consumer culture as atomizing and spiritually debilitating. Consumption can lead to a "painful, contagious, socially transmitted condition of overload, debt, anxiety, and waste resulting from the dogged pursuit of more," says *Yoga Journal* (Colin 113). On the other hand, LOHAS is squarely situated in the midst of consumer culture and industry, so it can't help but make as its mission the resurrection of latent and dormant ideas about consumption as a labor of collective consciousness. This is where the most important work of LOHAS occurs—at that point of tension between supporting market capitalism and calling for its reform.

Barbara Kingsolver asks in the LOHAS publication *Utne Reader* why consumption should be so privileged in society, noting that the one sphere where it was not dominant was religion. Religions, she said, encourage people—through tithing, charity work, refusal to collect interest, or even the decision to take vows of poverty—to give money away rather than to accumulate it. Calling to mind Baudrillard's critique about consumerism's effects on civic engagement, she says that "even one's patriotism and good sense may be called into doubt if one elects to earn less money or own fewer possessions than is humanly possible" (56).

Kingsolver suggests Americans "rein in the free market's tyranny over [the] family's tiny portion of America and install values that override the profit motive." Doing so, she believes, can make us "happier souls." In fact, Kingsolver says not only does she "sleep better at night" thanks to feeling more "connected to the things that help make a person whole" but also that the process has been for her a "spiritual conversion" (56).

In another article in the *Utne Reader*, Noelle Oxenhandler, an author on Buddhism and modern culture, writes about how she changed her thinking about money. She had long associated spirituality with poverty but had come to acknowledge the usefulness and the reality of moneymaking. She explained that for much of her young life she was under the impression that "it is harder for a rich man to enter the gates of heaven than for a camel to go through the eye of a needle," and had come to regard money as a dirty thing (Oxenhandler 104). As an adult, she became a devout follower of Buddhism and linked "being poor with feeling blessed" (104). No surprise then that she "missed the great bull market of the late twentieth century." As time wore on, she began to notice that her fellow baby boomers who had tended well to their financial lives were now middle aged and seeking out spiritual lessons, just as Oxenhandler was seeking out books on personal finance. "Sometimes when I think of the lack of concern that my [Buddhist] companions and I had for money, it does seem a kind of hubris, a blindness to a particular kind of Karma, to certain laws of cause and effect," Oxenhandler writes (106). "I have come to a belated admiration for people who have truly made their way in the world, to an appreciation of the discipline it took" (104). These types of texts may open up for consumers new perspectives on spending money.

At LOHAS Forum 9 in 2005, Weider's Barbara Harris made a plea for a "middle way." In her presentation at the conference, Harris quoted Vietnamese Buddhist teacher and monk Thich Nhat Hahn saying, "The more we consume the more we suffer and the more we make our society suffer." After letting that shocker sink into the trade-conference audience, she said the only way out is through mindful consumption. And "what is mindful consumption?" Harris asked the LOHAS Forum audience. She replied that it meant conscientious use of the earth's natural resources and of the mind. It meant being mindful of the thoughts one absorbs, including those received through media.

Mindful consumption is the LOHAS remedy to the critiques of consumerism. It counters "mindless" consumption—the urge or drive to purchase simply for the act of purchasing and the acquisition of something new and different. Mindless consumption is buying without considering the impact of the product's production and distribution. Mindful consumption, on the other hand, means assessing a product's lifecycle, not taking more than you need, and finding other avenues to self-fulfillment besides accumulation. It means supporting specific types of products and practices that in turn support cultures, worker rights, environments, and animal rights.

This middle way in LOHAS—offered up as the antidote to a frenetic Westernized life—is based on living more simply, what is often called "slow living." In the April 2007 *Vogue Australia*, an untitled article describes how one can identify the LOHAS lifestyle. It identifies a LOHASian as a person who adopts various eco and healthy practices, including "going slow" (*Vogue Australia*). "Millions of Americans have revised their notions of the good life," writes David E. Shi, "because they feel so overworked, stressed out, and vulnerable to sudden layoffs" (xi). No wonder one of the top-selling consumer magazines in the country is *Real Simple*, a publication focused on teaching us how to pare down our time, costs, and clutter.

Writing in *O magazine* about the Simple Living movement, which is based on the philosophy that less is more, Alison Glock writes, "Many of us are coming to recognize that time spent watching *Real Housewives of Atlanta* is not time that buffers the soul." Voluntary simplicity, according to an article in the LOHAS publication *Experience Life* magazine, can be a "means of fostering greater life freedom, personal integrity or social justice" (Hart 82). The idea is to "look beyond the dollar value of every purchase to its deeper value and leaving wasteful consumption patterns behind" (82). But at Simpleliving.net, simple living is defined as an "examined life," whereby you "decide what is important for you and discard the rest." That leaves a lot of negotiating room.

In LOHAS, simple living equals good living. Simplicity is presented in the clean lines of the straw-bale house, in the homegrown heirloom tomato, or in a meal of healthy foods shared with one's family. It is a lifestyle of comfort, abundance, and joy, not austerity, but it tries to come to terms with the hyper-production of goods and the constant messages in the culture that we should buy them, and keep on buying them. Simplicity is "avoiding the thoughtless worship of the new and doing daily tasks in the simplest ways"

(Spayde 58). Greed, even if you're greedily accumulating organic carrots, is not simple living, then. "Greed comes from a poverty mentality," admonishes yoga teacher and author Cyndi Lee in the *Yoga Journal* (qtd. in Moran 64). Lee explains that "a poverty mentality is feeling like you don't have enough, so you try to get more. . . . It causes a person to want more—more food, clothes, complements, attention, anything" (64). "Curiously, *affluence* [my emphasis] can breed this poverty mentality as efficiently as lack can, especially in a media-dominated society saturated with the message that acquisition and consumption are the keys to power and pleasure," says Victoria Moran (64), author of *Fit from Within: 101 Simple Secrets to Change Your Body and Your Life*.

The impulse to acquire is treated in LOHAS like other diseases of the body, and LOHAS texts contain plenty of "how-to" articles to correct the "Affluenza" (De Graaf, Wann, and Naylor) in the culture, the desire to have more and more. The message is clear: if we're going to live sustainably, we are going to need to think differently about accumulation.

Simple living is meant to "slow us down" (Korelitz 100) and to provide us with "natural pleasures" (Erney 88), while leaving "less of an ecological footprint" (Colin 113). These attributes are the building blocks of sustainable goods and services offered on the LOHAS buffet; they are implicit and explicit in the marketing of fair trade, organic, socially responsible, natural, cruelty-free, vegan, vegetarian, and holistic products. These help everyone to live a better life, the marketing claims.

An article in *Natural Solutions* titled "To Live Simply is to Live Well" cited Duane Elgin's 1981 book *Voluntary Simplicity*, calling it a "game plan for the modern world" (Crawford). "Taking inventory of one's life and clearing away the excess in the process, Elgin proposed, was a way to 'cultivate more meaningful work and a stronger sense of family and community, and to make a greater contribution to the world'" (Crawford). The article said, "One recent sign of this is the slow movement." The April 2007 *Vogue Australia* article on the LOHAS lifestyle names membership in the Slow Food Movement as an important part of slow or LOHAS living (*Vogue Australia* 135). The Italian food critic Carlo Petrini invented the term "slow food" in the mid-1980s, after hurling bowls of penne in protest at the opening of a McDonald's restaurant in Rome. While his fellow Italians were having happy thoughts about their forthcoming Happy Meals, Petrini saw the opening of the chain as another hammerhead on local traditions, local businesses and farms, and the condition and quality of food. He saw globalization represented in those golden arches, and it spelled social and environmental malfeasance. Petrini well understood what George Ritzer has called in his famous book of the same name the "McDonaldization" of society that "affects not only the restaurant business, but also education, work, the criminal justice system, health care, travel, leisure, dieting, politics, the family, religion and virtually every other aspect of society" (Ritzer 2).

Petrini was one Italian food critic who wasn't going to take his Big Mac sitting down. When he came up with the term *eco-gastronomy*, he decided to wage a battle against the encroaching homogenization of his culture and against what he saw as the undermining of the social, economic, and political fabric of Italy. The seeds were sown for the creation of the Slow Food Movement to combat "the uniformity of sensory perception, mass standardization, loss of identity, and unhealthy eating habits" (Petrini xxii).

The movement aimed to support local agricultural systems. This included supporting traditional foods, encouraging healthy and tasteful foods that result from natural and traditional agricultural methods and food preparation, encouraging ways of eating food that build community and good health, favoring locally owned and operated businesses over multinational corporations, revving up policy-making for the protection of endangered foods, educating people about nutrition and food traditions including food handling and preparation, and supporting the environment though biodiversity and other natural and organic agricultural methods (see Petrini; Ritzer).

The campaign has been successful by anyone's standards: In the twenty-plus years since Petrini launched the movement, Slow Food chapters have sprouted around the world. According to Slow Food International (http://www.slowfood.com), there are 100,000 members in 132 countries. In the United States, at the 2008 Slow Food Nation festival in San Francisco, 85,000 foodies celebrated the Slows. Speakers included celebrated food scholar, author, and columnist Michael Pollan, who joined Carlo Petrini along with a who's who of environmental and social activism: Vandana Shiva, Winona LaDuke, Marion Nestle, Carl Pope, and Wendell Berry.

Food intersects with almost every issue LOHAS takes on, including integrative health care, organic agriculture, fair trade, nutrition, the environment, worker rights, poverty, and animal cruelty. The idea of Slow Food holds the essential LOHAS principle that health and happiness are inseparable. And, when it comes to food, our health and happiness depend not only on how food is grown but also on how it is eaten. Slow Food supporters charge that Western culture has reduced food to the mere intake of calories to reduce the pain of hunger. Michael Pollan, for example, says the "fundamental act of choosing one's food . . . has become a simple calculation of price for most consumers in the United States" (qtd. in Rose). It has lost in the bargain ties to environmental stewardship, spirituality, and social cohesion—the core of the Slow Food Movement and also that of LOHAS.

These trends toward the fast and thoughtless may well be changing judging by the increase in membership in Slow Food, the rise in purchase of books about food politics and culture, and on restaurant trends. As to the latter, the LOHAS.com website states: "A new National Restaurant Association survey of more than 1,600 professional chefs—members of the American Culinary Federation (ACF)—revealed that 'nutrition and philosophy-driven food choices' will be the hottest trends on restaurant menus in 2009."

In an article on Slow Food, *Utne Reader* correspondent Nick Rose writes: "[Michael Pollan] tells *The Sun* that 'our relationship to food constitutes our most profound engagement with the natural world.' To sever that relationship with a trip to the supermarket, then, is not only a crime against the environment, it's a crime against yourself. When people start to become personally invested in what they eat, they enter into what Pollan calls 'a kind of landscape and kind of community.' While a whole litany of benefits result from the 'relationship' model, Pollan argues, the current system breeds nothing but problems: '[C]heapness and ignorance are mutually reinforcing.'"

Pollan's argument reflects similar ones in LOHAS. For example, Richard told me, "All of the Slow movements—food, money, thinking, fitness—incorporate the concepts of awareness, consciousness and concern for the greater good." Richard said these slow movements "understood the bigger picture of what is important, just like LOHAS." To him, "slow" meant being mindful, just as "LOHAS is about learning to be conscious of our every action and its impact on the world."

That consciousness informs other Slows, notably the Slow Money movement, which, like Slow Food, was initiated to support sustainable agriculture. The pioneer behind the ideas and principles of Slow Money, Woody Tasch, decided to name his new movement after Slow Food—Carlo Petrini even wrote the foreword to Tasch's book, *Inquiries into the Nature of Slow Money*. Today, Tasch is chairman and president of the Slow Money Alliance.

Slow Money reverses the priorities of investing from fast profit to social betterment. Shifting an economy based on "extraction and consumption" to "one of preservation and restoration" means, according to the Slow Money Alliance (http://www.slowmoneyalliance.org), "bringing money back down to earth" and the alliance means this quite literally. The Slow Money movement wants investment dollars to be spent locally as a way to sustain the essential elements of community. More specifically, money should be invested in processes related to food production, including farms, aquifers, ecosystems, schools, neighborhood retailers, urban gardens, and organic manufacturers. Saying there is nothing beautiful in the synthetic flavorings and colorings used in food, the alliance calls for investment as "if beauty mattered." The alliance says that community-supported agriculture (a cooperative whereby consumers and farmers share the costs and risks of farming in exchange for fresh food) is "beautiful" but that "red dye #4 is not."

An *Ode* magazine article about Slow Money and Woody Tasch states that the movement's emphasis on soil fertility has important environmental and social reasoning behind it. While soil fertility is an important factor in the protection against global warming (healthy soil stems erosion and promotes healthier plants), it will also help to "reconnect" people with the planet by tending to the source of their food supply and ultimately "connect the whole person with the sustainability problem" (Hawn, "Slow and Steady" 28). "We must dare to imagine that after the Age of Industrial Finance and Industrial Agriculture comes the Age of Earthworm Economics," states the Slow Money Alliance website.

This is a "patient capital" that lines up with LOHASian conscious capitalism (Hawn, "Slow and Steady" 28). *Whole Life Times* quoted Mahatma Gandhi on the usefulness of money: "capital as such is not evil; it is in its wrong use that is evil. Capital in some form or another will always be needed" (Shalmy 26). Just so, "Money is no longer the currency," says Tasch, adding, "Air and water and soil are the currencies of our future" (Hawn, "Slow and Steady" 30).

Perhaps. Or maybe the currency is actually our *consciousness* about the need to be slower, and this is the premise of another slow-based philosophy, the Slow Thinking Movement. It not only encompasses the principles of the other Slows, but it seems logical that it must serve as an umbrella for all things slow. The website for the Slow Thinking Movement says slow thinking is about spending time in discussion with others focused on what is "important" rather than what is "urgent." These communal sessions preferably occur over a slow meal, perhaps discussing the merits of slow money. What is key is making the "deliberate" act to not "do" anything but rather to simply think and speak with others, and take your time doing so. "Debate is the lifeblood of Slow Planet," a website devoted to all things slow (http://www.slowplanet.com).

Clearly, the Slows have been easily incorporated into LOHAS because they share a goal: shift the gears of consumer culture without demolishing it altogether. Wrapped up in popular notions about what constitutes quality of life, the Slows and LOHAS aim to give us more time, more healthy products, and more supportive communities. The movements bid us to "walk quietly" and to indulge in observation and consideration, tasting each amazing detail in the ordinary journey, says a Chinese company advertising slow "LOHAS vacations" at the Shanghai LOHAS Vacation Exhibit.

Slow and simple is all very well, Paloma said, as long as we don't lose the inherent *fun factor* in consumer culture. Paloma has spent her adult life in the natural and organic industry. She believes the LOHAS industries need to persuade people to *choose* sustainability rather than hit them over the head with it, because "this is capitalism not communism." People want choice, she said, adding that the market had to make sustainability "fun, sexy, and cool." "[Consumers] won't do it if it is hard, unpleasant, and requires renunciations," she said.

Paloma's concerns point out a serious challenge for LOHAS market organizations: as the market expands and attracts more consumers, it becomes trickier to navigate between pleasing consumers who are deeply knowledgeable about healthy and sustainable living and the LOHAS market and those who aren't. What this means is that the increasing diversity of consumers in the marketplace makes it exponentially more difficulty to create an appealing shopping environment. "Fun, sexy, and cool" clearly will take different shapes to different populations. Added to that problem is the fact that it's never been easy to discern what is acceptably slow and simple, sustainable and healthy, ethical and socially responsible, because the discourse around these concepts, practices, and products changes as do the sources of authority for defining them. Not that long ago, for example, customers seeking a more natural lifestyle relied heavily on the advice of their local health food store owner about what to buy, perhaps because that person was the only available source to the customer or because store owners followed informal but generally accepted industry "standards" regarding products to stock on the shelves. Customers were exposed to these ideals through in-store newsletters, magazines, radio shows, product labels, and shelf talkers that explained why a certain product was included in the mix. In the early days, consumers could assume that the store wouldn't stock any products containing artificial colors, synthetic fillers, or preservatives, and they could bet their composters that they wouldn't find tobacco, alcohol, or sugar on the shelf next to their soy milk, alfalfa powder, and organic carrots.

That's still the case for some stores nowadays, but mostly the mega-markets in the garden of "crossover" retailing that has sprung up around the country carry "conventional" as well as "organic" and "natural." This same crossover mentality is true for some of the media covering the healthy living and LOHAS marketplace in terms of the products they advertise and the ideas, practices, and products that appear in editorial or programming. For example, Charlotte told me that while her national magazine was based on a spiritual tradition that rejected use of tobacco and alcohol, the publication nonetheless occasionally took ads for wine, recognizing that the practices had to address the lives of "contemporary people," and that those people did indeed at times drink wine. And, when Dragonfly publications, a chain of regional magazines, took advertising from the natural tobacco company American Spirit, letters from readers poured in. Did tobacco fit with a mission of healthy living, they asked? Was it sustainable? Was it ethical?

The tide of new consumers and organizations flowing into the LOHAS space stresses the market's semiotic boundaries. On the one hand, it's important that the media and market organizations ensure there is a substantial difference between "LOHAS" and "mainstream" products. On the other hand, these organizations want to make sustainability the rule, not the exception, and to do so they need to be able to speak to the expanding heterogeneous consumer base. As a result, it behooves them to refrain from representing the "lifestyle" as onerous in its rigor, price, elitism, or inconvenience.

Paloma alluded to this when she told me that she resented what she saw as a minimalist attitude to life that had become de rigueur in parts of the LOHAS space. Paloma told me she felt the idea of healthy living had gone too far, creating an elitism around sustainability that had, in turn, made many LOHAS companies suspicious about their own and others' marketing and selling activities, thanks to the stereotypes that "big companies and profits are evil." In Paloma's mind, this approach only served to restrain the growth and expansion of the demand and market for sustainable goods. "It is almost a socialistic, communistic, puritanical approach," she told me. She rejected what she saw as the idea of "asceticism and the path of renunciation" that she felt described many of the companies in the space. "Why does it need to be that way?" she asked. "[Sustainability] can be sensual and fun. I applaud the large companies coming in and challenging anti-materialism."

In fact, the tendency in the natural and organic products and healthy living industries overall has been to remove barriers, real or perceived, between "mainstream" and "alternative" in order to stimulate rather than constrict the spread of sustainability ideas, products, and services. As a result, the boundaries of "health" and "sustainability" have become flexible as well as portable, which might entice more sectors of the market and the culture into the sustainability dialogue. When the LOHAS Forum moved for a few years from just outside of the healthy living mecca of Boulder, Colorado, to the environs of Los Angeles, for example, the company made it clear that the move was a way to fold the power of Hollywood into the batter. With the glitterati enlisted, it seemed the forum organizers were intent on demonstrating just how fun sustainability could be.

At one event, the LOHAS 9 conference, held April 25–27, 2005, in Marina del Rey, California, fashion designer Linda Loudermilk spoke about her clothing label Luxury Eco, which she said made "sustainability fun, beautiful, and hip." Her website says the company "redefines" sustainability, intimating it was anything but fun not so long ago. The website says the clothing line "outfits the movement, providing the uniform for this new kind of earth warrior—an infusion of hope for an abused but resilient planet" (Loudermilk). Facing the audience who may or may not have been wearing their earth-warrior clothes, Loudermilk explained the choice of eco-luxury: "We are given ego. It's a part of us." If the wealthy were going to buy luxury items, she reasoned, why not at least give them a sustainable choice? Her products were part of the LOHAS trade exhibit, products that Andy Marks of MATTER Entertainment, the LOHAS Forum show producer, described in his opening address as enhancing the "Zen-like atmosphere" of the conference.

LOHAS isn't simply a move to infuse sustainability with more playful appeal; it's also an attempt to create an aura of consciousness or spirituality around the materiality of sustainability, the everyday products that make up the concept and marketplace. This is achieved by clearly positioning products as representations of environmental and social values as well as of the good life. The tagline used by the Sustainable Style Foundation (SSF), a nonprofit organization promoting sustainable lifestyles and design, for example, reads: "Look fabulous, live well and do good." SSF, like Loudermilk and Paloma and many others in the space, believes that sustainability needs to be "sold"—that it must be made as appealing as possible in order to draw it into the flow of consumer culture, which is why SSF says it "has designs on making sustainability the next big thing, as well as a timeless trend by using the power of popular culture to influence consumer choices," according to the SSF website (http://www.sustainablestyle.org).

This is not your grandmother's or great-grandmother's sustainability, which might have leaned more toward something about rationing, canning, mending, and letting fields go fallow. This isn't a minimalistic worldview—Loudermilk's Luxury Eco isn't encouraging you to think of your wardrobe as having one day dress and another one for church. This sustainability is trying to steer the ship of consumerism between the reefs of hedonism on one side and planetary meltdown on the other.

Spiritualizing Consumption, Consuming Spirituality

By putting our collective dollars to work for social justice, environmentalism, and personal health—packaged as mindful consumption and slow and simple living—we generate a moral economy, one shaped by our deepest values. In the bargain, we find a touchstone for our own *spirituality*. But there is a tenacious suspicion alive in the culture about the commensurability of spirituality and commodification. The utilitarian aspect of everyday consumer goods and popular culture has often neutralized their ability to serve as transcendental go-betweens in history (McDannell 4–5). As one notable example, consider the snubbing of Warner Sallman's famous painting *The Head of Christ* by liberal critics at the time, who accused the piece of "standardization, reproducibility, sentimentality, effortless absorption, commercialism, mechanization, and dehumanization" (Promey 157). Religious leaders weren't alone in their repulsion at the sight of Christ afloat in a sea of commercialization—many in the art community had similar epithets for the painting, held as they were under the "power of the Protestant intelligentsia" (162).

What is or is not worthy to represent the sacred has occupied philosophers, pundits, and painters for centuries, but for purposes here, the most interesting arguments are those that circulate through theories of *"culture"*—that is, about what culture is and is not, what constitutes "good" vs. "poor" taste, what is "high" culture and what is "low" culture, and by what authority these decisions are rendered and made hegemonic. Thanks to social and cultural theorists of the past century, we've pried open that vault to reveal how authority operates in cultural practices and beliefs and why some voices, some artifacts, and some beliefs trump others.

Scholars such as Colleen McDannell have shown that under the social power strata that generate authoritative decisions about the suitability of some objects and not others to associate with religion, there have always been other, even oppositional ways of experiencing religion among various populations, ways that include commodities and mundane "profane" objects bought and paid for by barter or money. As McDannell says, "If we assume that whenever money is exchanged religion is debased, then we will miss the subtle ways that people create and maintain spiritual ideals through the exchange of goods and the construction of spaces" (6).

British cultural studies theorists in particular threw open a wide window onto this landscape, revealing, especially, how media, religion, and culture interface in people's everyday lives. Studies from British cultural studies provided new ways to understand how mass-produced goods, media, entertainment, and more served as channels through which to understand the sacred, helping people to forge new forms of collectivity and identity. These products and practices involved the sense organs in ways that enabled people to participate in their religious communities (McDannell 2).

Certainly in the "New Age," goods, especially media, figured prominently. The New Age seems almost synonymous with mass-produced, commodified cultural artifacts such as crystals, mandalas, incense, sweat lodges, candles, herbs, and tarot cards (Granqvist and Hagekull; Norlander et al.; Sutcliffe and Bowman; York, "New Age"). Media and artifacts *enabled* the expression of the New Age and its multivalent spiritual nature, as Mears and Ellison describe: "Given the clear emphasis of New Age movements on a wide variety of teachings, and the absence of a unified or organized New Age church, it is logical to expect that to a large extent the success of any New Age movement would rest upon the dissemination of relevant materials (e.g., how-to books, magazines, audio or videotapes)" (292).

In her studies of piety in popular culture, art historian Erica Doss researched collectors of Elvis Presley memorabilia and found that even though her informants resisted the idea of "religion" being tagged to their Elvis collections, the pieces were still integral to the processes of their meaning making on a very deep level (Doss). While it's doubtful that such modern LOHASian goods and concepts as investment portfolios, cork flooring, and spa vacations have figured prominently in theologians' minds as objects through which to inspire the awe and passion considered appropriate for religious life, these are the very channels through which LOHAS attempts to anchor, interpret, and manifest spirituality.

LOHAS is able to do this because the movement is built on a cultural wave of spiritual seeking, or the "spiritual marketplace" (Roof). "North American 'supply-side spirituality' has always carried the assumption that the individual is entitled to an endless supply of material satisfactions" says Steven Hunt (332). Hunt argues that this has included seeing the "well-being of spirit and body" as connected and as "interpreted in terms of inner happiness and material accomplishment which are viewed as intimately related and merged in a single religious order of reality" (332–33).

We've seen that LOHAS discourse advocates generating a holistic self of mind, body, and spirit through personal development work using practices and goods. The goal is an "enlightened self-interest," if you will—the obtainment of happiness, but not at any cost (Gerasimo 52). There is authentic happiness and there is the happiness that a misguided culture has foisted on you through excessive and mindless consumerism, say the texts.

"We are unfulfilled as a culture," Penny told me, explaining that Westerners suffer from a "broken mind" that is attracted to whatever new and pretty
thing put before it. But, she asked, what happens when your stomach is filled
and your house overflows with clutter and you still want more? Instead, my
informants told me, we need to fill our selves with more meaning, as Pilar
Gerasimo, writing in *Experience Life*, indicates: "If our rampant productivity
doesn't make us happy, doesn't allow for calm and creativity, doesn't give us
an opportunity to participate in a meaningful way—then, really, what's the
point?" she asks (52). "Thoreau talks about this, the ecstatic experience of
life," she writes. "What makes you happy? What is good for your well-being?
The key is to learn how to answer those questions—not just throw away your
credit card" (53).

Authentic happiness is understood in LOHAS as one's birthright, but one
that's been eroded, or eclipsed, by economic and political pressures. LOHAS
texts pound home the message that everyone can reclaim authentic happiness
from the grips of those who would destroy it—be they mortgage bankers,
land developers, politicians, or our own inattentive, consuming selves. We
simply need to spend money differently, support different causes, and bring
ourselves into a new, different consciousness so we can recognize our interdependent nature with the social and natural worlds.

What we need, says Sasha, a marketing consultant with a thirty-year career in the healthy-living and "green" economy, "is to heal ourselves and
our planet from the ills of overconsumption"—from skyrocketing debt load
to mountains of landfills. "The stores are full of useless tchotchkes that are
made in sweatshops overseas and then end up in landfills that are now closing because we have too many items that we're throwing away," she told
me. Sasha believes people have, however, come to an "awareness" of living
consciously, to be attuned to the sacred nature of the world and the need
to heal its wounds. Sasha said that healing "has to begin with people voting
with their pocketbooks."

The ordinary *is* the extraordinary journey in LOHAS; that is, the pathway
to healing one's self and the world is found through commitment to everyday,
mundane acts including, our purchases. This does two things: it legitimizes
the self as a spiritual authority, freed from formal religiosity to discover the
genuine nature of life, and it validates a specific sort of materiality as a spiritual conduit. "Simplicity leads to spirituality; spirituality leads to simplicity,"
according to *Natural Solutions* magazine (Crawford).

An article in *Spirituality & Health* says, "The pathway to a deeper life may
be hanging on your wall or waiting in the video store" (T. Moore, "Spiritual

Arts"). Or, it can also happen through your food: "What you eat, affects the planet," declares Wholeliving.com, the website of *Body+Soul*. In fact, the British newspaper the *Observer* stated, "Not since Jesus rustled up a feast from some fishes and a few loaves of bread . . . have we invested food with such spiritual qualities" (Gerard). "Has food become the faith of a decadent West?" asks the author, who proclaims the guru of food to be none other than the Slow Food movement's Carlo Petrini, who has claimed that the Slow Food movement represents nothing short of the "salvation of the planet" (Petrini qtd. in Gerard). Petrini demurred from the honorable title of guru offered to him by the *Observer* and instead named Britain's Prince Charles as the spiritual guide of the Slow Food Movement, hailing the prince for his vision and commitment to sustainability (Gerard).

In another example of the spiritualizing of our everyday lives, an article in a Georgia newspaper, again about the Slow Food Movement, quotes a local organic farmer who compares the simple sustainable life to the American idea of freedom: "It has been such a spiritual journey living seasonally and sustainably . . . and there is so much comfort and peace knowing we are not so dependent on the system. I mean, this is life as close to freedom as you can get in this country" (Reinhardt).

LOHAS's ethicizing and spiritualizing of the economy follows an argument made by Tufts economist Julie Nelson, whereby a selfish economy is bridged to a nurturing one. Nelson says we need to rethink our understandings about the economy, to stop viewing it as a distinct sphere in human life, sitting beyond human control because in fact, it does not; the economy is responsible and responsive to human endeavor, according to Nelson. In that vein, Hunter Lovins declared in her presentation at LOHAS Forum in 2009 that the economy needed to be dethroned. "Free markets make a lousy religion—they weren't intended to take care of our grandchildren; that is our job." She argued for the importance of infusing the market with our values, bending and shaping it to our will to do good, and, she said, it would be regular entrepreneurs like those at the LOHAS Forum, the "little people" who, just like the hobbits in the Tolkien trilogy *Lord of the Rings*, would save the world through their courage and their innovative ideas.

Lovins's and Nelson's arguments echo those of the twentieth-century economist Karl Polanyi, who claimed that the economy is culturally embedded, arising from its "social and ecological context" (qtd. in Langley and Mellor 62). Once we recognize that we have created its form, we can also understand that it can and must be manipulated to address our needs, and by doing so we recenter the role of "human creativity and responsibility" in economic modeling, Nelson says, reaffirming that the economic self isn't separate from the ethical self (394).

In LOHAS the self is more than "homo economicus," it is an ethical and spiritual entity who is mandated to overlay a moral code onto what is perceived as an amoral economy (Nelson). Through their self-actualization journey, consumers and producers become transformed into powerful agents of change in the world, able to push aside the illusory veil of consumer culture to find deeper values and truths. *Experience Life* gives an example: "Conscious consumers are not merely consumers, but engaged and concerned individuals who think in terms of lifecycles, who perceive the subtleties and complexities of interconnected systems" (Gerasimo 52). The article cites bestselling author Patricia Aburdene, author of *MegaTrends 2010,* who claims that these consumers are "more carefully weighing material and economic payoffs against moral and spiritual ones" (Gerasimo 52). "They are acting out of a sort of 'enlightened self interest,' one that is deeply rooted in concerns about sustainability in all its forms," Gerasimo says (52).

According to *Ode* magazine, "The perceived conflict between 'doing good' and 'making money' is on its way out" (Hawn, "Gospel" 40). According to the author, "the gospel according to Adam Smith" means doing good *is* compatible with money, as long as "consumers [use] their purchasing power to buy stuff from companies that espouse spiritual capitalism" (40). But beyond that, there are ways to inform any of our activities with environmental and social justice, values that reflect our authentic nature as holistic human beings. *Yoga Journal,* for example, tells readers how to incorporate "spiritual principles to enlighten their gift-giving and receiving" (Lane 18) through such practices as requesting wedding attendees to donate money to a favorite charity rather than buying a consumable for the happy couple.

How far can we venture in redeeming market-based activities and rebranding them as spiritual when there is still a cultural "sniff" test in place regarding the intermarriage of spirituality and consumerism? Even in the case of the commodified New Age, religion scholar Michael York argued that the movement's "guiding transcendent value" that claims the "universe as an interconnected field," which includes the marketplace, provided it with the "justifying rationale for attempts to spiritualize commodification and commercial exchange" ("New Age" 364). Similarly, criticism ensued when *Body+Soul* magazine was sold to Martha Stewart OmniMedia, raising questions about the organization's dedication and approach to spirituality.

Phyllis Fine, for example, hailed *Body+Soul*'s (recently again retitled, this time to *Whole Living*) original incarnation—*The New Age Journal*—because it took a "journalistic, sometimes skeptical approach" to topics that were considered on the "fringe" back in the New Age heyday of 1974, including to alternative health care, spirituality, and self-help. "I trusted the mag back then;" she says and adds, "I'm not so sure about it now." She complains that the magazine no longer interprets the "self-help gurus" but instead "channels them directly." She highlights this excerpt from the magazine: "Here's famed New Age guy Deepak Chopra: 'You only have to look for, and tune into, the timeless cosmic beat to recapture your vitality.'" Fine calls this too much "New Agey tripe and not enough substance." She asks why the editorial staff doesn't instead integrate the expertise of the "Martha empire in lifestyle magazines and position *Body + Soul* as more of a guide to the green goods and lifestyle?" (P. Fine).

In an article in *Yoga Journal*, the author expresses frustration with the binary nature of the magazine—as being both a spiritual magazine and a capitalist endeavor. "Is it my imagination, or has spiritual commercialism been getting more rampant lately?" she asks (Cushman). While she acknowledges that people have always marketed spirituality through "hawking papal indulgences, bones of the saints, and Ganges water in brass flasks," she says that it "seems to have reached new heights of glossy sophistication" (Cushman).

She isn't the first to note that consumerism has become "a kind of religion," but she is clearly astonished at the manner in which the "superficiality" of consumerism has invaded her world of Hatha yoga, "where spiritual advancement is often measured by how good you look in a leotard" (Cushman). "But who am I to criticize?" Cushman asks, calling herself "a scavenger on the same food chain." "How would we fill our magazine, if entrepreneurs didn't seasonally repackage the perennial wisdom?" she asks (Cushman).

LOHAS has to carefully negotiate between authenticity, particularly spiritual authenticity, and commodification, keeping a rigorous watch out for what I've come to call *spiritual-washing*. Similar in nature to the idea and practices of green-washing, whereby companies attempt to profit by marketing their products as green when they are really only minimally so, spiritual-washing occurs when the product or service is brushed with a gloss of virtue, giving it an enticing sheen, but one as shallow as egg glaze. There are plenty of opportunities for spiritual-washing in what is called Corporate Social Responsibility (CSR) and Cause-Related Marketing (CRM). These activities designate efforts within corporations to align themselves with causes, issue-related organizations, and other philanthropic events, people, and institutions (Einstein). "Corporations have discovered a wealth of categories from food to clothes to text messaging through which they can combine commerce with 'compassion,' and ultimately sell more products," says religion and marketing scholar Mara Einstein. Marketers tell consumers that by buying certain products they are feeding the poor, preserving indigenous traditions, providing livable wages, eradicating child labor and animal cruelty, and saving the environment. In fact, CSR is so integral to LOHAS, one assumes that any company within the fold has such a program in place. CSR tells consumers something about the integrity and deep values of the company. And while CSR offers many "strategic benefits to an organization," say Burke and Logsdon (495), CSR marketing and advertising can confuse and delude consumers by creating the perception that the product or company has nonprofit endorsement or another third-party seal of approval (Bower and Grau). As is the case with green-washing, it can be all too easy to create an image of an ethical, philanthropic, and sustainability-minded organization when it is anything but that.

That was the concern of the activist group Press for Change when it made a media splash in 1997 by exposing shoemaker Nike's abysmal treatment of its workers in Southeast Asia. At the same time, Nike was spending millions of dollars on its CSR campaigns and attending sustainability meetings around the world (Cockburn and St. Clair). Jeff Ballinger of Press for Change argued that Nike could have corrected the poor working conditions at a cost of 75 cents per shoe, or $210 million. Instead, the company opted to spend $12 million on CSR as a public relations effort.

Angela Eikenberry makes a strong case against "consumption philanthropy" in the *Stanford Social Innovation Review*. While "consumption philanthropy" might be an easy way for consumers to feel good and for producers to "bolster their reputations," it actually short-circuits the overall goal of social betterment, she says. She explains that while most critiques of cause marketing have focused on the "pesky problems of execution"—creating perceptions that aren't entirely or at all true—the real problem lurks deeper. "Consumption philanthropy individualizes solutions to collective social problems, distracting our attention and resources away from the neediest causes, the most effective interventions, and the act of critical questioning itself," she says on the *Stanford Social Innovation Review* website. Eikenberry argues that these consumption practices not only "devalue the moral core of philanthropy by making virtuous action easy and thoughtless," but also actually does more to "obscure" the relationships and other practices among "markets—their firms, products, and services—and the negative impacts they can have on human well-being."

This critique also surfaces in the LOHAS texts. In *Yoga Journal*, Bo Forbes, a Boston yoga teacher and clinical psychologist, says it's incumbent upon consumers to be honest with themselves: "You have to get informed about the changes that are possible for you to make, and ask yourself whether you're doing as much as you can." Forbes lays out a series of choices that the consumer should make, such as buying a fuel-efficient car and supporting organic agriculture, but he says that while it's okay to do these actions because they might save you money or improve your health, the real reason for taking sustainable action is "to remember the importance of selflessness and altruism in yoga" (qtd. in Wellner).

The *Utne Reader* takes a tougher stance. "So-called 'radical' environmentalists and little-read deep ecologists hark to our 'duty' to preserve and care for nature, poignantly calling for a profound paradigm shift that will allow the human race to see beyond its own wants, needs, and foibles to a Higher Love—a tall order for people who can't decide whether to use paper or plastic" (Millet 35).

When I interviewed Iris, a freelance writer and editor for numerous magazines in the LOHAS space, she recognized her own cynicism about the spiritual, moral, and ethical marketing in the LOHAS industries. But she felt if spiritual-washing occurred, it wasn't so much due to malicious duplicity on the part of industry organizations, but more because of the unavoidable dynamics of capitalism. "I think probably the underlying spirit of the healthy living movement is altruistic, environmental, mind/body/spirit-oriented," Iris said. "And then, you know, you still have to work within a system that's essentially wasteful, corrupt, usurious, and so then those two belief systems kind of clash."

But the important thing, Iris said, was that the LOHAS industries were filled with generous people—people gripped within the fist of capitalism that forced them to make hard choices such as between what they could afford financially and what they wanted to do spiritually. She explained, "if I'm gonna eat at a restaurant, which is the better thing for the environment or people: going to McDonald's or going to the Whole Foods Deli?" Obviously, the latter, she said, but for a family of four living paycheck-to-paycheck, that might not be a choice they could make.

The road to sustainability is "littered with good intentions," Iris said. After all, sustainability is still a hit or miss game—there are no regulations for the most part, and it changes all the time. People are doing what they can or what they think is right, she said. "You work within the system and you try and make it as good as you can, but when it's all tallied up at the end of the millennium, maybe we'll look back and say, 'Oh, this was the beginning of a whole new trend, a better way of being a more conscious culture,' or maybe it will be seen as a little blip of people fooling themselves into thinking they were doing better."

Iris was concerned that consumers might hold too tightly to high ideals and essentially strangle what could be the beginnings of deeply effective sustainability strategies. She mentioned Wal-Mart, saying, "Even if they're doing [sustainability] basically as a marketing scheme, well, what does it matter?" So what if their "motivation was selfish," and they were only out to "make the biggest buck they possibly can?" she asked; wasn't it better that Wal-Mart was attempting to become more sustainable, considering the tremendous impact of the company in terms of number of employees, quantity of goods sold, and consumer loyalty?

With its penetration of every inch of the lifeworld, consumerism may have become the most logical place for many people to express social and environmental activism. Margaret Scammel argues that despite proclamations to the contrary "citizenship is not dead, or dying, but found in new places, in life-politics, as Anthony Giddens (1991) calls it, and in consumption" (351).

Struggling with her own ambivalence, Iris was not convinced. At the end of the day, she said, "It's just another part of the lie like, you know, having a hybrid car—yes, it saves gasoline, but it's still a car." Isn't everything in the market constructed around some sort of "need," she asked, a need that was constructed by the culture in the first place? This, she laughed, is where "one goes on a bad day of thinking." "The fact of the matter is we're not going go back to living in sod houses on the prairie and being self-sufficient and living off the land," Iris said. She pondered the room we were sitting in at her home and pointed to a recently installed gas fireplace. "I push a button and the gas comes out and I have a fire to warm me," but, she said, it was a luxury. She justified purchasing and using it because "it's more efficient than the furnace and the company uses recycled metal and is careful about their carbon emissions and all of that stuff." Yet, at the end of the day, Iris said, "I don't have to have this to stay alive." She sighed and said, "Still, if you're going to have a 'luxury,' it's better to have a conscious luxury." For Iris, the moral debate was deep and complex, and "spiritual-washing" was not always simple to detect or to avoid.

Judging by Paul Ray's research, the Cultural Creatives must chafe at this ambiguity. Being authentic, meaning their "actions are consistent with what [they] believe and what [they] say," as Paul Ray and Sherry Ruth Anderson write (8), is nonnegotiable. Because they want to "make a difference in the world," they can only do so if they're armed with the right information and tools (10). It would stand, then, that this population would need nonrelative definitions of what is or isn't spiritual or sustainable in order to live authentically. Hints that their sources of information, including the companies they support, are flawed in this regard can seriously harm the relationships consumers build in the marketplace that are based on trust.

To avoid this, LOHAS-related market organizations require stringent, well-researched sustainability programs and standards, and a solid crisis-management strategy if things go afoul. It's essential that companies participate with other associations and organizations in order to create an industry-wide self-policing program and position themselves as trustworthy sources of information, particularly in areas that are not standardized or regulated by official policies that monitor marketing claims. Consider, for example, the furor over the use of the word "organic" on labels. While the use of "organic" is strictly regulated by federal policy, marketers have found a loophole. The word "organic" can be used on a product label, even if nothing in the product itself is certified organic, if the word forms part of the name of the product or company (for example, Acme Organic Vits). Whole Foods Market has recently started to self-regulate by excluding vendors that use the word "organic" that way, and some marketers have protested the store's position as gatekeeper. But Whole Foods Market occupies a position of credibility for consumers, as a reliable information provider about health and sustainability. And Whole Foods is in a position where it can afford to be picky about the vendors it chooses to work with or not. Many of the small media organizations in the LOHAS space do the same in terms of tightly controlling what types of advertisements they will accept, but other media in the space have shown a willingness to include advertisers the natural and organic products media would have once definitively turned down.

Evangelizing LOHAS: Media, Spirituality, and Culture

Garnering endorsement from visible and respected members of the community such as Whole Foods Market or celebrities can bolster a company's sustainability legitimacy. Celebrities, in particular, have surged to the cause of sustainability, and they make powerful allies for companies. As Debbie Levins, president of the Environmental Media Association (EMA) put it, "EMA's public service announcement, with superstars Cameron Diaz and Gwyneth Paltrow expounding the virtues of alternative energy vehicles and energy saving behaviors, is like Moses carrying down the 10 Commandments to their fans" (qtd. in Lampe, "Riding the Wave" 22).

Expanding on this to think about the role of media in general, I asked publishing exec Richard what he thought of the media's role in the LOHAS "movement," the word he had used earlier in our conversation to describe

LOHAS. He said, "The media have been instrumental in this because without a way to create information, without the vehicles to provide resources, and without being able to try and foster a community with a sense of purpose, this would still be something buried in the subconscious as opposed to becoming communities and marketplaces."

Richard's use of active verbs to *create* and to *foster* says something about the type of power he believes media hold. It also says something about how he perceives the media to have a duty to help people manifest their natural tendency to act in a sustainable manner. He says new communities have emerged as a result of this mediated work around the terms "health" and "sustainability," and that LOHAS media have raised new awareness of their meanings and applications.

What he describes here is *culture*, the shared values and practices that enable collective meaning making or understanding. British cultural studies theorist Raymond Williams famously said culture "is a dynamic process arising from relationships among all the elements of our lives to create a whole way of life," emphasizing the importance of communication in these processes (*Long Revolution* 46). Language and communication are *signifying* processes, acts of representation of reality or truth, articulating cultural meanings (Denzin, *Symbolic*). "Between consciousness and existence resides communication and culture" and "these two processes dialectically structure existence and consciousness," says Norman Denzin (*Symbolic* 164). In short, media institutions are involved in the making of culture and in performing creative and socially meaningful work constructing and mobilizing ideas, power, and movements. While they storehouse and transmit symbols and signs, the raw resources we peruse to make our identities and understandings about the world, they also "generate" these symbols through a complex interplay with the social world (Carey; Giddens, *Consequences*; Hoover, *Religion*; Thompson, *Media*).

Media hold an unusual situation in the social world by virtue of their sheer reach. Meaning is circulated through words, language, and imagery in global media and is, in the Foucauldian sense, an event of power. They are involved in the struggle to float a meaning that can supersede and overtake other meanings in the culture; in the case of LOHAS this struggle over meaning integrally centers around what it means to be a consumer and how that links up with what it means to be "conscious" or "spiritual."

The LOHAS discourse frames media and market organizations as leaders in a historic time. As public servants, then, media are not only capable of guiding the public toward a new world paradigm—toward consciousness about holistic ideals of health and what it takes to sustain health—but are also ethically bound to do so. Fran, for example, told me her publication helped readers find their way in the world. She explained that readers wanted to believe in a better world, but while "they believe, they also don't know what to believe." Fran said this was where LOHAS publications like hers helped individuals overcome a state of alienation, by showing them how they could create the world as they desired through their everyday choices.

Media help people to "connect the dots," said Margo. She saw this as one of the most exciting aspects of her work. "We open new worlds to people," she said, adding "we have the potential to be the bridge." Andy Marks, in his opening remarks at LOHAS Forum 2006, made it clear that LOHAS's success was going to rely on the those in the "know" educating others about health and sustainability. He said, "We are bridge-builders, not gatekeepers," referring to the LOHAS audience. "Take the LOHAS message out to the world and make a difference by the clothes you wear, the products you use and eat." With that, he deftly interpellated the LOHAS audience of manufacturers, consultants, yoga instructors, media executives, and managers as living prophets of sustainability, the LOHAS army of celebrities and ordinary people alike.

Moving the LOHAS Forums from their place of origin in Colorado to Los Angeles was done to enlist the support of media—of Hollywood in particular. The Environmental Media Association (EMA) was a strong presence at these L.A. forums. Founded by the producer Norman Lear and his wife, Lyn, and Cindy and Alan Horn in 1989, EMA's purpose is to link the power of celebrity to environmental awareness. According to the organization's website: "EMA believes that through television, film and music, the entertainment community can affect change in a positive way. EMA's work is widespread, from subtle messaging on the screen to promoting sustainable lifestyle choices and educating influential people on the power of 'green,' our goal is inspiring the path to a healthier planet" (http://www.ema-online.org).

Moderating a panel of movie stars (Raquel Welch, Wendie Malick, Ed Begley Jr., and Amy Smart) at LOHAS Forum 9, EMA president Debbie Levin guided her speakers through a discussion of environmental issues, asking how the media could help promote consciousness. Ed Begley was blunt. He said, "[T]he media treats us [actors and actresses] like royalty, so we have a responsibility to lead, to learn, and to try and do what we can. People listen to us, so we are responsible for reporting the stories not being heard." Amy Smart agreed with Begley, saying she tried to be a role model for other twenty-somethings. EMA member and actor Pierce Brosnan had a similar message in his keynote address to the "Investing in Media That Matters" conference, held in Sundance Village, Utah, just prior to the 2003 Sundance Film Festival:

"Films not only influence an audience, but also define [the] public agenda. Together, we can produce films that promote a sustainable future. We can shape dreams that affirm human values. We can cure the disease of cynicism that crushes hope and vision. Today, there is no better time for each of us to choose a cause and nurture this passion in our children" (qtd. in Lampe, "Mainstream Media" 35).

Brosnan points out a couple of themes woven throughout the LOHAS texts: that media can "set" the agenda for discussion and that media can turn negatives into positives to inspire people toward hope for a better future. Moisander and Pesonen have discussed how media, including marketing materials, are directly engaged in defining the terms of "moral behavior" in the green movement, behavior that "has usually been conceptualized in terms of an 'ethical choice,' one based on sound moral reasoning about the consequences of the choice of action for human wellbeing" (329).

Inspiring people is key to LOHAS media, which is why LOHAS Forums offered a preconference event called "The Inspirational Film Festival." A press release for the festival defined an "inspiration film" as one that "[i]nspires us, lifts our spirit, or transforms our lives. We identify with an *Inspiration Film*'s characters on a deep, emotional level, and are motivated by their stories to pursue positive change in our own lives. An *Inspiration Film* honors the belief that simple choices can change the world and inspires us to make a difference."

Inspirational films bring "socially conscious companies and the movie industry" together to "jointly . . . explore something beyond product placement," according to *The LOHAS Journal* (Lampe, "Mainstream Media" 32). This type of discourse also helps to veil the business side of media and its reliance on advertising dollars and to turn the consumer's attention to the media's work as storytellers, visionaries, and spiritual and moral guides to holistic, sustainable living.

For example, when I asked Richard to name the main editorial goals of his LOHAS publication, he said, "Educating our readership about the ideas behind LOHAS, providing factual information so that they can come to understand that it is a better system, and when I say better, I mean a more profitable system that will benefit all individual shareholders in a new company." He added that it was important to provide "inspiration" so that readers would be "more motivated to accept or learn" about the various themes, principles, and beliefs that were encompassed in the LOHAS idea.

Each media professional I interviewed believed LOHAS media should promote healthier minds and bodies, educate people about sustainability, stimulate and form community, give people the tools by which they could make meaningful acts, and, perhaps most importantly, inspire people by crafting the "right" sort of messages that stayed true to principles of sustainability.

This responsibility was made more urgent for my informants because of what they saw as a lack of attention to a deep (as opposed to a shallowly treated) sustainability in the mainstream media. They not only accepted their roles as what Gramsci called "organic intellectuals"—to educate, inform, and provide the means for action to heal both themselves and the world—but they also assumed duties once assigned solely to religious leaders, such as defining what constitutes "enlightened" or right behavior, interpreting events of the world for the faithful, and prescribing actions and thoughts.

This "sacred" work had to be carefully balanced with the "profane" need to serve market interests—to seek more users, more advertisers, and new content. Richard told me, for example, that while there was a "mercenary" side of his publishing work in selling advertising and in producing a return on investment for stakeholders, ultimately the company's mandate was to create healthier lifestyles for readers and for conference attendees. "There is a higher vision at work to try and create change," he said. "It's more than selling boxes."

Accordingly, I asked Frank Lampe why readers were attracted to *The LOHAS Journal*. He laughed and said, "It's a great idea!" He added, "I think [LOHAS] represents a higher calling on both the business and personal levels." When I asked him what he meant by a "higher calling," he said the concept showed people a connection "between their personal values and professional values— there are representatives of the LOHAS community who truly feel this is a spiritual mission for them to change society at some level."

LOHAS media and market organizations view their work as an important counterbalance to "negative" dialogue in the culture. Carl told me, for example, that he did not often personally use visual media (television or film). He was happy to spend his days editing articles for his magazine, which he found "fun and uplifting." But when he did occasionally turn on his television, he was appalled. "I think we are doing such great things [at his magazine], and then I go home and turn on the TV and go 'Oh, my God.'"

Being "fun and uplifting" falls in line with the therapeutic quantum spiritualities. At LOHAS 9, Barbara Harris from Weider Publications recited the quantum philosophy to the conference attendees, saying, "Our mind creates our body." She mentioned the quantum spirituality film *What the Bleep Do We Know!?*, which emphasized the power of intentionality: what you think and feel creates your reality. This is why, Harris said, it was important to focus on "positive" messages—presumably along the lines of those distributed by her publications. Although she voiced strong support of the right to free speech—saying filmmakers and television producers had the right to show the "darker" side of life, if they so chose—she was adamant that the challenge for mass media was to provide a means for people to achieve happier and healthier lifestyles by offering new visions of reality.

Along similar lines, Fran became quite heated when speaking to me about the "mainstream" media, pointing to what she considered unimportant stories such as "weeks and weeks of Michael Jackson's [child molestation] trial" in 2005, taking up valuable time and space to the exclusion of "positive" news and examination of social issues such as hunger and poverty. She was very discouraged about the media in general and stressed the "huge responsibility" of the media to inform people. "Just think—we were not allowed to see our dead soldiers [killed] in Iraq . . . when these people go and give their blood," she said angrily. "The [media] must show more to the people they serve. It is a tremendous disservice to the American people."

Positive messages become framed as a "service" because of their presumed power to inspire, and LOHAS marketing firm eCode Media says on its website that in order to communicate successfully with LOHAS consumers firms must do three things: a.) never green-wash, b.) tell a story about sustainable development, and c.) choose words that sell positivity, hope, and solution (http://ecodemedia.onereason.com.au/).

Positivity in LOHAS is constructed as healthy and sustainable, and this, in the words of Robert Owens Scott, former editor-in-chief of *Spirituality & Health* magazine, makes life worth living. In an editorial, he wrote, "At the risk of overdramatizing, I like to think that all our articles can help save our lives—not only by improving our physical health, but by focusing on what makes life worth living. When we do this, we move ever closer to wholeness, so that those who look at our baby pictures will see the seeds of beautiful lives" (Scott 6).

While Margo agreed LOHAS media must be inspiring, she said she was also realistic. She explained that while her publishing company inspired people through positive messages, even serving as the proverbial bridge to sustainability for new consumers, she also believed that her media organization and publication were probably not the "first doors" for people seeking information about sustainability. More likely, she said, consumers approached her publication after becoming familiar with ideals of holistic health and sustainability. Only after becoming educated on such matters were consumers probably ready to read her magazine, which delved more deeply into sustainability issues than the "mainstream publications that are dabbling in this area," Margo said.

Margo identified one of those dabblers as Oprah Winfrey and her *O magazine*. "Oprah is there [in the sustainable living space], but her ads are unrelated to the level of spiritual awareness she encourages in her readers," she said. I heard this complaint from other informants in LOHAS culture, even though some also admitted to blending "alternative" with "conventional" lifestyles in their media product in ways that were similar to what the mainstream media were doing. They explained, however, that the difference between their media companies and newcomers to the field, such as Oprah's *O*, lie in stringent advertising and editorial policies that regulated what sorts of products and organizations could be represented. As mentioned earlier, though, this is a point of contention among media professionals in the space and a quality my informants found lacking even among each other, their direct competitors in the LOHAS space.

While my informants accepted that more mainstream media seeking a "piece of the pie" were entering the LOHAS market, they worried about not only their own market competitiveness but also about the effect on the sanctity of sustainability ideals overall. Sasha explained it this way: on the one hand, more competitors expanded awareness about sustainability, but, on the other hand, it was often done in such a way that too many compromises had to be made, resulting in the dilution of ideals of sustainability. But if rigorous advertising and editorial criteria were in place that identified acceptable products and services, then my informants welcomed competition, saying the more players the more the market and the consciousness of sustainability could expand.

It sounds good in theory, but riding the expansion of the market while still attempting to uphold their own standards of integrity concerning sustainability seriously challenges organizations attempting to cater to multiple levels of sustainability knowledge among their heterogeneous audiences; it's tough to make everyone happy. Carl told me that even though he receives angry letters and cancellations over an article or program, he is often amazed that certain types of people pick up his magazine at all. "Where we succeed, what amazes me, is the breadth and diversity of people who read the magazine," he said. "We end up getting letters from people we offended, and I'm surprised that they picked up the magazine, because they are real fundamentalists."

LOHAS: A Spirituality of Sustainability

Newsweek described LOHASian spirituality as a bricolage, stating that LOHASians shop "widely for spiritual practices," adapting and adopting from the world's faith traditions and more:

> From Buddhism: meditation and admiration of "nothingness." From Hinduism: yoga, gurus, color and chanting. From paganism: an emphasis on honoring

nature. From Asian cultures: feng shui and acupuncture. Lohasians devour heaping doses of Western psychotherapy, plus the ideas of the recovery movement ("one day at a time"). They identify as "spiritual, not religious," and many believe in "synchronicity" or "meaningful coincidences" that might be guided by a spirit world. Does this sound like someone you know? If you have a yoga mat and "singing bowls," if you chant or do polarity therapy or energy healing, if you consume goji berries or biodynamic organic wines, you just might be a Lohasian. (Waldman and Reiss)

But my informants disagreed. The *Newsweek* quote doesn't capture the complexity of the articulation of spirituality in LOHAS. The discourse speaks to very pragmatic considerations about the planet's survival, considerations that go beyond the therapeutic self-actualization and metaphysical dimensions that *Newsweek* focuses on.

For example, Sam told me that his ownership of a chain of regional LOHAS-related publications represented a spiritual path for him. I asked him if he thought that the publications were also "spiritual" for readers. He responded by providing some history about his company and said when he started purchasing the regional publications that made up his chain, most of the magazines had a "New Age" focus and dealt with metaphysical issues, health, and personal growth.

"There is no doubt these readers, our readers, are on a path of self discovery and are actively looking beyond traditional avenues for spiritual meaning," Sam said. But under his ownership, editorial direction subtly changed. While the company retained a "degree of focus" on spiritual practice and personal growth, new areas were woven into the mix, including (and displacing what Sam called the "metaphysical" aspect) "environmental news, integrated medicine, alternative wellness, the world of economic justice and social justice, human rights, fair trade, electoral politics, renewable energy questions around sustainability, organic food and agriculture," he said.

This is sustainability, Sam said, and it is embodied in the LOHAS concept. That is why, he said, that LOHAS and the research on the Cultural Creatives (CCs) by Paul Ray were crucial to the restructuring of his company. "LOHAS and CCs are two ways to explain both the commercial and social places that our magazines reside in," Sam said. He explained that LOHAS had supplied the logic and knowledge to "aggregate seemingly separate areas together under one commercial impulse." "LOHAS was pertinent because it was pioneering work to identify these niches and to weave them together and whether that was imperfect is less important than the recognition of the interrelatedness of these seemingly separate business areas out there," Sam said. This is a spiritual work, said he added: "It is a question of interrelatedness."

LOHAS has worked diligently to generate a version of sustainability that rests on the theory of interrelatedness among the spheres of life. To that, AtKisson has argued that sustainability can only move forward through recognizing that interrelationship—through a partnership between science and religion and spiritual traditions and institutions, which are, he said, the only institutions that "have demonstrated continuity over millennia" (233). "So, while we must be intensely scientific, our future is also in need of a renewed sense of spirituality and the sacred," AtKisson says. But that spirituality needs to take a new form, one that "is inclusive of believers, nonbelievers, and those for whom belief itself is not the core of spiritual experience."

Sam's idea of interrelationship was based on his belief that there can be different "dimensions and consequences" of any action, from market-based labor to philanthropy to raising a family. Based on that, his "social mission" with his media company was to enable readers to discover new depths to their lives, to "more consistently integrate their values with their everyday lives." He said, "We give them the tools so they can make change in their own lives, based on sustainable, healthy living, and on service and engagement in the broader social world."

Is this the type of new spirituality, then, that might work in the sense AtKisson describes for sustainability? Can we think about LOHAS in this manner?

If we break down LOHAS into its component parts, we first see that this mediated and commodified phenomenon indeed serves as a symbolic system in the sense that New Age scholar Wouter Hanegraaff describes as composing religion: as "any symbolic system which influences human action by providing possibilities for ritually maintaining contact between the everyday world and a more general meta-empirical framework of meaning" ("New Age" 295). By symbolic system, Hanegraaff refers to "a system of 'carriers of meaning'" and to a domain of "objects, words, images, sounds, actions" all of which "form a whole which is meaningful" to the person (295). In the case of LOHAS, that larger framework of meaning, I propose, is the idea that health comprises a healed, holistic self, society, and nature. LOHAS goods and services are carriers of meaning that enable users to connect their everyday lives to that larger worldview.

Second, we can look to LOHAS's own historical relationship with spiritual movements from New Thought to New Age and contextualize LOHAS in terms of the evolution of religion, just as Jonathan Z. Smith, for example, argues that religion should not be treated as something fixed and natural, but something that can be spontaneous, responding to other social pressures and forces upon populations. Along with that, and pertinent to the case of LOHAS,

William Arnal suggests we should "deconstruct the category [of religion] and analyze its function within popular discourse rather than assuming that the category has content and seeking to specify what that content is" (30).

This interpretivist approach understands religion primarily as one of variations or differences rather than commonalities, and focuses on the context in which people claim it occurs, which is key to AtKisson's idealized new spirituality and well suits the heterogeneity of LOHAS consumers as well.

By offering a smorgasbord of symbolic resources in the form of everything from cars to candles to community-supported agriculture, the lifestyle LOHAS media become the carriers of meaning to which Hanegraaff refers. In what Wade Clark Roof has called the "spiritual marketplace" (1999), audiences shop for meaningful values, beliefs, and practices that are reassembled into customized systems of self-identity, truths, and values, all part of the "plausible ordering of existence" by individuals and groups, say Clark and Hoover (17). This popular culture-as-marketplace operates "as a particular religious practice of the self" (Hoover and Venturelli 255), and as what Hoover and Lundby refer to as a "kind of context of social dramaturgy against which individual and community consciousness is formed and shaped" (8). What is more significant, they say, is that this use of popular culture "can be religiously and ritually significant," because "constructive processes that result in new conceptions of truth, value, meaning, notions of 'the good' and the 'right' and so forth are intrinsically religious matters" (8). People learn, then, through popular culture about what they can or want to label as spiritual, just as Mears and Ellison found that New Agers looked to specific media forms to learn about various practices and beliefs that could be incorporated into a personalized bricolage considered the hallmark of New Age spirituality (see also Barker; Hanegraaff, "New Age"; Heelas, *New Age*; Riches).

The media and the commodities of LOHAS serve as the vehicles not only of learning but also as the very sites and substance of spiritual expression. Christopher Helland, in his well-known essay "Online Religion/Religion Online," discusses the differences between finding religious information online and experiencing faith and community online, for example. Likewise, Shawn Landres showed how art murals are interpreted as sacred space in Los Angeles for Asian American groups, and Lynn Schofield Clark has demonstrated how American teens use mediated texts about the supernatural to define their own positions with regard to their social networks and private beliefs (Clark, *From Aliens*; Landres).

Because media are in a constant flow of change, much like market capitalism itself, this lack of fixity, when brought into engagement with spirituality, becomes a contentious stance for some people, particularly when it invokes the old arguments about the ways in which commodification and mediation degrade more meaningful, religious practices. After all, "consumers choose their religion, enjoy it, and once it has served its purpose—usually to achieve self-fulfillment—they discard it," says Kline. That might be true, but there have been no extended studies on conscious consumers to indicate that this is indeed the case, either in the author's first claim of consuming religion for self-fulfillment solely or in the second, of discarding it once they reach their goal. In either case, it is debatable that "discarding," if it does indeed occur, bears any reflection on the meaningfulness of their experience spiritually. What we do know is that the LOHAS texts indicate that the opposite might be the case: rather than dilute users' understanding or expression of spirituality, it seems just as possible that media have increased both by providing more opportunities to link actions to results, for example, linking up support of a fair trade product with the visible increase in farmers' wages, and by providing more opportunities and sites at which consumers can interact with others or be exposed to spiritual lessons, topics, and debate.

LOHAS offers up a competing claim about the contents of spirituality, a claim that's been validated by the legitimation within the broader culture of its components—self-development, environmentalism, and social justice—and the framing of these concerns as ethical and moral (see Adams and Raisborough 2008; Brown 2008; Nichols and Opal 2004). Sustainability, media, and spirituality link up in LOHAS texts in very visible and public ways, and the discourse works to open up possibilities about what it means to be spiritual, and about where and how spirituality can be experienced in late modernity. As an example, consider the April 27, 2009, edition of *The LOHASian* (thelohasian.com) that focused on a public art concept featured at Salon del Mobile, the international furniture fair in Milan. The piece by San Francisco design company Knoend was titled *Passage of Peace*: "This groundbreaking project not only pushes the boundaries of the definition of 'furniture' but also extends the socio-eco definitions of sustainability to include the spiritual wellness of the world. Furthermore, it utilizes wireless technology to connect people in a physical way rather than virtually, and thus provides a new medium for personal interconnectivity."

LOHAS discourse is constructing sustainability as a set of distinctly spiritualized practices that tie personal well-being and self-actualization to collective and civic action, forming an amalgam of beliefs, practices, and materials that the discourse calls *consciousness*.

7. The Collective Conscience

The publisher of *The LOHAS Journal* hoped to use the magazine, the conference, and the concept to create new arterial networks among disparate industries that would allow each to share knowledge and build the market for healthy and sustainable goods and services through partnership. In effect, the mission was to cohere a community or a collective around specific sets of values.

The first mission statement of *The LOHAS Journal* in 2000 read: "*LOHAS Journal* is dedicated to the promotion of sustainable business as a way to fundamentally alter the landscape for economic, social and environmental change. Our mission is to educate our readers about the growing LOHAS industry and to inspire innovation, creativity and dialogue between the companies and individuals that make up this diverse market, fostering a new paradigm of sustainable-business practices that can help create positive change" (LOHAS Journal media kit, 2000).

But the population the publishers based LOHAS on—the Cultural Creatives (the CCs)—was anything but cohesive, at least according to the market research. In fact, research noted that CCs experienced a strong sense of disconnectedness. CC researcher Paul Ray believed that the CCs felt culturally isolated and didn't understand how many people shared their values. This prevented them from acting upon the potential of their collective power in the cultural and political spheres. But if they could be made to see the sheer quantity of their numbers they would unleash a powerful political, social, and economic force that would change the world.

Natural Business Communications and that organization's backers thought LOHAS was the perfect tool for convening the Cultural Creatives as a way to enable them to recognize themselves and to understand they weren't alone. If *The LOHAS Journal* and LOHAS Forums could convince trade members that an enormous CC population existed, waiting to be tapped, market forces would quickly begin to interpellate the CCs as "conscious consumers," and the population would gain a sense of themselves as part of a whole, unleashing the potential of their collective power.

Fast forward to 2007. In May of that year, at LOHAS Forum 11, internationally recognized chef Deborah Madison declared in her panel, "It is all about community." "Together we can do this, using government, agencies, schools, etc., we can use connectivity to get things done," she said. What type of community, if any, evolved during those ensuing years around the LOHAS concept?

The scholarly literature defines community as the outgrowth of shared interests, goals, or values; as something small in size and the site of physical interactions; as necessarily democratic; as an association; as more than an association; and as particularist and thus antithetical to universalism and wider concerns of social equality. In the midst of these competing definitions, Robert Bellah put it more simply, saying a community rests on its members' "shared concern with the question 'what will make this group a good group?'"

Bellah's definition works well for LOHAS because the texts seem less interested in the formal rules of association and more so in articulating the *substance* of "consciousness." As a set of values that orbit around ideas of health and sustainability, LOHAS's definition of consciousness could fairly easily be pinned onto a taxonomy of practices and beliefs—but it would be a lot tougher to similarly organize its tactics, the means used to manifest those practices and beliefs, because they vary so widely from text to text in the discourse. LOHAS's focus has always been on showing how different industries and external resources are logically connected by common goals, on cross-fertilizing ideas and industries, and on increasing awareness of how difference and diversity can improve sustainability business. In short, the concept celebrates heterogeneity of organizations, ideas, people, and environments; whether it is actually successful in doing so is another matter. Still, Natural Business Communications intended the concept of LOHAS to serve as a type of "bridging" entity, to borrow a concept from Robert Putnam (21). LOHAS discourse underscores the importance of relationship, of bridging differences in productive ways, and examines the types of relations that can be built among people (Jean-Luc Nancy qtd. in Willson 156). This has been especially important in LOHAS because of organizers' attempts to bring together mainstream and alternative organizations and ideas.

The early organizers of LOHAS made it clear in the mission statements of the journal and the forum that LOHAS was intended as a set of practices and language that could generate a collective of new partnerships as well as dialogues among disparate industries and populations, including the "mainstream." But this desired LOHAS community hasn't been easy to accomplish for a number of reasons, including the nature of competition among market organizations and the challenge of juggling the debate between collectivity and individualism. The LOHAS discourse positions individualism as the roux that flavors the stew of a happily heterogeneous community. Consider the following excerpt from *Body+Soul* by dance therapist Gabrielle Roth: "I feel like a lone wolf surveying my pack, high on a ridge above the plateau. And yet I can see each individual distinctly, like grains of sand on a silver desert. Each reflects the moonlight in her or his original way. As the music carries through the rhythms of our lives, we explore what gives us our unique identity, how we bring that identity to one another, and how we serve within the larger whole" (96).

The differences that make us not only perfect consumers of market capitalism are constructed as also "healthy" for community. While the discourse is urging individuals to heal themselves by bringing their bodies, souls, and minds into holistic alignment, it is also reminding them that such healing occurs within and in conjunction with the formation of community, where we learn to interact and live in balance. Community keeps us healthy, says Clores in *Body+Soul*, because we learn to share. "By keeping it all inside . . . you don't share your needs, desires or experiences with anyone, [and] there is a chance the stress and alienation will cause psychic and bodily harm," Clores says (108). The more we honor our individual differences, the more we honor the *true* essence of life. Somehow and somewhere these differences synchronize and harmonize, although the texts are less clear about how that exactly happens.

In the business context, the idea of community is developed as a web of relationships with other companies and with customers. As to the latter, industry is encouraged to recognize and to treat customers and clients as comrades in the movement for a sustainable world instead of as breathing pocketbooks. Parker Palmer, for example, writing in *Spirituality & Health* magazine, says businesses throughout the twentieth century broke trust with the consumer and, as a result, also with society, disabling the formation of community. This, Palmer says, is *unnatural*. He says the workers at "Enron, Arthur Andersen, Merrill Lynch, WorldCom, and the Roman Catholic Church, to name a few," must have "heard an inner call to wholeness," but had become "separated from their own souls, betraying the trust of citizens, stockholders, and the faithful—and making our democracy, our economy, and our religious institutions less trustworthy in the process" (40). The "social costs" of such betrayals are "immense," Palmer writes. "The poet Rumi said with ruthless candor 800 years ago: If you are here unfaithfully with us you're causing terrible damage," Palmer adds (40). Being with others "faithfully" means adhering to a sustainability and health gospel, if you will, even though it isn't a very clearly delineated gospel.

Paul Ray brought the two ends of individual and corporate well-being together by explaining to trade audiences at various LOHAS Forums that Cultural Creatives yearn for more personal relationships with companies. CCs are put off by superficial marketing hype; they aren't easily duped and will support companies that prove they hold a genuine commitment to making the planet a better place. Making this point at LOHAS Forum 9, Ray said to the audience, "[CCs] are looking for what's underneath the surface. . . . [I]n the LOHAS space the best thing you can do is to use your website to spell out the information and to communicate your passion." He continued, "Consumers want to know who your company is, so tell them about your process." According to the LOHAS firm Sdialogue.com's white paper, media are the perfect tools to help because they are "breaking down barriers between managers and stakeholders, forcing a more transparent conversation." The company adds, "time will show social media to be a catalyst for changing how companies engage their multiple stakeholders and nurture long-standing relationships" (Sdialogue.com, Sept. 25, 2009, on LOHAS.com).

The focus on relationship building in LOHAS centrally involves both the communicative process and the media. When Martín-Barbero suggested media scholars shift their focus from "media" to "mediation" in his groundbreaking work, he provided a way to rethink media and information communication technologies in a way that went far beyond their roles as transmitters of information. By introducing the cultural aspect of media's work, Martín-Barbero showed the manner in which media *mediate* between individuals and culture. Mediation enables a better understanding of how "individuals locate themselves in social and cultural space and time," says Stewart Hoover (*Religion* 34), and the centrality of media in social life forces us also to consider how "audiences come to recognize their collective cultural identity in media discourse," as Georgette Wang says (11).

In the case of LOHAS, media form the ligature of community because there are no other traditional nuclei or markers of community in the LOHAS marketplace. There is no central "LOHAS" headquarters, no recognized LOHAS president, no spiritual leader, and no constitution or other governing policy to serve as a centripetal force even though some involved in the LOHAS marketplace might like to have those historical signs of community. (LOHAS businesspeople and consumers from Japan have several times made a pilgrimage to Boulder, Colorado, just to meet the founders of Natural Business Communication and to visit the local natural and organic product manufacturers where the term "LOHAS" first was made public, for example.)

In the absence of these sorts of community polestars, LOHAS has its mediated events and texts. At LOHAS Forum 2006, Nina Utne of *Utne Reader* joined a panel discussing the importance of media in social change, including the formation of community. "The future of the planet is yet to be written and it is possible to make potent change, which is what we must do," she said. Change was going to occur through the emergence of new forms of collectivity, and here she cited her publication. She said *Utne Reader* strove to forge connectivity among readers, particularly "supernodes—the people who take the ideas they see in our magazine and then pump them into the future."

This highlights one traditional function of media as transmitting information, but there's a more complex and nuanced way to regard what media do in creating connections and community, and that is through the notion of "ritual." Communication scholar James Carey proposed that communication has two metaphoric models: a *transmission* view, where the key purpose of communication is to transport messages through space for the purpose of control, and a *ritual* view, where media are geared toward the transformation, modification, maintenance, and creation of a shared culture.

Carey rejected the notion of thought as predominantly a private activity and instead framed it as a public and social activity that "depends on a publicly available stock of symbols" that can both present and create reality (28–29). This dual nature of symbols in communication, Carey says, is no different from what one finds within a religious ritual. "In one mode it represents the nature of human life, its condition and meaning, and in another mode . . . it induces the dispositions it pretends merely to portray" (29). While media perform the transmission role through the circulation of messages "for purposes of control," Carey said, they also perform *ritually* by virtue of their ability to "draw persons together in fellowship and commonality," in ways that mirror the "sacred ceremony" of other ritual forms (43).

Although Carey's argument overlooks the fact that communication is not necessarily always benign, nor is it always a social project, rational or socially cohesive in nature, his work, like Martín-Barbero's, spawned new thinking about the media as sites and channels through which tales of reality are exchanged and created, informing the practices and beliefs rising in their name. Media, religion, and culture scholar Lynn Schofield Clark notes media can serve as a site of collective ritual through the articulation, regeneration, and construction of social mythology, performing discursive work that can bind together an imagined community or discourse community of social actors ("The Turn").

LOHAS Communities

Various types of LOHAS-minded collectives are developing through the LOHAS mediascape, including through print and broadcast media, social media, and events.

In the 1980s the *Utne Reader* developed "Utne Salons." These were local gatherings organized by individual readers in their homes and modeled after the European salons of the nineteenth century where eclecticism ruled, in the types of attendees and topics of debate. For its salons, *Utne Reader* provided readers with guidelines on how to form and maintain a salon and what topics to discuss. With the development of the World Wide Web and Internet, the *Utne* salons evolved into Café Utne on the company's website, billed as "A place in cyberspace where ideas and community intersect." This product complemented its flagship *Utne Reader* while finding a way to utilize emerging online technologies.

Zaadz.com was one of the first of the social media sites to emerge in the LOHAS space that focused solely on the goal of community organizing. Social media—online and mobile technologies, including Twitter, YouTube, and Facebook, that allow for user-generated content and social interaction through dialogue and images—enable people to connect around shared interests.

Started in 2006, Zaadz claimed itself "the Web's first social networking site all about changing the world." The name came from the Dutch word for seed, as a reminder of the potential that people hold within themselves to become socially powerful through the development of their individual skills—a very LOHASian idea. By fulfilling their own "calls," individuals could inspire and empower others who were also on their paths toward personal and social transformation. Sharing their stories, information, and ideas through the site's many thematic *pods*—discussion groups organized around a topic—members were encouraged to regard their jobs, leisure activities, voting, shopping, studying, procreation, thought, and prayer as channels through which world change is made possible. Through these pods, Zaadzsters were instructed to lean on and learn from one another, network about business opportunities, debate issues, and swap ideas and information.

Parallel to the LOHAS discourse overall, Zaadz management was enthusiastic about the role of capitalism and spirituality in social change. Capitalism figured prominently in the company mission statement and listed right after "capitalism" in the company's national ad describing the organization's plan of action was "spirituality."

"Imagine social networking with a purpose," that ad stated. "A community of seekers and conscious entrepreneurs circulating wisdom and inspiration and wealth—This is a community of inspired souls passionate about growth, life, love and all that good stuff," said CEO Brian Johnson, whose full title was Philosopher and CEO. "We like to think of Zaadz as an oasis, a sanctuary—a place to re-charge, connect with your highest self and others who are passionate about life." As part of this, company materials stated that it is important for individuals to be paid for doing what they love and helping others do the same, because "life is about more than the 9-to-5, the house, and the car: it's meant to be lived in service, love and spirit." Zaadz.com was later sold to lifestyle media and retail firm Gaiam, Inc., also the owner of *The LOHAS Journal* and Forums, and renamed Gaia Community.

It wasn't that long ago, but since Zaadz burst out of the social media ether, its format rocketed in popularity in ways perhaps few expected. Social media present an intricate and complex web of communication, not only because of the multi-dimensionality of the technologies and their speed and reach, but also because of their favorable cultural positioning. There are LOHAS "groups," some with numbers of participants in the thousands, on LinkedIn and Facebook. They use terms to identify themselves such as "kindred spirits" and "Cultural Creatives," and members include both veterans of the LOHAS movement and "newbies" to the area of healthy and sustainable living. They are business people, retirees, students, activists, parents, and consumers.

Participants share ideas about how to both mobilize resources to expand the market and their own interests. They exchange information about products and practices, people and organizations, beliefs and values; and they argue for what they believe should or should not be considered part of LOHAS. They promote their private interests. They ask for advice. They seek opportunities for work. They advocate LOHAS principles such as environmentalism and fair trade.

In 2009, nine years after the launch of *The LOHAS Journal,* I interviewed Frank Lampe again and asked him how today's media environment, especially social media, might have affected the mission and strategies of the organization. He said: "If we'd had the kind of online technology that we have today, things like Facebook, Twitter, and LinkedIn, I think the LOHAS idea would have developed differently, not in intention—it was always to develop new networks of dialogue and partnership—but we would have probably emphasized these technologies, as a way to ramp up bringing people into conversation. It might have sped up the process of building community."

Penny told me she believed media were instrumental in helping people visualize the greater community they belonged to, whether they knew they did or not. "Media [can] open new worlds to people," she said, explaining that media products changed people's lives by making them aware of their health options and the fact that others were also engaged in holistic lifestyles. In this way, they came to understand how powerful they were individually and together, as a group.

Carl said his magazine built that sort of community by creating interconnections among people, and that, he said, remained the most important facet of his work as editor-in-chief of a LOHAS publication: "We are reaching a lot of people who interact with other people. As large media corporations become more monolithic with no one's best interest at heart, there are also some thirty thousand blogs opening. The world is becoming connected so quickly in such unimaginable ways, it's impossible to know which of those we should be paying attention to—the big media being gobbled up by giants or the people suddenly talking to each other as they never have before. I suspect the more significant event is people talking to each other."

In 2009 Ted Ning, the director of Conscious Wave, owner of LOHAS Forums and the *LOHAS Journal,* wrote on his blog that "conscious consumers tend to be very social and participatory in communication," and he added, "LOHAS consumers are more likely than ALL others to engage in social media" ("Social Media").

Because the seed of LOHAS is manifesting real change, not just creating the wired version of pen pals, the deeper questions about LOHAS with regard to communities forming in its name are what types of communication are produced, where, and with what results? If the goal really is to do nothing short of reforming capitalism, ending social injustice, and restoring cultures and environments, then we are talking about activism. And this centrally situates media once again.

Between the 1960s and the present, social justice movements have gone from being perceived as an eruption in the fabric of society to being considered part of that fabric of Western societies, according to Della Porta and Diani. They argue that perhaps what we have now is a *protest* society where resistance movements are unmoored from older forms, particularly in the manner in which they are unaligned with political parties, for example, and are instead embedded within the culture. An example is the way in which a consumer commits selective acts of consumption, patronizing specific companies and products assumed to reflect the consumer's "greater moral and ethical standards" to "affect the balance of economic power" locally and globally (Della Porta and Diani 2).

Emerging social movement theories since the Seattle protests in 1999 against the WTO (and against neoliberalism in general) have had to account for these shifts as well as for the heterogeneity of participants and interests that link together in social justice movements (Della Porta and Diani). Media play an important role in allowing and facilitating these changes, particularly as contextualized within globalization. Carroll and Hackett say, "In the networks of activism that criss-cross various groups, media activists may play the role of 'cosmopolitans,' spanning different sectors and improving the prospects for counter-hegemonic coalition formation" (Carroll and Hackett 94).

Focusing on sustainability, Tábara and Giner write that media are essential to facilitate the paradigm shift of sustainability. According to them, for "information, to become sustainability 'knowledge,' it has to form part of the body of the cultural reference system so that each diverse society and individual can link them either by direct experiences or by reflection to their daily practices in a meaningful way" (272). The media are crucial to this process because media can translate the larger issues of sustainability into local contexts, "reflecting local lives and concerns; and where action is as important as language" (Tábara and Giner 272). But the media have unparalleled abilities to show how cross-fertilized global sustainability issues really are, and in that way they also are able to reveal to consumers and producers how their singular acts are actually global in nature, combined with others' to serve as resistance to or support of various regimes, ideas, beliefs, and practices, showing in fact how "all social locations become sites for resistance to power" (Carroll and Hackett 95, citing Buechler).

Claes de Vreese writes about the new centrality of media use in civic and political engagement among young people, for example. According to de Vreese, the Internet in particular—and counter to popular theories of the ways in which media have eroding effects on civic life—has become a key portal to and site of political engagement for younger people, affecting the way in which political acts occur and political issues are understood. LOHAS firm Sdialogue.com says, "Social media are having a powerful impact on the sustainability dialogue" (Sdialogue.com, Sept. 25, 2009, on LOHAS.com) and that "there is a natural intersection between social media and sustainability as both require authenticity, accountability and engagement with their audience to be effective."

But effectiveness if measured as productive acts in the public sphere relies on *participatory communication* not simply a sort of reflective communication, where one's desires and thoughts are reflected back uncritically, for example, as isolated entries on a website or as part of a marketing strategy.

The LOHAS media should serve as "the place[s] where we communicate with others, deliberate, come to agreements about standards and norms, pursue in common an effort to create a valuable form of life, in short . . . the world of community," in the manner that Jürgen Habermas had in mind (qtd. in Bellah). At LOHAS Forum 2007, Peter Russell described this model when he said there was a movement toward self-awakening occurring around the globe, one that involves others in a "collective learning system" as we adapt, learn, and share with others our new knowledge. "That is what this movement is accelerating," Russell said, referring to LOHAS.

Russell also hit on the idea of what Karol Jakubowicz terms "communicative democracy" (83). Differentiating communicative democracy from democratic communication, Jakubowicz says where communicative democracy emphasizes action in the public sphere and communication is facilitating engagement, democratic communication focuses primarily on the process of participation in communication itself and only secondarily on its impact on democracy in a wider sense.

To accomplish action in the arena of sustainability, say Tábara and Giner, the media needs to do better in providing audiences with "particular cultural frames to interpret environmental realities and change" by focusing less on bad news and more on social agency and praxis (279), and, there's nothing the LOHAS media are better equipped to do considering their emphasis on positive thinking and agency as "lifestyle," or, as Fran described it, providing a "little buffet" of ideas of what each of us can do. The individual is hailed in LOHAS media to accept his or her responsibility (and importance) to social change: "If you stand up for something, others will as well," states *Utne Reader* (Creedon 86). And, convincing people to stand up, Penny said, was media's strength.

Communication in the communicative democracy model results in the social circulation of ideas and influence upon political and social decision-making, and this deliberation provides the means and content of resistance to hegemonic and elite ideas, values, and culture (Pelczynski). But the core of this model depends on inclusivity. To accomplish this, LOHAS groups will need to address a tendency already circulating in the LOHAS culture. Like many communities, LOHAS is susceptible to the "community as communion" phenomenon, where communities form around an essentialized and stable identity, and membership becomes a process of receiving ablution and anointment based on how well one performs with relation to a predetermined set of values and arguments (Jean-Luc Nancy, in Willson 155)—a mutual admiration society, in other words. This is exacerbated in LOHAS culture by the tendency in the texts to gloss over the fact that not everyone is able to place themselves on the map of LOHAS or on any chart of sustainability at all. Like the Slow Movements it embraces, LOHAS has been accused of elitism, an exclusivity that will certainly short-circuit the opportunities for real participatory communication and potentially derail global goals of social change. Considering the enormousness of the scope, spatially and ideologically, of the issues that LOHAS embraces, it's crucial to avoid essentializing tendencies in community identity, to keep the doors open to all and to their inevitably differing views about or abilities to undertake sustainability. Managing this inclination depends in great part on the level of provocative discussion LOHAS members both stimulate and tolerate.

What should help with this is the very polysemy of LOHAS—its multivalent identity as a concept attached to self-development, holistic health, environmentalism, social responsibility, and natural capitalism. The community that identifies as "LOHAS" will need to allow for the logical synthesis of numerous identities, and a fluid identity among participants will make clear the very relational nature of these issues and concerns, say Carroll and Hackett. This is what LOHAS organizers had in mind: to reveal and to construct the relational nature of commodities within a holistic lifestyle using the power of media.

Class Issues, Taste, and Distinction in LOHAS

Media, marketing, and advertising serve as cultural intermediaries. They provide "symbolic goods and services" (Zukin and Maguire 182), and the "production of signs and social relations" drives New Social Movements today, say Carroll and Hackett (92). These market and media organizations can reinforce, challenge, and reconstruct notions of taste and form ideas about *distinction* among individuals. Does the articulation of good taste, style and social distinction in LOHAS challenge consumers to move beyond their learned and patterned ways of being to explore anew (Bourdieu, *Distinction* 359; cited in Zukin and Maguire 182), or do they set up blockades that prevent access to and even the desire for sustainability action, for example?

The *Wall Street Journal* ran an article about LOHAS and said, "It's all part of a move to cater to the growing niche of shoppers willing to spend more money for products that let them feel they are acting in a socially responsible fashion. There's even a name for these people, 'LOHAS consumers'" (Mclaughlin). The writer makes her sniff of distrust apparent, and *she's* certainly not alone in feeling a tad suspicious of LOHAS. Iris, a book and magazine editor and freelance writer in the LOHAS space, said the consumer lifestyle publication for which she worked as an editor "sold dreams." "People want to live on the map of natural living, even if they can't really afford to do so," she said with a shrug.

Through the years, critics have leveled accusations of elitism (and price gouging) at the industries under the LOHAS canopy. Organic food, for example, continues to battle the perception of being overpriced, and supporters continue to explain why it often is, saying that complicated factors obscure the reasons behind pricing not just of organic but also of mainstream goods as well. The economies of scale greatly differ between the small, independent organic farm and the large, corporate or factory farm. Not only that, but organic agriculture is also more labor-intensive, requiring more hands-on cultivation and often more expensive inputs to ensure soil, water, and air quality. LOHAS industries have responded to charges of high prices by pointing out that while conventional products may be less expensive than natural/organic/sustainable ones at the point of purchase, they actually carry a much steeper price tag to society because of the way they are grown, manufactured, distributed, or packaged, costing societies billions of dollars in environmental and human health problems. For organic marketers, the goal is to get consumers to care about problems that they perhaps do not see as an immediate threat to themselves.

Despite sophisticated marketing campaigns by organic products producers, there remain unflattering perceptions about organic products: that natural, organic, and "green" are just marketing ploys to give consumers the feel-good sensation of having done something personally, socially, and environmentally righteous but which has probably done little in that regard. One needn't look far to find such commentary about "alternative" goods and practices.

As one example, as I shopped a national chain department store, I saw organic sheets for sale and stopped to examine the labeling. A young couple with their shopping cart passed behind me. "Give me a break," said the man, snorting in derision. "Organic sheets?" he laughed as they pushed their cart down the aisle. Trying to explain the social importance of these products, of sustainability, is the marketing conundrum for LOHAS companies that struggle to find ways to communicate the benefits. Compact fluorescent lightbulbs, for example, aren't just good for the environment—they also save you money by saving on electricity power usage. Sheets and clothes made of organic fibers help reduce the overall amount of pesticides used in the environment, and cotton, a primary fiber crop, is also the most heavily sprayed.

Clearly, the *Wall Street Journal* writer is not convinced that "socially responsible" shopping actually culminates in the promised results. She seems sympathetic with the charge that LOHAS industries replace real philanthropy and social activism with consumption, yet this also implies that consumers are sheer dupes ready for the picking by advertising. If consumers *are* being duped, it isn't only the commodities and commodity providers doing the fooling; it indicts the greater cohort of "texts" in which these ideas and organizations are situated. And that forces us to engage with class issues.

Class in America has been stalwartly denied, as a contradiction in terms to democracy, and acknowledged as "disparity" but with its markers of inequality attributed to flaws in individuals' character rather than to the macrodynamics of capitalism. Both are in play in LOHAS. Individuals are hailed as having the "consciousness" to choose the right products with little attention given to the other aspects involved that activated and enabled that decision, such as income, education, and access to goods. "Consciousness" becomes another word for "taste" and "distinction."

Liu, Maes, and Davenport have coined a wonderful term, "taste fabric," by which they refer to a person's preferences, which become articulated as a result of new information and the processing of information. The notion of "taste"—of one's power to discern among the plethora of social elements represented in a specific milieu—is what niche media expertly generate and reinforce. Their competiveness or distinctiveness in the marketplace depends on how well they do that, how well they elucidate the preference parameters of their specific interest market for their audiences. French theorist Pierre Bourdieu examined how constructions of "taste" and "style" reinforced and informed "class" and structures of power. Bourdieu proposed that ideals about good taste are developed and acquired through interactions among social classes, as part of a process of creating lines of distinction among people and groups. In *Distinction*, Bourdieu says, "[T]aste transforms objectively classified practices, in which a class condition signifies itself (through taste), into classifying practices, that is, into a symbolic expression of class position, by perceiving them in their mutual relations and in terms of social classificatory schemes" (175).

Let's apply a LOHAS example here. First, consumers and producers are interpellated as "conscious" based on the understanding that they adhere to certain principles about the right way to live on the planet—those prescribed conditions inherent in the discourse about health and sustainability. A distinction is made between the LOHAS consumer and producer and those who are non-LOHAS, or mainstream. One is conscious; one is not. This distinction is inscribed upon the food one eats, the clothing one wears, the transport one uses, the groups one associates with, and the causes one supports, and these qualities are generated and reinforced through the cultural intermediaries of market and media. This becomes the taste fabric of a LOHAS sustainability.

As an example, in 2009 on a well-known social network site, a newcomer to the LOHAS marketplace put forth a question to more seasoned LOHAS group members. She asked, "Should a LOHAS fan be using leather products?" Since we know there is no official LOHAS rulebook, one can only imagine the types of responses she received—from promotion of veganism to an argument for humane animal husbandry. For purposes here, however, it is the manner of the exchange itself that deserves our scrutiny: the discussion among self-defined LOHASians on a non–trade oriented social networking site about the composition of the LOHAS disposition, or the construction of the LOHAS taste fabric.

The construction of the taste fabric becomes an expression of power in the world, where power is "the ability to act in pursuit of one's aims and interests, the ability to intervene in the course of events and to affect their outcome" (Thompson, *Media* 13). LOHAS discourse encourages individuals to enact a power that has arrived to them via their righteous labor in becoming conscious, or enlightened about the ills of the world and how they were caused.

Sameer Reddy in *Newsweek* magazine writes, "The age of the eco status symbol is upon us, even at a time of worldwide financial crisis." Writing about new hydrogen-based automobile technology, Reddy notes that the price tags of these cars, sometimes over a hundred thousand dollars, don't deter the target market. "For wealthy auto enthusiasts, the sticker shock isn't an impediment," Reddy says. "If anything, it's the opposite—the extreme price tag makes these cars seem even more appealing as a way to stand out while making a progressive statement." These conscious consumers and producers are told that they can effect change by intervening in systems that have created inequalities without reproducing those imbalances and they are offered resources with which to do so. The texts tell users that they are conscious, wise, alert, and savvy while also being progressive, modern, chic, and cutting-edge.

Media provide ways for people to "consider" these processes and products, and such consideration in turn develops "values" (Bourdieu, *Practical*). What this directly implicates is the power of media because mediated discourse is created through the selection or rejection of ideas, values, meanings, and practices—a "covert exercise of power," Cronon says ("Place" 1350). It isn't a complete power, of course. People have other means of learning and assessing information than just the media. And, while words and meanings have a "determining role in forging human consciousness," it is not an absolute one

(Higgins 40). The media's "strong constitutive force can be challenged and the vocabulary then appropriated by the people themselves if that inheritance is made at once conscious and critical," says Higgins (40).

Again looking to Bourdieu, this time regarding the social relations of power, we can understand this process as one operating through his two key concepts, "habitus" and "field." Habitus refers to the unconscious, internalized structuring mechanisms inscribed in our bodies, as our dispositions—patterns, thoughts, beliefs, and practices that while transposable are also durable and exert influence externally and internally at the same time. This is what is meant by their "structuring" effect. The habitus is a product of history, Bourdieu says (*Outline* 82). It reflects objective conditions of the social world that we have internalized, and, as a result, they structure or determine us, meaning that these dispositions and sensibilities limit what we can do in the world; they counter free will to some extent.

In his use of "field," Bourdieu referred to the social world where we (social actors) and our social positions are located. Here, we struggle and compete for resources, which take the form of "capital." We are accustomed in the West to thinking of that form as monetary, but Bourdieu's capital can be economic, cultural (knowledge, for example), or social (such as is the case with prestige). The struggle over capital, in all its various forms, is our struggle for power on the field. The amount and type of capital we accumulate locates us within social and cultural settings, but some of these we don't like and want to be free of and others are desirable but not necessarily open to us. We struggle to free ourselves from some settings and struggle to gain access into others, in other words.

An important point in Bourdieu's work in application to LOHAS is that "symbolic capital"—such as prestige—can be exchanged for (or transformed into) other kinds of capital such as wealth or a better education or a juicy job. But here's the catch: the dynamics of that transaction are not always transparent, and therein lies a key to understanding the social nature of power. It's rather a sneaky process because situations that might, on the surface, seem quite simply the result of one's own initiative and hard work at becoming conscious actually are brought about by a host of other, predetermining factors. The symbolic nature of power operates like a subway under the infrastructure of daily life.

For example, let's imagine that a woman studies her sustainability marketing coursework diligently during her university years. She graduates with honors and lands a high-paying, high-profile job with Whole Foods Market and, later on, becomes a sustainability book author. Everyone, especially mom and dad, are very pleased. While our student-cum-author may appear to have gained these things through her own "hard work," and indeed she did work hard, let's add some elements to the story. Let's say she is also related to a family who made a fortune during the robber-baron days of capitalism. Subsequent generations managed and grew their money through the hiring of lawyers and accountants, to the point that descendents have each received small fortunes of their own as trust funds. The family culture expects children to obtain a college degree or two at an acceptable institution, marry within their class, and to go on to reproduce the lifestyle and *good* taste of that culture.

This can work in myriad ways. Let's take another example, this time a person who is heralded as someone who has "taken good care of himself" so that he looks younger than one might at a certain age. That individual might also have had the good fortune to buy top-quality food and expensive dietary supplements and had the time to engage in yoga classes and take regular spa vacations. These are matters of income, education, access, and initiative, but this nexus of forces isn't always evident. To continue with our example, however, because of these practices, our gentleman is "read" as someone who is respectful of his body and mindful of his health. This translates into other "readings" of him. He subsequently is articulated as a good parent and dutiful spouse because he is attendant to his health.

As a real life example, in 2006, *Newsweek* ran a food issue in which it was declared that Americans were experiencing a "new interest in food" and that they were "demanding—and paying for—the freshest and least chemically treated products available" (Winne). But in a protest about this article, Mark Winne, author of *Closing the Food Gap*, writes in the online magazine *AlterNet* that this statement obscures and obfuscates the real struggles among Americans for access to the means of good health. Winne said, "Whole Foods' John Mackey told the *Wall Street Journal*, 'the organic-food lifestyle is not a fad . . . it's a value system, a belief system. It's penetrating into the mainstream.'" This completely hides the factors that prevent many people from ascribing to these values and makes it appear as if they have simply chosen not to do so. That is, it makes people who are unhealthy look like victims of their *own* lack of motivation to attain the right values rather than as victims of social pressures such as poverty and racism.

Winne mentions a story in the *New York Times* about families who had moved from New York City to the Hudson River valley and changed their lifestyles to accommodate healthier living. One family started eating "strictly organic foods"; another family, according to the husband, had moved because the "wife was pregnant with their second child and had decided that their 'children needed to be in nature'" (Winne). Winne remarks that this all sounds lovely—"In fact, it just may be the latest incarnation of the American dream," he says. "But what about those who can't escape or afford to eat 'strictly organic' or for whom 'buying local' means the past-code date, packaged baloney at the neighborhood bodega? How do we fulfill the desire for healthy and sustainably produced food that is increasingly shared by all?" (Winne). The "choice" to be healthful, in LOHAS or otherwise, is dependent on one's ability to access the means of healthfulness—and *means* cannot be reduced to *character*. That is, there are real forces—historically rooted, politically bound, and culturally informed—that bear down on populations that bar them access to certain products, practices, institutions, and so forth. What is not acceptable is the virtual pat on the shoulder to these populations that commend them for doing "what they can" rather than understanding that perhaps they want to do much more and working to make that possible.

Bourdieu's concept of capital provides a way to understand and to *see* in these examples the expression (and how and why it was attempted to make them invisible) of the mechanics of power, letting us view power as a product of social class that occurs through very material forms instead of thinking of it only as an abstract force. Using his concepts of cultural, social, and economic capital as our lens, we can also view the practices and products that make up the LOHAS market as cultural indicia—rather than just isolated things or behaviors—and these can tell us something of what trends and data these market and media producers believe they have tapped into.

All of this may sound as if populations are determined from the onset as to what they can achieve in life—a complete contradiction to American mythologies of freedom, equality, and liberty. But that is not the intent here—it is also true that people can be creative and innovative, that they can make meaning, struggle for resources, and surpass barriers put before them. While habitus is embodied in individuals in ways that encourage us to act in a patterned, social, and recognizable manner, we each also have our own particularized ways of internalizing the external world and expressing that outwardly. That is, we can also "improvise and coordinate and cope with unforeseen and changing situations" (Garnham and Williams 119). Bourdieu did not envision freedom broadly, however. We remain constrained by the internalized structures resulting from our own practices (habitus) that become externalized in the shape of social structures such as class order.

An interesting study by Julie Guthman on the construction of alternative food practices is a good example. Her work reveals that a strong "white" cultural narrative infiltrates the practices known as biodynamic, organic, locally grown, and natural. In her article, she examines the notion of "food deserts"—a term coined to describe the dearth or absence of venues in urban environments that sell "healthful fruits, vegetables, meats, and grain products," and instead "sell snack foods and highly processed ready-to-eat meals." These so-called deserts are the result of economic and social forces including "racist insurance and lending practices (red-lining), which have historically made it difficult to develop and sustain businesses in certain areas," says Guthman (431). She also notes the effect of "white flight" and high unemployment in urban areas via the "neoliberal restructuring of those spaces," and the "net loss of supermarkets to suburbs with larger sites, fewer zoning impediments, and customers with higher purchasing power" (432).

Guthman describes a food project undertaken by her Community Studies students. The students were assigned to work with low-income African American populations to introduce organic food, organic gardening, and other alternative food practices to the community. But the people did not react the way students had hoped. The alternative food practices, including the food products, were often received with suspicion, contempt, and disagreement, much to the students' disappointment. This is because alternative food practices are coded with "whitened cultural histories, such as the value of putting one's hands in the soil," Guthman writes (431). It isn't enough to have good intention in activism; one must understand the cultural symbols and histories of populations. "Current activism reflects white desires more than those of the communities they putatively serve," Guthman concluded (431).

In the case of Guthman's study, the word "organic" had become synonymous with "useless" for these communities; many didn't know how to prepare or use the foods presented to them. Others associated it with undesirable forms of labor. Because of this, are these populations to be left out of the consideration of sustainability, forced to accept whatever others decide will or will not be sustainable living without a voice in the matter? Instead, Guthman's study underscores the importance of staying alert to the ways in which words, images, and practices have been imbued with meaning from various discursive practices. As a result, they become unacceptable, unattainable, or otherwise undesirable to various populations.

The importance attached to words and language is of vital concern to an organizational field such as LOHAS that depends on the construction of terms and concepts and the strength of their representation in the greater public. Paloma, for example, told me about the difficulty she had in deciding upon a title for her publication. She had rejected "sustainability," saying, "we tend not to use the word, not because it isn't a good word, but because it isn't a sexy word." Instead her team tried such words as environmentally conscious, authentic, pure, and "other words that were inspiring." Even while her consumer research showed the word "sustainable" scoring higher than even the widely used term "organic," her company's researchers believed that most people did not know what "sustainable" actually meant. "Some may think of agriculture when they hear it, and some might think it pertains to supporting their family," Paloma said.

What she really wanted to do with the title was to escape all of the usual terms common to the LOHAS industries and use something "more emotive," such as the words "happiness or joy." Partly, she said, she did not want terms that forced readers into having to analyze too much: "What we want is to give readers is something more pleasurable and relaxing." The distinctions among verbiage are vital, particularly when we consider the global nature of LOHAS discourse.

Understanding language norms and meanings is important for LOHAS advertisers, manufacturers, retailers, and media professionals, of course, to be able to "target" audiences, people whom they believe will be willing and able to select their products. Moisander and Pesonen say the "socially acceptable green consumer is constructed as an autonomous, prudent and well-informed choosing individual, who performs his/her received role in society as a powerful market actor by meticulously monitoring and controlling his/her consumption-related activities" (332). The "ideal green consumer," they say, "is a decent, or rather exemplary, citizen who tirelessly but with a relatively 'low profile' works towards sustainable development, doing small but momentous good deeds, guided and motivated by a rigid personal ethic and a firm confidence in his/her ability to 'make a difference'" (332). But those who are able to "make a difference" are making that difference in ways that affect others, whether those others have a voice in the matter or not.

Obviously, the ideal green consumer for a LOHAS company is the one who can afford to buy the company's goods. Despite that, or because of it, the LOHAS discourse calls for the establishment of an egalitarian society where the needs of all are considered and met. Comments such as "businesses are restructuring management to be more egalitarian" (*LOHAS Weekly*, Nov. 1, 2000); "LOHAS is uber-egalitarian" (blog comment, http://hokai .info/2008/01/discussion-ad-hominem.html); and "ethical fashion should be truly egalitarian" (http://www.lohas-guide.de), flow through these texts. Even Paul Ray noted that the demand for more egalitarianism was a marker trait of the Cultural Creatives (Dykema).

Egalitarianism is implied in the construct of *holism*—in the idea that self, society, and the natural world are interdependent. In Riches's work on the New Age, he writes that the construct of holism in the New Ager is related to a desire for "egalitarian social values," but he distinguishes between two types of egalitarianism that are also useful for the study of LOHAS (670). The first is an egalitarianism of *opportunity* whereby everyone in a community has equal access to the materials necessary to enable individual action. The second type is an egalitarianism of *outcome*, whereby "social equivalence is stipulated as the result desired from individual transactions" (Riches 670). In other words, while the first, at least in theory, allows for all individuals to have equal opportunity to get ahead, the second prefers that all actually participate in an equal result. According to Riches, the idea of the *holistic* person in the modern West rose through the replacement of the notion of egalitarianism of opportunity with the idea about egalitarianism of outcome.

These distinctions are useful to apply to LOHAS because they again lure out questions about taste, distinction, and power. We know, for example, that the "opportunity" model describes the mythology underlying the "American way of life"—everyone has an equal chance to pull themselves up by the proverbial bootstraps to achieve their goals. We also know the American Dream is supported, even if rearticulated, in the LOHAS discourse. But the egalitarianism that runs through the "Dream" contradicts the articulations in LOHAS of health and sustainability, because these concepts imply that personal, social, and environmental "resources" are distributed unequally, effectively barring many from being able to change their lives.

Outcome-based egalitarianism in LOHAS is the acknowledgement that all people, for example, have common health needs. But this shared nature of our being must also celebrate and accommodate diversity and difference, not only among people and cultures but also among organisms, animals, and ecosystems. This thought is indispensible to the liberal democratic state. Where things get sticky is in the logistics of how to accommodate difference and which types of difference are allowable, meaning which ones are considered "unsustainable" or "unhealthy" and thus unacceptable. Who decides? If we are to follow our individual bliss, on the one hand, how do we do that without impinging on the bliss of someone else lying downwind and downstream? Whose values and needs and differences trump? While one is worrying about how to work in enough "salmon, sardines, herring, and tuna" (*Natural Solutions*, Dec. 2008, 55) into their daily diet to achieve the right amount of healthy fats, how do they also accommodate the fact that "the ocean called: it's out of fish" (*Good*, cover Sept/Oct. 2008)?

The LOHAS texts have not been able to avoid wrestling this conundrum. In the October 15, 2009, issue of *Sustainable Brands Weekly* (http://www .sustainable-media.com), the author cheerfully asks, "what if luxury and sustainability could not just co-exist, but actually thrive together?" (Manconi). "What if sustainable luxury items could become the vehicle to make sustainability an inspirational added value of a product? Or spearhead technological innovation that tomorrow will be adopted by the masses?" Manconi asks and adds, "This is what luxury yacht maker Ferretti is betting on." Buying one of those yachts will set a person back "little over $4 million."

The article attempts to exonerate these rarefied products by framing them as portals into sustainability for some wealthy people who might not otherwise ever accept a sustainable lifestyle. This is dubious logic for a number of reasons, but it raises serious questions about how sustainability meanings are constructed and conveyed, particularly within Bourdieu's notion of the social relations of power and how meanings are constructed in ways that favor some people/systems/beliefs and not others.

Reddy raises these concerns in *Newsweek,* writing, "There's nothing like a fat bank account to make it easy being green." Reddy continues, saying, "Fortunately for the lovers and purveyors of old-fashioned luxury standbys—like 30-carat canary yellow diamonds and Lamborghinis—the market for eco friendly luxury is still in its nascent stage." Reddy adds: "Its cost premiums require buyers to appreciate the idea of sustainability in order to accept higher prices. But in the coming years, especially if economic hard times improve, the market will likely boom as luxury consumers express their concern the way they know best: with their credit cards."

How does the acceptance of yachts and yellow diamonds as a legitimate part of the sustainability dialogue affect understandings of sustainability and, subsequently, influence practices, regulations, policies, innovations, distribution, all of which carry implications for people and environments? How do we reconcile the presence of these products—the conditions of their manufacture, marketing, and purchase—with advice to others on "how to generate your own electricity, revolutionize energy supply and forever shift the balance of power," as offered on the cover of the September 2008 issue of *Ode* magazine?

Consumption studies show that consumers try to imitate the consumption practices and choices of those a "rung or two" above them on the social ladder. But now consumers are aiming for the lifestyles of those at the top of the social ladder, thanks to more awareness of those lifestyles through the media (Shah et al. 7). This is a strange egalitarianism. It's even stranger when we consider that in LOHAS culture consumers are also being encouraged to imitate the lifestyles of those who may be "rungs" below them in terms of wealth. This happens when lower-income, indigenous, or other populations are interpreted as having much more of the new precious commodities—time, happiness, and quality of life.

Such counter-marketing can result in a type of eroticizing, consciously or unconsciously, of indigenous people and their cultures and cultural artifacts and a sort of erasure of the complications of poverty. The imagined "simple" lifestyles of other populations manifested through their handmade cultural artifacts are commodities exported through media and inventoried by market organizations for socially conscious consumption. Carolyn Betensky writes about this, saying a certain "prestige of the oppressed" can occur whereby remote, threatened, and esoteric products gain a certain cachet or purchase in the global commodity marketplace by virtue of being "Othered," as Edward Said called it.

These "othered" products, unmoored from their cultural or geographic origins, transform into the Western consumer's symbolic capital, as something "traditional" (highly valued in a culture of newness), as something produced through non-Western scientific wisdom (something more natural and indicative of other ways of knowing), and unique (appealing for purposes of identity building and distinction). Decorating one's home using the principles of Wabi-Sabi, for example, or adorning one's self with handcrafted jewelry from an indigenous artisans' cooperative and ingesting a rainforest remedy once known only to Amazonian shamans have a peculiar status in the West's market culture (Betensky). "Whenever the recognition of oppression—responsibility established, consciousness raised—is viewed as valuable unto itself, whenever symbolic empowerment is asserted to be empowerment *tout court*, 'capital' is allowed to stand in, however temporarily, for Capital," Betensky says (209).

While LOHAS market organizations frame these practices and products as fair trade, culturally sensitive, and environmentally sustainable, sustainability is still framed in economic terms without considering deeper social questions such as what one economy potentially gives up to serve the other in this exchange. Did, for example, the shaman lose symbolic, cultural, or social capital when his knowledge was exported to outsiders by causing a real or perceived erosion of sacred power? And, how does a shaman in the rainforest actually give informed consent to a Western scientist in the first place? (Emerich). These questions are difficult for lifestyle media to address and are left to the more news-oriented media in the LOHAS space such as *Utne Reader* and *Ode*. In great part, this lack of exploration on the part of lifestyle media is a problem of the advertising model of lifestyle media. Imagine the displeasure of a manufacturer of a line of expensive natural skin care products when a radio program that is financially supported by the manufacturer's advertising dollars presents programming arguing that impoverished women and men are not able to access the latest technologies in natural skin care and hence have higher levels of skin cancer.

Language is constructive of reality. Thus, we have to remember that when we read, for example, that a young mother chooses to eliminate the television from her home in order to stimulate her children's creativity it is but one solution for one population: it simply isn't the sustainability solution for those consumers for whom television is the safest or most accessible window onto the world, including the world of sustainability issues (Korelitz 105). Sustainability needs to be contextualized within a host mitigating factors such as class, taste fabric, income, and location.

Stitching together a logical argument about sustainability—which is, by its nature, a critique on the processes of late modernity and late capitalism—within the logic of late capitalism can't help but be fraught with contradictions. If the rights of global elites to their exceptionalism—their cultural difference in the form of yachts, natural hair dyes, their ability to purchase *unique* gifts of indigenous art, and hybrid vehicles—is to be safeguarded with the same vigilance as the rights of hill tribes around the world to clean water and grazing lands, who is to monitor the possible infringements of one group upon the other? This becomes more confounding when another form of symbolic capital is introduced into the sustainability dialogue: spirituality. LOHAS culture is comfortable with using the term "spirituality," so much so it can easily stand in for "sustainable" and "healthy." Sasha, for example, told me that "God is sustainability; whatever we define as God is sustainable."

Verter argues that if "religious capital is conceived a la Bourdieu as something that is produced and accumulated within a hierocratic institutional framework, spiritual capital may be regarded as a more widely diffused commodity, governed by more complex patterns of production, distribution, exchange, and consumption" (158). Spiritual capital, like Bourdieu's other types of capital, is part of the complex field of power through its construction and its exchange among holders and seekers. Spirituality becomes another public badge of sustainability consciousness and, as such, because of the nature of spirituality, it also becomes a sort of divine stamp of approval on the LOHAS worldview.

Sasha's linking of God with sustainability—while leaving the definition of "God" as open-ended as possible—is axiomatic in the LOHAS space. Terms such as "sacred," "God," and "spirit" along with images of altars, icons, holy lands, and people praying or meditating are put to use in nontraditional pairings in LOHAS media—with everything from holistic business management to the home arts. These couplings are unlinked from theology, denomination, liturgy, and institutional infrastructure but still retain their metaphysical strength and ability to serve as signposts to moral reasoning. The power of the LOHAS discourse lies in its ability to transport those signs to other sites and spheres without a loss of meaning or legitimacy, to effect a transformation in the meaning of the mundane and ordinary objects and practices in these sites, elevating them to the level of the sacred.

LOHAS media and market assume their consumers or users have "the linguistic facility to discuss" (Verter 152) spirituality in these terms and that they are able and free to associate spirituality with other markers of sustainable living. The ability of users to do so, however, only means that they have accumulated a "knowledge of status codes"—that they've become adept with the terms of the ideals in LOHAS or healthy living discourses overall—and that they view these discourses as sources of legitimacy on issues of spirituality (152). This literacy, in turn, is what facilitates the establishment of a type of distinction or identification as LOHASian (Zukin and Maguire).

The spiritualizing of consciousness in LOHAS is accomplished through the use of familiar religious and spiritual symbolic language, but done in as diaphanous a way as possible. This allows "spirituality" to be lightly overlaid onto any number of personalized practices, and this treatment is celebrated as one of the advantages of the new consciousness of holism and sustainability in the discourse. Carl, editor-in-chief of a national consumer publication, for example, says his magazine works hard to be inclusive of multiple faith traditions in a way that allows practitioners to feel comfortable with the publications. "The common ground is in experience, practice," he said. "We don't get involved with liturgical controversies. It is about the experience of the sacred. And what's interesting is that [the sacred] is universal, even if the language is different."

It sounds simple to use spirituality this way, to speak about religious values without having to be constrained by religion's dictates regarding identity and social mores—positions handed down through and enforced by community, family, and cultural institutions (see Flere and Kirbiš). But like other keywords of the LOHAS discourse, the term "spirituality" only works in this ideal manner, as put forth by Carl, when it isn't too narrowly defined. Once definitions are attempted, things can become uncomfortable. At LOHAS Forum 13 in 2009, Andrew Cohen, editor and founder of the spiritually focused magazine *EnlightenNext*, conducted a seminar titled "Evolution of Enlightenment—Do You Want to Just Survive or Do You Want to Evolve?" Seated in the audience was Steve Keisling, the editor-in-chief of *Spirituality & Health*. Cohen, who opened with the intriguing line "I don't know anything about sustainability," told the audience God should be thought of as a maturation of human consciousness or evolution. "There is no cosmic being outside process," he said. "We are in the tipping point—are we going to take responsibility for what's happening here?" He then added that humans needed to stop seeing themselves as just human and instead as a part of the cosmos, as one with "the creative process—God."

Keisling suddenly shot up his hand in the middle of Cohen's presentation. When Cohen did not call on him, Keisling called out, "What if all this is wrong?" He was not pleased with Cohen's representation of God as a concept solely expressive of human consciousness. He argued instead for the equal, if not supreme, consciousness of organisms and animals. Science, he said, does not back Cohen's claim of consciousness, and he argued that Cohen's theory was not helpful to creating a model of change that would take care of all species.

Cohen did not choose to answer Keisling, but Keisling's question might just as easily be applied to any of the truth claims made within the discourse. For example, there could have been quite a lengthy and dynamic conversation when, at LOHAS Forum 2006, an audience member asked the panel on stage, "what if capitalism is not compatible with sustainability?" It is the elephant in the living room, and it could have led to a vibrant and fruitful discussion. Instead, this intrepid person received less an answer than he did a dismissal when the panel moderator essentially called the question passé and off the point. These questions get at the bedrock of LOHAS and are ultimately about whose version of truth becomes legitimized in public discourse, but trying to define any of the terms seems discomfiting to individuals.

When I asked Margo, for example, if she thought there was a spiritual dimension to sustainability, she hesitated to answer. She said she did not want to imply that the work for sustainability on the levels of self, social, or natural world *should* be interpreted with the words "moral" or "ethical." That in and of itself is a spiritual question, she said. It felt judgmental to her. "Anything, whether it is mainstream religion or any kind of practice, if it's a dogma, it is not spirituality," she said. "I don't think anything like that is genuinely spiritual because it leads to the quality of judgmentalism and rigidity, and that is antithetical to spirituality." Instead, she explained her work in sustainability this way: "What keeps me doing what I'm doing is the number of people who tell us that they've changed their lives and how they see the world and have gone on to change the world around them."

In another interview, this time with Richard, I asked what the word "holistic" meant to him. He said sustainability was holism: "The word holistic to me refers to an awareness of and mindfulness of the entire system, as opposed to specific components of a system; it is a 'big-picture' outlook and it is inclusive." I then asked him if there was a quality of spirituality involved in the concept of sustainability. He paused and then said, "On the surface, no. I believe the concepts of sustainability as we have discussed them don't require an element of spirituality for completeness."

But he added, "Having said that I've become more aware that a good spiritual base is crucial for manifesting all these other areas [of sustainability and health]." Richard felt that people who have a deep spiritual base are better equipped to lead the charge in creating sustainability. Quickly he said, "That is not to say they have to have it, but those that do—I think they understand the concepts of sustainability deeper than those who do not and are better advocates for making it happen." I asked Richard what he meant by spirituality or a "spiritual base," as he had called it. Richard thought for a minute before replying, "I can't speak for all people who have spiritual bases, but when I look at what Christianity means, it means taking care of your fellow human beings, and that would indicate a lot of the things we've talked about [in our interview], but many of the people who call themselves Christians don't look at things that way." He paused again and said, "If you look at the born-agains or the fundamentalists who are waiting for the rapture, well, clearly they're not dialed into [sustainability]." He seemed frustrated with his answer, and added, "I don't how to get my hands around your question."

It's little wonder. Spirituality is used in the broader culture as "an extrainstitutional, resolutely individualistic, and often highly eclectic personal theology self-consciously resistant to dogma," says Verter (158), and that is about as narrow as LOHAS culture can tolerate, which makes sense: spirituality is a descriptive of sustainability and health and these terms are, as we have seen throughout this book, deliberately kept as open-ended as possible. No wonder Keisling had trouble with Cohen's attempt to identify spirituality; if spirituality only refers to a human conscience, as Cohen said, then on what basis do we argue for limitations on human use of the natural environment, for example? How do we accommodate Kiesling's view that the natural world holds wisdom that we must learn?

For now, the flexibility of "consciousness" or spirituality in LOHAS allows for inclusivity, for a diverse population to "locate" themselves on the map of LOHAS. This is good for building a larger consumer base for LOHAS. One can argue that this floating meaning serves to welcome more individuals to join the vanguard of social change—to allow, in effect, an individual to see him- or herself as a "self-managing, enterprising, choosing self and the model citizen of neoliberal societies who shoulders the responsibility for maintaining social order through his or her 'good' choices," as Zukin and Maguire say (183). The badge of spirituality confers ability and righteousness, as we see in an article by Leif Utne writing in the *Utne Reader* saying that people are made more effective when the "spiritually inclined" are taught "how to be more engaged in political and social-change work" (90).

By embedding the idea of spirituality in the everyday bits and pieces of life, the LOHAS discourse reconstitutes goods and practices as something other than what they seem. A refrigerator becomes an energy-saving device, a bamboo T-shirt becomes a renewable resource, and coffee beans become lifelines for indigenous farmer families and their villages. Like religion and media and market organizations—particularly those linked to "lifestyle consumption" and "collective identity" such as we see with global brands (Jeep or iPod, for example)—have a vested interest in constructing a discourse that goes beyond the mere advertisement of products, to construct narratives that integrate products and practices with other values and other sensory stimulation (Shah et al).

But for consumers and producers caught in the logic of late capitalism, LOHAS may prove to be the language and practice that allows individuals to work to resolve the contradictions in their lives brought about by the forces of late modern. LOHAS ameliorates conversations that have stayed regnant within the fabric of the counterculture such as the New Age, positive thinking, social justice, and environmentalism, and it weaves these with the market to tell people how to be virtuous without being violating.

Toward an Integrative Spirituality of Sustainability

> "That longing for spiritual uplift and communion, along with the sense of being let down, have no doubt driven the popularity of New Age beliefs in the U.S. and elsewhere in recent decades. It may also have contributed to the rise in eco-consciousness and the emergence of a 'Lifestyles of Health and Sustainability' (LOHAS) demographic."
> —M. Brunton, *Ode Magazine* 2009.

How are we to live? The question brings to mind both spiritual and lifestyle considerations, concerns that are merged in the LOHAS movement as a way to mobilize an answer to that pervasive question of the ages through the discursive construction of two concepts: "health"—represented as a state of balance—and "sustainability," the acts and beliefs it takes to maintain that balance. Health serves as the representation of the sacred in LOHAS. It not only makes reference to the socially constructed and physically imperative needs of the self, but it also frames these as interdependent with the needs of others and the needs of the natural world. This is holism, the LOHAS worldview, a *sacred* tripartite of self, society, and natural world.

LOHAS may be the perfect postmodern spirituality. Bricolage is its nature; LOHAS texts speak to the importance of connecting our spiritual selves with our consuming selves, of linking disparate spheres of existence, and of bringing together histories, narratives, social movements, geographies, the senses, cultures, and rituals. LOHAS culture serves as a type of logic that can be used to navigate the pressures and contradictions of late modernity, all brought to our doorsteps in Technicolor via the twenty-four-hour media and the continually evolving information communication technologies (Badaracco; Giddens, *Consequences* and *Modernity*; Thompson, *Ideology*, "Mass Communication," and *Media*)

Media and market have forced awareness of the world as a shrinking space; new revelations arrive each day about the interrelationships of our governments, ecosystems, economies, cultures, workforces, lifestyles, and more. We can see, as an article on LOHAS put it, that "your lifestyle choice *is* my concern—your *diet* is my concern, your *means of transportation* is my concern, your *politics* are my concern, your *religion* is my concern" (Burgess), even while the increased movements of people and capital expose our differences more than ever (Keane). Too, media and market have forced open a view onto our own histories in such a way that we are able to regard the implications not only for ourselves but also for societies, and for environments we've never seen. Armed with that knowledge, we can situate ourselves on local and global maps with an eye to where we want to be in the future, whether we have the means to bring that into being or not.

It is no wonder that lifestyles of health and sustainability are appealing—LOHAS tells us, first of all, that we have power to effect change in the state of affairs we find ourselves facing and that we do not have to wait for institutions to take action, if these organizations even could or would. Second, LOHAS tells us we are more than homo economicus, that we can experience a renewed wholeness of mind, body, and spirit, as Wade Clark Roof has said, even while we continue to enjoy the fruits of capitalism and consumer culture. It allows us to go forward, without feeling paralyzed by our own inability to escape market economics.

Third, LOHAS provides us with a site and a liturgy through which we can recognize, repent, and assuage guilt about our complicity with the suffering wrought by modernization, industrialization, and neoliberalism. Fourth, LOHAS attempts to make peace between that uncomfortable realization and the bedrock of American values—it salvages the American Dream and the tenets of liberalism and allows us to reconcile those histories with our imagination about the "ethical possibles" of the future (Y. King). It assures us that we can reinvigorate civil society even as we retain the self-focus inherited from our American spiritualities of "healthy-mindedness" and the resulting therapeutic traditions (Badaracco; Peck). By working on the "self," through our commitment to develop our consciousness, and through our belief in conscious consumption, we can reenchant the world, allowing the irrationality of mystery, intuition, and spirituality to conjoin with our intellect, our pragmatism, even our positivism. We can be materialistic and compassionate, forward-looking and reflective, redeemed and forgiven.

LOHAS tells us that capitalism is innovative, powerful in ways social institutions including religion are not, and that it is cooperative and pliable and responds to the driver's hands upon its wheel, which is why it is up to us to direct it wisely. In essence, LOHAS presents a way in which to think about late capitalism as both ruination and remedy.

Rationality and a "Reflexive Spirituality"

Capitalism is a master bloodhound. The market can sniff even a fairy dusting of consumer discontent, and it is able to quickly turn any potential non-profitable trends into opportunities by creating desires that seem to arise in us so organically that we assume them to be natural and only waiting to be revealed to us.

In the case of LOHAS, rising discontent among consumers with main-stream products across the spectrum told early LOHAS organizers that seismic shifts were occurring around ideas about living more sustainably, simply, and healthfully. As even more evidence, they noted the recent work by sociologist Paul Ray on the Cultural Creatives, convinced he had discovered something unusual about Americans, something other demographic and psychographic measures had missed.

The staff at Natural Business Communications believed Ray's research showed that so-called alternative ways of living that emphasized environmentalism, spirituality, and natural medicine, for example, that had been stewing in the culture throughout the twentieth century were now materializing for consumers in new ways. For those industries involved in natural and organic products, LOHAS was an easy and logical transition because these firms were already sympathetic to these interests, but for others such as the automotive industry, for example, interest in LOHAS rose less from allegiance to social movements and alternative lifestyles and more from the convincing arguments Ray and LOHAS organizers were making about a virtual tsunami of consumers. These consumers wanted a more holistic, sustainable, and healthy lifestyle and were looking for companies that fell into line with their values. But it wasn't just the types of products that consumers were purchasing that caught the interest of these more mainstream industries—it was also the way in which consumers were synthesizing these into a lifestyle.

These consumers, according to market researchers, were disenchanted with the fruits of "progress." They were fed up with mindless accumulation, unhealthful products and practices, and the further erosion of their private time. They were suspicious of capitalism even as they were caught up in it. "Multinational" had become synonymous with "corrupt." They wanted more value from products than cost savings. They wanted a longer-term savings that represented improved health for people and planet for all time, ensuring the continuation of generations to come. Value became articulated in emotional, spiritual, moral, intellectual, and physical qualities. They wanted industries to be worthy to step into new roles of leadership and vision

LOHAS producers realized they had to simultaneously nod to new intimations of austerity in the marketplace while also gently revealing how other types of consumer goods could represent these different values. They also needed to convince fellow industry members that the time was ripe for businesses to move into the spaces held by government and social institutions, and that the early industry members who did would be rewarded. LOHAS media had to explain that reward would not just come in the form of quick company profits: Industry needed to cultivate new relationships with their value-driven consumers by developing products that reflected these different measurements of eco-consciousness, social responsibility, and holistic health. This would result in a "triple bottom line," as it is called, which reflects equal concern for people, planet, and profits. Value had to be equated with a rising global consciousness that would address the increasing pressures of social and environmental problems.

The media serving the market for alternative lifestyles found a plethora of new advertisers and new consumers joining their fold throughout the 1990s. The mission became a question of how to build bridges among these new consumers, industries and practitioners. The media needed to find terms that would welcome new populations but not turn away existing customers. They found that they already had useful tools for this work, in the narratives already extant in much of the texts, including ideas about personal development, health and wellness, mind/body/spirit, environmentalism, and even about America as the promised land providing a superior "quality of life." These tropes could be newly articulated in the media through liberalism and through the therapeutic traditions that already resonated not only through alternative America but throughout mainstream America as well. Still, some terms particular to the more alternative side of things, especially "New Age," had to be renegotiated. That term implied more of an interest in spirituality than the mainstream could probably handle, but there were useful parts of it to salvage in the construction of LOHAS sensibilities.

The New Age represented "the inner realm" that supposedly served "as the [sole] source of authentic vitality, creativity, love, tranquility, wisdom, power, authority and all those other qualities that are held to comprise the perfect life," as Paul Heelas put it (*New Age*, 19, qtd. in Houtman and Aupers 307). But while Cultural Creatives were sympathetic to those themes, Ray showed they also wanted to do more than work on themselves; they wanted to tie their inner work to the activism they had encountered in the 1960s, to an awareness of the external world brought home to them through the media. Paul Ray and

Sherry Ruth Anderson quote Sarah van Gelder, editor of *Yes!* magazine, who had written to Ray and Anderson to say she was "tired of the dichotomy that pits inner change against changing the culture" (Ray and Anderson 93). She said: "The New Age stereotype is that it's all about changing ourselves internally and the world will take care of itself. The political activists' stereotype is that we ignore our inner selves to save the world. Neither works! . . . The Cultural Creatives are about leaving that dichotomy behind and integrating the evolution of the self and the work on the whole" (93).

Her comment mirrors an argument by Rosemary Bechler who says there is a crucial difference between individualism and selfish individualism. Bechler says this is a "confusion that anyone who wants to see social progress in the world reproduces at their peril since it is a conflation on which capitalism and capitalist power increasingly relies." Individualism allows people to regard their own self interest, which is a "precondition," Bechler says, for "all progressive social change." Selfish individualism is concerned for its own being and happiness, whereas individualism understands the strength of collectivity and its interests with regard to participation in contemporary societies that are marked by diversity rather than homogeneity. Referring to Hannah Arendt and Charles Taylor in their writings on civic republican thinking, Bechler says that these scholars recognized that "in these circumstances, political community must be based on communication rather than the assumption of commonality."

LOHAS grows from this seed of distinction. Participants and organizers have a choice to make about the future development of the movement, to salvage it from the ever-grasping embrace of capitalist power and the tail-chasing type of individualism that consumerism encourages in the interest of commodifying all social needs and interests. The discourse has already once recognized the selfishness of the individualism espoused through capitalism when the inner realm of the New Age was retranslated in the idea of LOHAS as "personal development." Our own bodies—mind, body, and spirit—serve as the sites through which we first become conscious of our fellowship with other people, with animals, with environments. What the emerging LOHAS discourse promised in the beginning were bridges between the spheres of rationality and spirituality, between the inner and outer realms, and between mainstream and the alternative markets.

The LOHAS Journal team contributed to this by reordering the marketplace for sustainable and healthy goods and services, creating new "categories" that would allow mainstream and other newly interested businesses to locate themselves in the healthy living space. The categories also made clear how the inner and outer realms of experience integrated. Our personal health was linked to the health of other people, places and environments, which served as a holistic worldview or spirituality.

These categories married everyday experiences (from changing lightbulbs to choosing a mutual fund), with transcendental meanings (salvation, compassion, the divine), and both yet again with civic engagement. It appealed to consumers whom Ray said were tired of the increasing compartmentalization of their lives, the idea that they could only "do" good when they were active in philanthropy or civic engagement. They wanted everything they did in the capitalist marketplace to line up even as they were tired of the encroachment of rationalization into all parts of the life world that "substituted mastery for mystery" (Roof 62). It appealed to people who were "aching for a sense of wholeness," to borrow a phrase from Wade Clark Roof (62), and suddenly spirituality didn't have to be a choice between formal religion and New Age "woo-woo."

LOHAS evolved into what Kelly Besecke calls "reflexive spirituality." This occurs through the injection of an elemental spiritual question into any number of consumer goods, from clothing to cars: how does this purchase add or subtract from suffering? In this way, spirituality becomes a cultural resource in a consumer culture that enables some individuals to speak of transcendent meaning in a rationalized modern society, while also allowing them to engage with rationality, as Besecke argues.

These practices also continue the type of individualized spiritual quest in rationalized societies that is "marked by reflexivity and pluralism," which Besecke and others have argued is a mark of contemporary society. But it attempts to stem the potential of selfish individualism in that quest, or at least the potential such spiritual seeking is feared to hold. Instead, it is just as possible that this spirituality of sustainability in LOHAS performs as the moral aspect of society, as Durkheim said, that can cohere people. Besecke says, "What is needed, in order to re-ground modern society in some kind of shared transcendent meaning, is a way of talking about transcendent meaning without sacrificing a broad-based commitment to the modernist project of a rational society" (366). What could be more sacred than the question of our own purpose and how to save our species along with that of the organisms, people, lands, and cultures with which we share the planet?

The LOHAS discourse reflects the understanding that "a metaphysics of consumerism" had "become a kind of default philosophy for all modern life" (Campbell 41–42, qtd. in Bauman 29), but also offers a patch for the parts in disrepair. LOHAS informs consumerism with *consciousness*, using products and practices from self-actualization to social and environmental activism. LOHAS had to find some higher appeal to legitimate the attempt to set controls on consumerism—the commodification of sociocultural needs (Teeple). Sustaining life is the new common realization, an inherently spiritual process, and it may be the best levee to hold against the reductive and particularizing power of late capitalism, allowing individuals speedy and available means to interact with an increasingly complex political and social global landscape.

And this is to say that LOHAS participants perceive they have a great responsibility to hold the levee firm.

With the rise of popular interest in LOHAS, there has been, unsurprisingly, an accompanying rise in critiques of the LOHAS concept. There is more than a hint of distrust for the New Age bricolage that still lingers there and for the insidiousness of commodification. As an example, in the online forum *Slate Magazine*, Ron Rosenbaum says, "There's nothing worse than narcissism posing as humility." He points out that if the LOHAS preference for Eastern religious traditions including Buddhism emphasize compassion, then "why not skip the scented bath, skip making amends with the self, skip realization of 'the opportunity to embrace *aparigraha* or non-grasping?'" and instead lend a hand at a soup kitchen or homeless shelter "rather than continuing the endless processes of anointing yourself with overly scented candlelit self-love?" It's a question that forces to the forefront the types of issues raised in the last section. Does LOHAS stimulate new forms of self-absorption and spiritual- and green-washing? Does it generate a new global imperialism cloaked in the benignancy of "health and sustainability?" Rosenbaum's particular charge insinuates that the deploying of spirituality is superfluous and gratuitous. The job of this book, as with any critique, is to open up spaces for debate, to reveal challenges, and to challenge perpetrators.

To Rosenbaum's point, we have to understand that LOHAS is not and never claimed to be a philanthropic endeavor. Of course the capitalist imperative is at work in LOHAS: these media and market organizations wouldn't survive without advertising or readership. Spirituality and consciousness, the glue in LOHAS that holds together its polysemic narratives about sustainability, have not escaped commodification. You can view LOHAS one of two ways: either it was created as an attempt to change the direction and nature of market capitalism, or it was an entrepreneurial venture that took full opportunity of the winds of change in the marketplace. Undeniably, there are organizations that, in their attempt to meet and shape consumer demands for goods, use spirituality to sell more widgets. The texts of LOHAS acknowledge this is a problem, even as they pose "conscious capitalism" as the solution. This is why spiritual- and green-washing, when called out as such, are treated with such repulsion in LOHAS—participants understand that such practices have betrayed and undermined the symbolic sacred language of sustainability, the worldview so diligently crafted by the discourse.

Without a doubt, assigning moral and ethical coding to dubious products and practices is an attempt to give these things an ideological stamp of approval. Sustainability is axiomatic in the culture. Janice Peck writes that "the therapeutic work of helping people 'reconnect' with the spiritual values, and then helping them actualize those values or truths as 'saving the planet' is part of an American trend in the press's treatment of public issues. . . . So firmly has this orientation implanted itself in American culture, according to James Nolan, that in the past fifteen years it has become institutionalized within the operation of the sate" (17). Spirituality, ethics, and morality are powerfully legitimating: Max Weber viewed religion as a tool of legitimacy by serving as the "ideological instrument by which the state legitimizes its domination through social and political institutions" (Verter 153).

The spiritualizing of sustainability is powerful in another way, too, because it adds a new form of disciplining power to the social norm of sustainability, enforcing narratives and discourses and the panoply of rules and regulations about health and sustainability (see Bohman; Etzioni). It may add a dimension of internalization to products and practices that invoke a sense of shame or guilt in ways other pressures cannot, nudging or forcing people toward living more sustainably. That might be good or bad. It could be good if it persuaded elites, those who wield the most economic clout, to live more sustainably or if it brought about pressure on wildly polluting companies that willfully turn a blind eye toward sustainability measures. It could be bad for the impoverished who cannot afford sustainable goods and services and have no opportunities to change their behaviors.

Ideology can also encourage us to accept what should never be accepted. For example, while there is a democratic dimension to shaming—shame may reflect the community's values and pressure offenders to modify behavior— we do well to remember that communities are not always benign. Consider, for example, the events of September 11, 2001. When a community upholds the notion of becoming a martyr as in the case of Islamic extremists, then there is no shame for that community member when he or she kills more than three thousand people in the World Trade Center, says Etzioni.

LOHAS is an ideology—it contains and distributes a worldview. Participants need to be alert to the fact that simply because certain ideals of sustainability and health are made normative in its discourse—that is, given power via the circulation and acceptance within the community—it does not follow that those ideals are also the best that we can come up with.

Through participatory communication that welcomes difference, especially differences in the stages and appearances of sustainability efforts, we work to avoid a hollow sustainability whereby industrialists take the talking cure (Peck), admit their unsustainable deeds, plead guilty, and demonstrate their willingness to change to meet the community's expectation. They need to follow through with more than providing a recyclable bottle for their noxious household cleaner. We need to ask them tough questions and encourage them on the path. Spirituality can be used to make us feel better without really changing anything, as Rosenbaum intimates, while serving as a sort of invisibility cloak (to borrow a Harry Potter image) thrown over the dynamics of capitalism so that we don't have to admit it has co-opted, with our blessing, the ideals of sustainability to serve its ends. As Stanczak and Miller noted, spirituality has been deployed "as an internal motivation and sanctifying presence in labor movements, immigrant rights coalitions, ecological protests and political campaigns" (80).

Some of the most egregious examples of spiritual-washing in the discourse occur through the seemingly innocuous evocation of "healing." At its best, the word connotes a restorative act whereby individuals find relief, health, or happiness. LOHAS discourse also speaks about healing as the process of restoring us to a natural state of holism, where mind, body, and spirit are balanced and reunited with the social and natural worlds. This articulation could serve to motivate individuals to commit to social action where other pleas have failed because it constructs the practices of preserving cultures and environments as matters not just of doing good, but also of doing acts because they are imperative to our own well-being—appealing to a selfish individualism, if you will. It could also serve to enable people to overcome the "compassion fatigue" in the culture that has resulted from of an overexposure to crises covered by the media. Healing captures the American imagination. It is a central pillar in the Obama administration that aims to heal a nation beset by economic criminals, Islamophobia, and Katrina-sized social inequities, restoring the founding fathers' American Dream. An ad for the Obama campaign, and a subsequent YouTube hit, was called "Heal This Nation," and featured celebrities and ordinary people giving examples of how to set about doing just that. It was a hopeful and optimistic message.

But healing could also be used as an insidious way in which to make real social, structural constraints on people invisible—that is, to make those constraints appear instead as solely the fault of the individual and his or her failures of character. Peck, in her work on the Oprah Winfrey empire, right-fully points out that when we should be looking to these complex cultural and social pressures bearing down on us, from racism to ageism, we instead look within, as if our failures to attain peace, happiness, freedom, and wealth were solely a matter of not applying ourselves correctly. And, in this same vein, the articulations of healing in LOHAS are not ones equally available to all. This is a serious problem with the commodification of sustainability. If health is holism, then everyone and everything needs to be enrolled or the structure of a holistic concept is shallow and its logic collapses.

Spirituality can be a footman in this work, cloaking class and privilege as well as the terrible suffering caused by war, poverty, persecution, and tyr-anny. There have been abysmal examples of this type of selfish individualism with regard to healing. Here I offer up the "quantum media" that encourage people to set their "intentions" as a way to create their reality. My critique is not meant to belittle these modes: many people have and continue to find solace and inspiration in these products. My intent, as with my treatment of LOHAS overall, is to challenge a bland acceptance of these narratives in hopes that we can continue to improve on sustainability narratives, practices, and products. In the quantum media, my example here, there is an overt and explicit emphasis on individual responsibility that reaches a desperately non-sensical and dangerous level for civil society. For example, when I attended a lecture by Sandra Taylor in 2006, accompanied by two representatives from the LOHAS media, a member of the audience asked how we are to understand such atrocities as rape or genocide in the context of positive thinking and self-directed reality. Taylor responded with a theory of "consciousness-coded Karma" whereby certain individuals and groups of individuals reincarnate their unfortunate selves into specific situations to learn a sort of necessary lesson brought on by actions in the previous life or dimension. My informants did not find this to be troubling, even in light of the other conversations we had had regarding their organizations' role in social change. By allowing ourselves to consider the awful plights of other populations as some sort of spiritual pact made in another time and place in order to incarnate into specific situations that will move them further along the evolutionary wheel, we pad ourselves from horror and give ourselves permission to do nothing tangible to repair the suffering we see.

I believe that this type of reasoning is the result of a non-holistic under-standing of health—a contradiction to the very argument that is core to these products. If mind, body, and spirit are indeed inseparable, each powerful in its own way, the overextension of rights to the mind is indeed most imbalanced. This type of discourse can only lull individuals into thinking about social change as a sort of new edition in the Jack Canfield book series *Chicken Soup for the Soul,* as a sort of Chicken Soup for the World, sending their positive thoughts toward visualizations of a happy planet without generating change through the application of physical labor including the donation of dollars.

Only by refusing to indulge in this abstraction of real problems can LOHAS retain any hope of being the sort of productive and effective social movement its texts proclaim it can be and which I believe it should be. Spirituality is too valuable a tool to allow it to be diluted through overuse and misuse. Spirituality is the well from which springs our deepest concerns, and here LOHAS culture has an opportunity. Participants can continue to channel the useful history of self-actualization toward social activism or further entrench the rather ridiculous notion that all we need to do to make a better world is to "think" our way to it—without deliberation, without dialogue, without action in the external world. It seems, truly, the last refuge, the desperate sigh of the oppressed, as Karl Marx said.

What it comes down to, says environmental scholar James Gustave Speth, is that there has to be more than just a transformation of consciousness. As important as that is, it must be coupled with a transformation in the realm of politics as well to make any real gains toward sustainability (222). Helping people become better citizens, not just better consumers for markets, is what LOHAS must do because, as the late Anita Roddick, founder of the Body Shop retail chain said in *The LOHAS Journal,* business has become more powerful than nations, and as such it is responsible for the welfare of people and planet (see Middendorf, "Business").

As a form of "lifestyle consumption"—a type of identity formed around specific interests such as "wine tastings, biker bars, fair trade cafes, and gift giving" (Shah et al. 8)—it's important that LOHAS not descend into focusing solely on self-adornment, more concerned with the "excessive consumption of elites [rather] than the underconsumption of the poor" (Speth xv). The market has to be on guard against becoming just another rendition of "status-conscious consumption" extending to participants a "badge of belonging" (Shah et al. 8). You don't have to look very long or very hard in LOHAS texts to find examples of supremely shallow efforts at sustainability that serve the media's need for advertisers and the manufacturer's (or other trade member's) need for a wash of green to reach potential new markets.

We are *all* caught in the web of capitalism, trying to understand what we can do to make a difference. At LOHAS Forum 9, Barbara Harris of Weider Publications alluded to this capitalist imperative in her presentation when she said, "Media is the most powerful tool to create critical mass, but it is a business. You have to get ratings." Those interviewed for this project were sympathetic with this problem because they had all experienced it, but they were also convinced that even yachts and haute couture had their place in effecting change. These materials could be the channels through which elites arrive at a consciousness about the need for sustainability, they said. As the reasoning goes, since elites are the ones who have caused the most damage in the first place with their excessive consumption, any vehicle that forces them to rethink their behavior is a good thing. I agree with that, but there have to be limits on excessive consumption (and how that is defined is another problem) or else the disciplining can flow in the wrong direction, meaning that instead of sustainability discourse effecting change in elites' behavior, elites' power can shape the sustainability narrative.

Business, my informants tell me, is a creative, innovative, and respon-sive mechanism, much more so than social institutions, but change happens slowly. Around the time I started interviewing in 2005, during George W. Bush's second term, an article in *The Nation* argued business was one of the "few avenues still open for creative progressive initiative," thanks to the domi-nation by the religious right of all three branches of the federal government (Shuman and Fuller 13).

Scholar Terry Eagleton shares that hopefulness from a different perspec-tive, arguing that since capitalism has enabled us to become a "universally communicative species," it should also enable a "global order in which the needs of every individual can be satisfied" (*After Theory* 161). Eagleton says, "The global village must become the co-operative commonwealth," and not just a "moral prescription," because the resources exist to make it possible. These are the same resources, he says, that "brought a global existence into being" and that "have made possible in principle a new form of political existence" (161).

Can the market be truly capable of self-modulation and self-policing? I doubt it and so does Ted Trainer, who says, "The market can't be the main determinant of what is produced and how production is distributed"—it needs restraint and that is achieved through equal consideration given to social and environmental benefits (146). But, as the global economy has no global government, as Amy Domini, founder of Domini Social Investments, said, perhaps spiritualized appeals are the only way left to us to shame busi-ness and consumers into doing the "right" things.

While I agree with Shah and his coauthors when they write that "[c]ritics who make invidious distinctions between the roles of citizens and consum-ers" have overlooked the fact that "both political and consumer behavior can be motivated by either enhancing the public good or satisfying egocentric needs" (13), I am not convinced it's a good thing that we can no longer "cut the deck neatly between citizenship and civic duty, on one side, and consumption and self interest, on the other," as Shah and his colleagues say (8). "Patterns of consumption" become normativized (and hence inscrutable) as "spiritual," "healthy," or "sustainable"—fobbed off as markers of an essentialized, universalized truth of beingness when in fact they are markers of class. These articulations become "tastes." Zukin and Maguire write, "If rich, well-educated consumers prefer one kind of art, bread or travel to that preferred by workers, farmers, or cultured but less-affluent professors, then lifestyles reconfigure (and disguise)—rather than replace—class positions as patterns of consumption" (183). Somewhere in the LOHAS schemata, "consciousness" needs to be married to real sustainability regulation because time is running out for the planet. This idea isn't completely without support in LOHAS: In *The LOHAS Journal*, Bill Coors of Coors Brewing Company said relying on the consciousness of the public to create social and environmental change is not enough. "Much as I hate to say it, I think we have to have regulations," he said (qtd. in Nachman-Hunt, "Bill Coors" 31). "We have to be pushed and forced and driven in the right direction" (31).

To move toward that goal, it is vital that LOHAS media and events continue to encourage broader participation in the conversation by the more politically inclined media and speakers. Some that are already in the space shaking the tree are such publications as *Ode* magazine and *Utne Reader* and speakers such as anthropologist Wade Davis, *Natural Capitalism* author Hunter Lovins, and activist-scholar Vandana Shiva. Media and market organizations have a nimbleness that can be useful, even given the dangerous erosion of media anti-trust and ownership rules and regulations. The media are powerful, as LOHAS participants know. Anthony Giddens once said media do not only "mirror realities but in some part form them" through the "collage effect" and "the intrusion of distant events into everyday consciousness" (*Modernity* 26–27). The media professionals in the healthy living space express the quintessential frustration of the advocacy journalist caught in the for-profit world: that line between advertising and editorial is becoming more and more indistinct. There are too many tales of venerable publications in the space trouncing that line, leaving their employees astonished at the blatant disregard of "values" in interest of profit.

My informants are well aware of the power of their organizations and how capable these are of affecting ideals of sustainability and health, and how individuals in these organizations could, if they were allowed to do so, promote and stimulate the sustainability discourse through spiritually motivating referents. As an example of the potential importance of spirituality in this dialogue, Stanczak and Miller, in their ethnographic-based study on the role of spiritual life in individuals' work for social change, found that individuals "learn to connect the meaning of spirituality with values of social transformation through the significant others in their lives such as friends, family, religious leaders, organizational leaders, or co-workers" (8). I would add here that they missed two key players in these meaning-making processes—the media and the marketplace.

"It's as if the world is first and foremost a world of words," writes G. Stuart Adam in his foreword to the collection of essays *Communication as Culture*, by the distinguished media scholar, James Carey (Adam x). We "use symbols to construct a culture in which [we] can live together" Adam says (x). So embedded are media in the construction and exchange of symbolic forms that their role in meaning making is rarely challenged any longer and, Hoover says—as cultural intermediaries they form a part of the "warp and woof" of everyday life (10). The mediating influence they exert between people and their cultures serve in the same way as do language, traditions, religion, politics, landscapes, and artifacts in enabling people to locate themselves in relationship to their families, communities, the world, and even their gods (Hoover, *Religion*).

Even though religion remained stubbornly resistant to association with the "profane" media, thanks in great part to the media's open embrace of mass-market advertising, these old barriers have been breached in visible and public ways, particularly with the global saturation of consumerism and the penetration of late capitalism.

Media and religion are both invested in the construction of "meaningful narratives and 'truths' using the cultural capital of symbols, sounds, and subtle evocations of rational and emotional response in the audience," as Stewart Hoover and Lynn Schofield Clark have said, but they also do so in tandem with industry and market organizations (*Practicing Religion*, 15). In a dialectical relationship with receivers or users, these organizations shape and reflect sustainability values, enabling the construction and clarification and the reinforcement and reification of these values in new ways. LOHAS media and market offer up plausible reorderings of an existence that accommodate the pressures of late capitalism and late modernity (17). In the manner of religion, these organizations are also relaying mythologies and social norms of the times, reinforcing values, anointing leaders and visionaries, and revealing other ideologies even as they are generating new ones. Knut Lundby says media "play a crucial role in establishing, maintaining, and changing collective representations—concepts, categories, myths, beliefs, symbols—and language" (146). This is the "ritual" effect of media, as James Carey termed it.

The social media and online retail stores that promote conscious consumption have become key sites of practice for sustainability engagement, promoting discussions, and providing points of reference to sustainability and health. The LOHAS media and market organizations have shown users how sites within the natural and social worlds serve as "integrative spaces" where we are revealed to be inextricably and reciprocally linked to the "other," both human and nonhuman (Bartowski and Swearingen 313). They articulate the LOHASian as one of those sites, as the most localized manifestation of sustainability and which can reflect the experience of the community's development (Mellor and Shilling). Using Durkheim's theory of "collective effervescence," Mellor and Shilling argue the "immanence of powerful passions and emotions of a collective, sacred character" effect transformation not only of people's "experience of their fleshy selves" but of their environment as well (1). In this same manner, Stanczak and Miller found individuals employed in occupations related to social change perceived that they were able to achieve different results by incorporating spirituality into their work than if they used secular means alone. Yet, the authors say "spirituality only becomes enacted for social transformation when the interpretation and personal meaning constructed around spiritual experiences fuse with interpretations and personal meanings constructed of a world or society in need of change" (Stanczak and Miller 7). This revelation of meaning through a fusion of the inner and outer realm is the role LOHAS media and market organizations have claimed for themselves. These organizations want to explain to participants how the path to sustainability winds through the sphere of materiality, and how that material world can be put to use to "socially constitute . . . the body in relation to self," as Gilchrist says.

By narrativizing the self as the portal through which a globally rising sustainability consciousness becomes manifest, the LOHAS texts articulate a truth claim that says we live in times where a dawning collective realization about our common needs and our finite reservoir of solutions is evolving. It is through an analysis of the symbolic forms that allow us to communicate that we can view and understand this, at last, as a cultural transformation, as John Thompson says (*Media and Modernity*).

Spreading the Word

When I started working with the *LOHAS Journal* team at Natural Business Communications in Broomfield, Colorado, in 1999, I remember having a sinking feeling that "Lifestyles of Health and Sustainability" was too wordy a title to really catch on in the popular imagination and that its abbreviated version, LOHAS, was utterly meaningless and clumsy to boot. I was wrong. I never imagined just how appealing and portable the concept would become. LOHAS has snaked its way from trade jargon into the social media. It has sprouted around the world, forming the basis of clubs in Japan, advertising companies in Australia, bamboo and charcoal car air fresheners in China, skin care lines in Germany, tourism campaigns in Greece, and a new pitch for healthy food in Korea. If you'd told me these things in 1999, I would have laughed.

But a global dialogue as well as global communities are springing up in the name of LOHAS. My informants in LOHAS media and market organizations view themselves as the torchbearers of a new paradigm, as the carriers of "truths." They understand that they have the power to select topics and voices, and they also see themselves as somehow standing outside of the veil of illusion that, seemingly, can cloud the judgment of other consumers and producers about the marketplace. Probably a better way to regard them is that they believe in the truth claims of LOHAS to the point that they also see themselves as freed from the illusions, but what their conversations have revealed is that they firmly believe in their and their organizations' right and ability to take on leadership roles, making a de facto challenge to other, traditional sources of authority, including that of religious, cultural, and political institutions.

While we know receivers of the LOHAS texts, the "consumers," also hold interpretive power and praxis, my goal has to been to turn the focus to the power of media- and market-produced discourse, to examine "the ways in which symbolic forms intersect with relations of power," (Thompson, *Ideology*). The LOHAS texts mobilize meaning in the social world about the "lifestyles of health and sustainability," and certain interpretations of health they circulate have already become cultural myths—"common sense" narratives in a culture that are not "naturalistic but naturalized" (Hall, "The Rediscovery" 75). "Conscious capitalism" is a key operative among these myths and is positioned as a crucial ingredient in a recuperative and reparative elixir to an unsustainable world.

There are several major strands of thought about conscious capitalism that I have found in LOHAS. First, people can be moral through consumption and production. Second, people can be spiritual through commodified practices. Third, individuals can be global and local at the same time and are compelled morally to be so. Fourth, people can resolve, through consumption and personal development, a sense of living in an increased *risk society* (Tomlinson) as well as restore their failing trust in global institutions. Fifth, people can be both resistive to and complicit with capitalism simultaneously.

As conscious capitalism becomes more popular, it will take serious efforts to defend its boundaries so that conscious doesn't become co-opted and watered down into yet more meaningless marketing hype and ad copy. There are enough consumers and producers who feel strongly about holding firm to certain values and definitions with regard to what natural, organic, healthy, and sustainable can and should mean that some vanguard will no doubt form to protect the narratives of conscious capitalism from folding in on themselves. That guard duty could be taken on in the name of or under the canopy of LOHAS—whether by the media or an association.

To do so, LOHAS participants must continue to expand participatory communication to ensure that dissent and debate is recognized and welcomed, in all its forms, allowing for venues where different and differing voices can speak, particularly voices that aren't married to a product or company interest. Without this, we risk reducing "social justice to the freedom to choose between products," to borrow a phrase from Zukin and Maguire (183). If this doesn't occur, LOHAS as a concept risks being eclipsed as a credible option in the sustainability market and movement.

Even though LOHAS is an amalgam of various oppositional identities to "mainstream" culture, it is swimming in a vast and competitive sea of sustainability, and to retain its visionary edge, its contestation to the status quo, the discourse is going to have to watch its borders, literally and figuratively. Finding our way through the global economic, environmental, political, and social complexities that face us will require tough decisions on the part of business and consumers. It will require that we commit to recognize our differences, to see those as necessary to a holistic model of health but also to recognize how those differences can prevent some populations from equally participating in sustainability and healthy living practices and dialogues.

We have to take risks, a word with a dual meaning in capitalism. Risk spurs innovation and can produce optimal "returns," but risk holds in it the potential for spectacular failure as well. Accepting risk means accepting opportunity for growth through change, and LOHAS media and market organizations evolved through some of the most notable risk-receptive movements in American history. If it can stay true to those visions, I believe LOHAS could become a viable partner in the sustainability movement by representing and educating market interests, building on a platform of integrative spirituality of sustainability as proof of our creative thinking.

Case Studies

Ethnographic Interviews
with Sustainability Consumers

I conducted in-home interviews with consumers as part of the Media, Home, and Family project at the Center for Media, Religion, and Culture, University of Colorado. The interviews supplied deep insights into how individuals reconcile inconsistencies in the cultural dialogues about sustainable living, rearranging those narratives to suit the conditions of their situations. So important were these insights to the development of this book, I thought it vital to include them here.

The people I interviewed exhibited wide differences in their understanding about sustainability. They were dispersed along the lines of income, location, education, race, age, and gender, which also meant that their ability to participate in the sustainability marketplace also varied, as did their perception about access to that market and its desirability.

The sample was not selected because of an interest in "sustainability." Rather, these were individuals selected through a snowball method and who were asked to participate in a study of media, family, and religion. Names and locations have been masked. They were told they would be asked questions about their media use, their family values and practices including those concerning environmental and sustainability, and their religious beliefs and practices. We were interested in understanding how informants participated in these three areas in their midst of their private lives.

Avis Grantman

Avis Grantman is a single mother of three. She has never been married, and her children range in age from thirty to fourteen. She is of Native American and African American heritage and lives in the inner city in a predominantly black and Hispanic neighborhood with a reputation for having high crime rates. She lives on less than thirty thousand dollars a year in a one-bedroom walk-up with her youngest daughter.

Avis struggled for years with a crack addiction. She's been on and off government support, but several years previously she found the Baptist faith, and she credits that with changing her life. She now has a steady job working for a local nonprofit.

Avis, her daughter, and I sat in the apartment on a summer day talking. The television was on in the small living room. Throughout our interview, Avis referred to the television, from the wonderful things she learned there about nature to her fondness for singing along with televised choirs during televangelical programs.

We had been talking for an hour about her life. I decided to ask Avis if she ever chose not to buy a certain product because of something she had heard about the company's policies toward people or environments. Avis nodded vehemently and said she tried never to buy things that were stolen. Also, she did not buy Nike athletic shoes for her teenaged daughter because she believed the company used "sweatshop" labor. Avis said her Baptist faith and the Golden Rule guided her annual hundred-dollar budget for athletic shoes—do unto others as you would have them do unto you.

I asked her then if she did anything she considered to be good for the environment, and she said, "I try not to run the water too much. It's disrespectful." To whom was it disrespectful, I asked? She replied "To God. To Mother earth." I asked Avis if she saw a link between her spirituality and her concern for the environment. She nodded and said, "For one thing, being Native American, some things are ingrained in us. I really feel things. I feel the change of the seasons before they happen. Oh, they say, nah, it's not changing until such and such date, but I already felt it and like, when it's raining or windy and the wind is high and it's going, oh, I feel like I'm on a natural high! I love the moons and the stars. So I'm really in tune with the earth, I think."

I then asked if she felt concern about environmental issues such as air and water pollution. She said she did: "I know that where there are areas of high population of people of color, a lot of times it seems that is where a lot of environmental problems will be."

Avis said: "There are a lot of liquor stores and a lot of drugs in these areas. Lot of pollution. Lot of factories. They making that hole a little bit bigger in the ozone which makes the global warming which is throwing everything out of kilter. I try to be more responsible in making sure that stuff that is recyclable that I put in the recycle bin, and I'm trying to remember that when I get food to go I take my old containers."

Avis defined herself as a "couch potato" and loved watching television, particularly programs about nature and animals. The media, she said, helped her reconnect to her Native American heritage, specifically her spiritual link to the natural world. While she rarely had the opportunity to be in wilderness, she bemoaned the actions of those who desecrated nature and killed animals. Living in tune with that spirituality meant enrolling her daughter in an excursion outside the city limits so that she could camp and hike, reclaiming her Native American roots. The daughter told me she had found this exercise stressful in the extreme, because she was frightened of deer and hated to walk. Nonetheless, she understood her family's position as "Native American" and that it entailed an appreciation of nature.

Norma Walsh

Norma Walsh is a Caucasian single mother living on a less than thirty-thousand-dollar annual income in a poorer section of a city in the Northwest. Norma prided herself on living a "simple" life, by which she meant a life rooted in family life, God, honest work, and very little media use. These were markers of her evangelical spiritual life along with living in a manner that was respectful of the earth, of others, and of her health. First and foremost, she said, was her relationship to food. Wasting food when others were hungry was a sin against God, as was buying products encased in unrecyclable packaging that polluted God's environment, she told me. Norma, who lived in a sparsely furnished home, believed consumption was an addiction, and as a result, it divided people from their relationship with God. She proudly pointed to her old television set that did not have a very good picture, her lack of cable TV, and the way in which her "fun" was derived from activities other than shopping, such as fishing, camping, and hiking. "I don't want to be into the latest gizmo because to me it isn't what's important," she said. For Norma, she simply had enough and liked her simple life as a result, she said.

She did not wish for more consumer goods, or to replace those old ones she had. She said her family was frugal. "We are not wasteful people," she said. "I don't like waste—not only are the bills high but to waste paper products and not recycle . . . within our household we are environmentalists," Norma said, adding "we don't compost or do things that are more work, I guess, because we are lazy sometimes."

Norma was adamant that being environmentally minded was "pleasing to the Lord. "He does not want you to drive a big huge truck and to waste His resources." She said that "oil spills and things like that are very displeasing to the Lord." As for the media, Norma saw little of value there, except in television shows about nature and in Christian music and books. She was not aware of ever learning about sustainability through media.

Priscilla and Butch Castello

On the other side of American economics, Priscilla and Butch Castello, an Italian Latino family living in the suburbs of a large city in the southwestern United States, live on one paycheck now that Priscilla has opted to stay home with their two young children. While this meant less money in the family bank account, it was important to be able to give the children the type of values they felt were important. Less money meant they needed to be more inventive. They'd not be buying ski passes this year, they said, and would instead opt to "be out in the fresh air and sunshine, camping and fishing." Priscilla and Butch were adamant that many consumer goods, particularly media, discouraged creativity and original thinking. They said the private school their children attended emphasized handicrafts, woodworking, and even homemade clothing. The school discouraged the use of television not only on campus but also in students' homes as well. Living simply was part of their Buddhist faith, they said.

Conclusion

Norma, Avis, and the Castellos mapped themselves onto the terrain of sustainability using different tools, but each householder was creative with regard to not only dealing with the actual constraints upon them, but also in the ways in which they constructed narratives about their social situations. Their ideas of sustainability had to be reconciled with the other pressures in their lives. Norma understands luxury goods as an insult to God; Avis's "power" over Nike also depends on what other sneakers she can afford to buy; for the Castellos, sustainability is found through activities such as skiing or spending time walking the creek paths. In each of these cases, I found an articulation of spirituality as a symbolic capital in the negotiation of sustainability consciousness.

It's plausible that this type of "spiritual knowledge, competencies, and preferences," as Verter says, will come to also be "understood as valuable assets in the economy of symbolic goods" (153).

Works Cited

Adam, G. Stuart. Foreword to James Carey, *Communication as Culture: Essays on Media and Culture*. New York: Taylor and Francis, 2008.

Adams, Matthew, and Jayne Raisborough. "What Can Sociology Say about Fair Trade?: Class, Reflexivity and Ethical Consumption?" *Sociology* 42.6 (2008): 1165–82.

Adler, Jerry. "Going Green." *Newsweek*, 17 July 2006, 42.

Albanese, Catherine. "Fisher Kings and Public Places: The Old New Age in the 1990s." *Annals of the American Academy of Political and Social Science* 527 (1993): 131–43.

———. *Nature Religion in America*. Chicago: University of Chicago Press, 1990.

Anderson, Alan. "The New Thought Movement: A Link between East and West." Proceedings of the Parliament of the World's Religions. Chicago, 3 Sept. 1993. 18 Apr. 2006. http://www.websyte.com/alan/parl.htm1993.

Anderson, Ray. *Mid-Course Correction: Toward a Sustainable Enterprise: The Interface Model*. Atlanta: Peregrinzilla Press, 1998.

Appadurai, Arjun. "Disjuncture and Difference in the Global Cultural Economy." *Public Culture* 2.2 (1990): 1–24.

Arnal, William. "Definition." In *Guide to the Study of Religion*. Eds. Willi Braun and Russell. T. McCutcheon. New York: Cassell, 2000. 21–34.

Arntz, William, Betsey Chasse, and Mark Vicente, producers. *What the Bleep Do We Know!?* Lord of the Wind Films. 2005. www.whattheBleep.com.

AtKisson, Alan. "Sustainability is Dead—Long Live Sustainability." In *The Future of Sustainability*. Ed. Marco Keiner. Zurich: Springer Netherlands, 2006. 231–45.

Badaracco, Claire Hoertz. *Prescribing Faith: Medicine, Media and Religion in American Culture*. Waco, Tex.: Baylor University Press, 2007.

Baer, Hans. "The Work of Andrew Weil and Deepak Chopra—Two Holistic Health/New Age Gurus: A Critique of the Holistic Health/New Age Movements." *Medical Anthropology Quarterly* 17.2 (2003): 233–50.

Baker, Andy. "The Growth of LOHAS Internationally." *LOHAS Journal* 9.1 (2008):7–8, 53. 27 Nov. 2009. http://www.lohas.com/sites/default/files/lohasintrntlgrowth_sm.pdf.

Barker, Ellen. "The Roots of ASANAS." Conference on Alternative Spirituality and New Age Studies, Open University, Milton Keynes, 2003.

Bartkowski, John P., and Scott. W. Swearingen. "God Meets Gaia in Austin, Texas: A Case Study of Environmentalism as Implicit Religion." *Review of Religious Research* 38.4 (1997): 308–24.

Baudrillard, Jean. *The Consumer Society*. London: Sage, 1998.

Bauman, Zygmaut. "Collateral Casualties of Consumerism." *Journal of Consumer Culture* 7 (2007): 25–56.

BBMG. *The Conscious Consumer Report: Redefining Value in a New Economy*. New York: BBMG.com, 2009.

Becker, Dana, and Jeanne Maracek. "History in the Remaking." *Theory and Psychology* 18.5 (2008): 591–604.

Bechler, Rosemary. "Democracy and the Individual." *Open Democracy.net* 22.17 (10 Sept. 2009). 10 Sept. 2009. http://www.opendemocracy.net/ourkingdom/rosemary_Bechler/plurality_and_the_individual.

Belk, Russell, Melanie Wallendorf, and John F. Sherry. "The Sacred and the Profane in Consumer Behavior: Theodicy on the Odyssey." *Journal of Consumer Research* 16 (June 1989): 1—38.

Bellah, Robert. "Community Properly Understood: A Defense of Democratic Communitarianism." *Responsive Community* 6.1 (Winter 1996). 18 November 2009. http://dspace.wrlc.org/bitstream/1961/584/1/bellah-community-1995.pdf.

Benjamin, Walter. "The Work of Art in the Age of Mechanical Reproduction." *Illumination*. Ed. Hannah Arendt. New York: Schocken, 1968, 217–51.

Berger, Peter, and Thomas Luckmann. *The Social Construction of Reality*. Garden City, N.Y.: Anchor Books, 1966.

Besecke, Kelly. "Speaking of Meaning in Modernity: Reflexive Spirituality as a Cultural Resource." *Sociology of Religion* 62.3 (2001): 365–81.

Betensky, Carolyn. "The Prestige of the Oppressed: Symbolic Capital in a Guilt Economy." In *Pierre Bourdieu: Fieldwork in Culture*. Eds. Nicholas Brown and Imre Szema. Lanham, Md.: Rowman & Littlefield, 2000. 207–14.

Biehl, Janet. Introduction to *The Murray Bookchin Reader*. Ed. Janet Biehl. London: Cassell, 1997. 1–12.

Blackmore, Jill, and S. Thorpe. "Media/ting Change: The Print Media's Role in Mediating Education Policy in a Period of Radical Reform in Victoria, Australia." *Journal of Education Policy* 18.6 (2003): 577–95.

Bloom, William. "Does Everyone Really Create Their Own Reality?" 22 June 2007. http://greatmystery.org:80//newsletters/william-bloom.html.

Boggs, Carl. "The Green Alternative and the Struggle for a Post-Marxist Discourse." *Theory and Society* 15 (1986): 869–99.

Bohman, James. "Deliberative Democracy and Effective Social Freedom: Capabilities, Resources and Opportunities." In *Deliberative Democracy: Essays on Reason and Politics*. Eds. James Bohman and William Rehg. Cambridge, Mass.: MIT Press, 1997. 321–48.

Bookchin, Murray. *The Murray Bookchin Reader*. Ed. Janet Biehl. London: Cassell, 1997.

Bourdieu, Pierre. *Distinction*. Cambridge: Cambridge University Press, 1984.

———. *Outline of a Theory of a Practice*. Cambridge: Cambridge University Press, 1977.

———. *Practical Reason*. Stanford: Stanford University Press, 1998.

Bower, Amanda, and Landreth Grau. "Explicit Donations and Inferred Endorsements: Do Corporate Social Responsibility Initiatives Suggest a Nonprofit Organization Endorsement?" *Journal of Advertising* 38.3 (2009): 113–26.

Brach, Tara. "A More Perfect Union." *Yoga Journal*, Sept.–Oct. 2004, 120–23, 175–78.

Braden, Gregg. *The Gregg Braden Effect*. Oasis Television. Nov. 2005.

Brantlinger, Patrick. *Bread and Circuses: Theories of Mass Culture as Social Decay*. Ithaca, N.Y.: Cornell University Press, 1983.

Brown, Keith R. "The Commodification of Altruism: Fair Trade and the Ethos of Ethical Consumption." PhD. diss. University of Pennsylvania, 2008. http://repository.upenn .edu/dissertations/AAI3309402.

Bruce, Janesse. "Editorial." *Body+Soul,* Nov.–Dec. 2004, 6.

Brunton, Michael. "The Reason of Faith. *Ode Magazine*, Sept.–Oct. 2009. 1 Nov. 2009. www.odemagazine.com/doc/66/reason-of-faith/4.

Burgess, Cameron. "Why LOHAS Isn't Going to Save the World." *Elephant Journal*, 12 Sept. 2009. 29 Oct. 2009. http://www.elephantjournal.com/2009/09/why-lohas -isn%E2%80%99t-going-to-save-the-world-cameron-burgess.

Burke, Lee, and Jeanne M. Logsdon. "How Corporate Social Responsibility Pays Off." *Long Range Planning* 29.4 (1996): 495—502.

Cahill, Michael. "The Implications of Consumerism for the Transition to a Sustainable Society." *Social Policy and Administration* 35.5 (2001): 627–39.

Campbell, Colin. "I Shop Therefore I Know That I Am." In *Elusive Consumption*. Eds. Karin M. Ekström and Helen Brembeck. Oxford: Berg, 2004. 27–44.

Capra, Fritjof. "Deep Ecology: A New Paradigm." In *Deep Ecology for the 21st Century*. Ed. George Sessions. Boston: Shambhala Press, 1995. 19–25.

Carey, James. *Communication as Culture: Essays on Media and Society*. Boston: Unwin— Hyman, 1988.

Carlisle, Sandra and Phil Hanlon. "Well-Being and Consumer Culture: A Different Kind of Public Health Problem?" *Health Promotion International*, 17 Aug 2007. 20 Aug. 2009. http://www.ncbi.nlm.nih.gov/pubmed/17704097?dopt=Abstract.

Carroll, William K., and Robert A. Hackett. "Democratic Media Activism through the Lens of Social Movement Theory." *Media, Culture, Society* 28.1 (2006): 83–104.

Chittister, Joan. "Be the Light." *Spirituality & Health*, Dec. 2004, 44–49.

Clark, Lynn Schofield. *From Aliens to Angels*. Oxford: Oxford University Press, 2003.

———. "The Turn to Popular Communication in the Humanities, Sociology, and Anthropology: Emergent Directions for Audience Studies." Paper presented at the International Communication Association, New Orleans, May 2004.

Clark, Lynn Schofield, and Stewart Hoover. "At the Intersection of Media, Culture and Religion." In *Rethinking Media, Religion and Culture*. Eds. Stewart Hoover and Knut Lundby. Newbury Park: Sage, 1997, 15–36.

Clores, Suzanne. "How Spirit Blooms." *Body+Soul,* September 2004, 76–79, 108–110.

Cockburn, Alexander, and Jeffrey St. Clair. "Why Corporate Social Responsibility Programs Are a Fraud." *CounterPunch* 25 May, 2007. 15 Nov. 2009. http://www.counterpunch.org.

Cohen, Lizabeth. "Reflections and Reviews: A Consumers' Republic: The Politics of Mass Consumption in Postwar America." *Journal of Consumer Research* 31 (2004): 236–39.

Colin, Chris. "Just Be." *Yoga Journal, Balanced Living, Special Issue,* Winter 2004, 74–77, 113–14.

Condor, Bob. "Fair Enough." *Conscious Choice,* June 2004, 20–22.

Cortese, Amy. "They Care about the World (and They Shop, Too)." *New York Times,* 20 July, 2003: section 3, 4.

Cosgrove, Denis. *Social Formation and Symbolic Landscape.* Madison: University of Wisconsin Press, 1998.

Crawford, Leslie. "To Live Simply Is to Live Well." *Natural Solutions: Vibrant Health, Balanced Living,* 1 Feb. 2005. 28 Sept. 2009. http://www.naturalsolutionsmag.com.

Creedon, Jeremiah. "Increase Your Energy IQ. *Utne Reader,* July–August 2004, 86–88.

Cronon, William. "A Place for Stories: Nature, History, and Narrative." *Journal of American History* 78.4 (1992): 1347–76.

———. *Uncommon Ground: Toward Reinventing Nature.* New York: W. W. Norton, 1996.

Csikszentmihalyi, Mihaly. "Why We Need Things." In *History from Things: Essays on Material Culture.* Eds. Steven Lubar and W. David Kingsley. Washington, D.C.: Smithsonian Institution Press, 1993. 20–29.

Cunningham, Rosemary. "42 Ways to Nourish Your Soul." *Spirituality & Health* July–Aug. 2004. 21 Jan. 2005. http://www.spiritualityhealth.com/newsh/items/article/item9138.html.

Cushman, Anne. "Marketing the Soul." *Yoga Journal,* 7 June 2004. www.yogajournal.com/views/282.cfm.

Dangle, Benjamin. "Put Down That Coors: Why We Should Be Boycotting Big Beer." *AlterNet* 15 Aug. 2009. 16 Aug. 2009. http://www.alternet.org/workplace/141953/put_down_that_coors:_why_we_should_be_boycoting_big_beer.

de Certeau, Michel. *The Practice of Everyday Life.* Trans. Steven Rendall. Berkeley: University of California Press, 1984.

De Graaf, John, David Wann, and Thomas H. Naylor. *Affluenza: The All-Consuming Epidemic.* San Francisco: Berritt-Koehler Publishers, Inc., 2001.

Della Porta, Donatella, and Mario Diani. *Social Movements—An Introduction.* Oxford: Blackwell, 1999.

Denzin, Norman. "Performing (Auto) Ethnography Politically." *Review of Education, Pedagogy, and Cultural Studies* 25 (2003): 257–78.

———. *Symbolic Interactionism and Cultural Studies.* Oxford: Blackwell, 1992.

de Vreese, Claes H. "Digital Renaissance: Young Consumer and Citizen?" *Annals of the American Academy of Political and Social Science* 611 (2007): 207–16.

Dodge, Chris. "Reconnecting with Mother Earth." *Utne Reader,* May–June 2008. 1 Nov. 2009. http://www.utne.com/2008–05–01/Environment/Reconnecting-with-Mother-Earth.aspx.

Doss, Erika. "Popular Piety in Material Culture." In *Practicing Religion in the Age of Media.* Eds. Stewart Hoover and Lynn Schofield Clark. New York: Columbia University Press, 2002. 63–86.

Dowdle, Hillarie. "Life's a Stretch." *Yoga Journal,* Sept.–Oct. 2004, 8.

Dryzek, John S. "Transnational Democracy." *Journal of Political Philosophy* 7.1 (1999): 30–51.

Duclow, Donald F. "William James, Mind-Cure, and the Religion of Healthy-Mindedness." *Journal of Religion and Health* 41.1 (Spring 2002): 45–56.

Dykema, Ravi. "An Interview with Paul Ray." *Nexus,* Mar.–Apr. 2001. 17 Oct, 2009. http://www.nexuspub.com/articles_2001/creatives_2001_ma.php.

Eagleton, Terry. *After Theory.* New York: Basic Books, 2003.

———. *Ideology.* London: Verso, 1991

Ehrenberg, John, *Civil Society: The Critical History of an Idea.* New York: New York University Press, 1999.

Eikenberry, Angela. "The Hidden Costs of Cause Marketing." *Stanford Social Innovation Review.* Summer 2009. 30 Sept. 2009. http://www.ssireview.org/articles/entry/the_hidden_costs_of_cause_marketing/.

Eilperin, Juliet. "Warming Draws Evangelicals into Environmentalist Fold." *Washington Post,* 8 Aug. 2008. 28 Nov 2009. http://www.washingtonpost.com/wp-dyn/content/article/2007/08/07/AR2007080701910.html?nav=emailpage.

Einstein, Mara. *Brands of Faith: Marketing Religion in a Commercial Age.* London: Routledge, 2008.

Emerich, Monica. "What You Should Know about Rainforest Remedies." *Delicious! Magazine,* March 1998, 42–45, 75–76.

Erney, Diana. "The Eco-Conscience." *Organic Style,* Dec. 2004, 88.

Etzioni, Amitai. *The Monochrome Society.* Princeton, N.J.: Princeton University Press, 2003.

Fine, Ben. "Examining the Ideas of Globalisation and Development Critically: What Role for Political Economy?" *New Political Economy* 9.2 (2004): 213–31.

Fine, Phyllis. "Body and Soul." *Magazine Rack,* 24 Feb. 2006. 1 Mar. 2006. http://publications.mediapost.com/index.cfm?fuseaction=PublicationsSearch.showSearchResults.

Fjellman, Stephen. *Vinyl Leaves.* Boulder, Colo: Westview Press, 1992.

Fleming, Richard. "Patagonia's Journey to Sustainability." *LOHAS Journal* 2.3 (2001): 18–21, 29.

———. "True Values, Guaranteed." *LOHAS Journal* 3.1 (2002): 40–43.

Flere, Sergej, and Andrej Kirbiš. "Comment on Houtman and Aupers." *Journal for the Scientific Study of Religion* 48.1 (2009): S161–84.

Foley, Doug E. "Critical Ethnography: The Reflexive Turn." *International Journal of Qualitative Studies in Education* 15. 4 (2002): 469–90.

Ford, Frank. "Preface." In Marjorie Winn, Susan Hillyard, and Mary Faulk Koock. *Deaf Smith County Cookbook: Natural Foods for Family Kitchens.* 1972. London: Collier MacMillan. xi.

Foucault, M. 1982. "Afterword: The Subject and Power." In *Michel Foucault: Beyond Structuralism and Hermeneutics.* Ed. H. Dreyfus and P. Rabinow, 206–26. Chicago: University of Chicago Press.

Fox, Richard Wrightman, and T. J. Jackson Lears. 1983. "Introduction." In *The Culture of Consumption.* Ed. R. W. Fox and T. J. J. Lears. New York: Pantheon.

Friedman, Emily. "Health Care Stirs Up Whole Foods CEO John Mackey, Customers

Boycott Organic Grocery Store." *ABC News,* 14 Aug. 2009. 3 Sept. 2009. http://abcnews .go.com/Business/story?id=8322658&page=1.

Garcia, Anne. "Eco-Manufacturing Under an African Sky." *LOHAS Journal* 2.2 (2001): 6.

———. "International Effort Leads to a Grass-Roots Agreement on Sustainability." *LOHAS Journal* 2.3 (2001): 5.

———. "Personal Development Can't Be Just Business." *LOHAS Journal* 2.4 (2001): 20–23.

Garland, Emily. "Style Point: Fashion, Sustainability Do Mix." *Evergreen Monthly,* July 2004, 13.

Garnham, Nicholas, and Raymond Williams. "Pierre Bourdieu and the Sociology of Culture: An introduction." In *Media, Culture and Society: A Critical Reader.* Eds. Richard Collins, Nicholas Garnham, and James Curran. Thousand Oaks, Calif.: Sage, 1986. 116–30.

Georges, Robert A., and Michael Owen Jones. *People Studying People.* Berkeley: University of California Press, 1980.

Gerard, Jasper. "Slow Food Guru Spreads Gospel in High Places." *The Observer,* June 17, 2007. 10 July 2009. http://www.slowfood.org.uk/userfiles/file/press/TheObserver_17-06-07 .pdf.

Gerasimo, Pilar. "The Better Good Life: An Essay on Personal Sustainability." *Experience Life,* April 2009, 49–54.

Giddens, Anthony. *The Consequences of Modernity.* Stanford, Calif.: University of Stanford Press, 1990.

———. *Modernity and Self-Identity: Self and Society in the Late-Modern Age.* Stanford, Calif.: Stanford University Press, 1991.

Gili, Enrique. "TreePeople Roots for L.A." *Whole Life Times* 26.7 (July 2004): 20–22.

Gladwell, Malcolm. *The Tipping Point.* Boston: Back Bay Books, 2002.

Glock, Allison. "Back to Basics: Living with Voluntary Simplicity." *O magazine,* Jan. 2009. 16 Sept. 2009. http://www.oprah.com/article/omagazine/200901_omag_simple_living.

Goodman, Douglas J., and Mirelle Cohen. *Consumer Culture: A Reference Handbook.* Santa Barbara, Calif.: ABC—CLIO, 2004.

Gottlieb, Roger. *A Greener Faith.* Oxford: Oxford University Press, 2006.

Granqvist, Pehr, and Berit Hagekull. "Seeking Security in the New Age: On Attachment and Emotional Compensation." *Journal for the Scientific Study of Religion* 40.3 (2001): 527–46.

Greenspan, Miriam. "The Wisdom of the Dark Emotions." *Spirituality & Health,* Dec. 2004, 36–40.

Griffith, R. Marie. "Body Salvation: New Thought, Father Divine, and the Feast of Material Pleasures." *Religion and American Culture* 11.7 (2001): 119–53.

Gulden, Paul. "CEO Watch ." *LOHAS Journal* 2.1 (2001): 15.

Gunaratne, Shelton. "Globalization: A Non-Western Perspective: The Bias of Social Science/ Communication Oligopoly." *Communication, Culture, and Critique* 2 (2009): 60–82.

Guthman, Julie. "Bringing Good Food to Others: Investigating the Subjects of Alternative Food Practice." *Cultural Geographies* 15 (2008): 431–47.

Hall. Stuart. "The Problem of Ideology: Marxism without Guarantees." In *Stuart Hall: Critical Dialogues .* Eds. David Morley and Kuan-Hsing Chen. London: Routledge, 1996. 25–46.

———. "The Rediscovery of Ideology." In *Culture, Society and the Media*. Eds. Micahel Gurevitch, Tony Bennett, James Curran and Janet Woollacott. London: Methuen & Co., 1982. 56–90.

Hamer, Dean. "Rate Your Spirituality." *Body+Soul*, Sept. 2004, 110.

Hamilton, Linda. "Faith in the Land." *Utne Reader,* July–Aug. 2004, 48–52.

Hanegraaff, Wouter. "New Age and Secularization." *Numen: International Review for the History of Religions* 47. 3 (2000): 288–312.

———. "Spectral Evidence of New Age Religion: On the Substance of Ghosts and the Use of Concepts." *Journal of Alternative Spiritualities and New Age Studies*, 2005, 35–58.

Hart, Joseph. "When Less Is Enough." *Experience Life*, April 2009, 82–84.

The Hartman Group. *The Hartman Report on Sustainability: Understanding the Consumer Perspective.* 10 July 2007. http://www.hartman-group.com/products/report-Sustainability2007.html.

Hatch, Nathan O. *The Democratization of American Christianity*. New Haven, Conn.: Yale University Press, 1989.

Havel, Vaclav. "Concerns and Hopes on the Threshold of the New Millennium." Paper presented at Forum 2000, Prague. 3–6 Sept. 1997. 13 March 2006. www.forum2000.cz/conferences/1997/speeches/40pen.php#2.

Hawken, Paul, Hunter Lovins, and Amory Lovins. *Natural Capitalism: Creating the Next Industrial Revolution*. New York: Little, Brown and Co., 1999. 20 Nov. 2005. http://www.natcap.org.

Hawn, Carleen. "The Gospel According to Adam Smith." *Ode Magazine,* June 2008. 24 Nov. 2009. http://www.odemagazine.com/doc/54/the-gospel-according-to-adam-smith/all.

———. "Slow and Steady Wins the Race." *Ode Magazine,* Nov. 2008, 27–30.

Heelas, Paul. "The New Age in Cultural Context: The Premodern, the Modern and the Postmodern." *Religion* 23 (1993): 103–16.

———. *The New Age Movement: The Celebration of the Self and the Sacrilization of Modernity*. Cambridge: Blackwell Publishers, 1996.

Heelas, Paul, and Linda Woodhead. *The Spiritual Revolution: Why Religion Is Giving Way to Spirituality*. Malden, Mass.: Blackwell Publishing, 2005.

Helland, Christopher. "Religion Online/Online Religion and Virtual Communitas." In *Religion on the Internet: Research Prospects and Promises*. Eds. Jeffrey Hadden and Douglas Cowan. New York: Elsevier Science Inc, 2000. 205–24.

Helwig, Terry. "Materialize Your Visions." *Spirituality & Health,* July–Aug. 2004. 21 Jan. 2005. http://www.spiritualityhealth.com/newsh/items/article/item_9105.html.

Higgins, John. "The Legacy of Raymond Williams." *English Academy Review* 14 (December 1997): 30–48.

Holt, Georgiana, and Matthew Reed. *The Sociological Aspects of Organic Agriculture: from Pioneer to Policy*. Gateshead: Athenaeum Press, 2006.

Hoover, Stewart. *Religion in the Media Age*. London: Routledge, 2006.

———. "Visual Religion in Media Culture." In *The Visual Culture of American Religions*. Eds. David Morgan and Sally Promey. Berkeley: University of California Press, 2001. 146–59.

Hoover, Stewart, and Lynn Schofield Clark. "Controversy and Cultural Symbolism: Press Relations and the Formation of Public Discourse in the Case of the Re-Imgaging Event." *Critical Studies in Mass Communication* 4.4 (Dec. 1997): 310–31.

——. *Practicing Religion in the Age of the Media: Explorations in Media, Religion, and Culture*. New York: Columbia University Press, 2002.

Hoover, Stewart, and Knut Lundby. *Rethinking Media, Religion and Culture*. Newbury Park, Calif.: Sage, 1997.

Hoover, Stewart, and Shalini Venturelli. "The Category of the Religious: The Blindspot of Contemporary Media Theory?" *Critical Studies in Mass Communication* 13 (1996): 251–65.

Horkheimer, Max. *Eclipse of Reason*. New York: Continuum, 1974. (Orig. pub. 1947.)

Horkheimer, Max, and Adorno, Theodor. *Dialectic of Enlightenment*. New York: Continuum, 1987.

Houtman, Dick, and Stef Aupers. "The Spiritual Turn and the Decline of Tradition:The Spread of Post-Christian Spirituality in 14 Western Countries, 1981–2000." *Journal for the Scientific Study of Religion* 46.3 (2007): 305–20.

Hunt, Stephen. "'Winning Ways': Globalisation and the Impact of the Health and Wealth Gospel." *Journal of Contemporary Religion* 15.3 (2000): 331–47.

Ingram, Julia. "Beware of New Age Bullies." *Conscious Choice*, Sept. 2004, 34–35.

Isaacs, Nora. "Vision Quest." *Yoga Journal*, Sept.–Oct. 2004, 21.

Jackson, Peter. *Maps of Meaning*. London: Unwin Hyman, 1989.

Jacobson, David. *Place and Belonging in America*. Baltimore: John Hopkins University Press, 2002.

Jakubowicz, Karol. "Civil Society, Independent Public Sphere, and Information Society." In *Information Society and Civil Society*." Eds. Slavko Splichal, Andrew Calabrese and Colin Sparks. West Lafayette, Ind.: Purdue University Press, 1994. 78–103.

James, William. *Varieties of Religious Experience*. New York: Simon & Schuster, 1997.

Jameson, Frederic. "Postmodernism, or, the Cultural Logic of Late Capitalism." *New Left Review* 146 (1984): 53–94.

Kaptchuk, Ted, and David Eisenberg. "Health Food or Granola?: It's Truth and Consequences." In *Examining Complementary Medicine*. Ed. Andrew Vickers. Cheltenham: Nelson Thornes, 2003, 17–28.

Keane, John. *Civil Society: Old Images, New Visions*. Stanford, Calif.: Stanford University Press, 1998.

Kemp, Jurrian. "Editorial." *Ode Magazine*, Nov. 2008, 8.

Kempton, Sally. "Guided by Voices." *Yoga Journal*, Sept.–Oct. 2004, 87–94.

——. "Real Joy, Right Now." *Yoga Journal, Balanced Living, Special Issue,* Winter 2004, 62–65, 104–9.

King, Ursula. Introduction to *Spirituality and Society in the New Millennium*. Ed. Ursula King. Brighton: Sussex Press, 2001. 1–18.

King, Ynestra. "Healing the Wounds: Feminism, Ecology, and the Nature/Culture Dualism." In *Reweaving the World: The Emergence of Ecofeminism,* Eds. Irene Diamond and Gloria Feman Orenstein. San Francisco: Sierra Club Books, 1990. 106–21.

Kingsolver, Barbara. "The Good Farmer." *Utne Reader,* July–Aug. 2004, 53–56.

Kinsley, David. *Ecology and Religion*. Englewood Cliffs, N.J.: Prentice Hall, 1994.

Klassen, Pamela E. "Textual Healing: Mainstream Protestants and the Therapeutic Text, 1900–1925." *American Society of Church History* 75.4 (Dec. 2006): 809–48.

Kline, Stephen. "The Morality and Politics of Consumer Religion: How Consumer Religion Fuels the Culture Wars in the United States." *Journal of Religion and Popular Culture* 17 (2007). 28 Nov. http://www.usask.ca/relst/jrpc/art17-consumerreligion.html.

Kopczuk, Wojciech, Emmannuel Saez, and Jae Song. "Uncovering the American Dream: Inequality and Mobility in Social Security Earnings Data since 1937." National Bureau of Economic Research, Working Paper 13345, August 2007. http://www.nber.org/papers/w13345. Accessed 30 Sept. 2009.

Korelitz, Jean Hanff. "It's a Wonderful Life." *Organic Style,* June 2004, 98–106,126.

Laclau, Ernst, and Chantal Mouffe. "Post-Marxism without Apologies." *New Left Review* 166 (1987): 79–109.

LaFleur, William. "Body." In *Critical Terms for Religious Studies.* Ed. Mark C. Taylor. Chicago: University of Chicago Press, 1998. 36–54.

Lampe, Frank. "Brown Calls for Advent of Eco-Economy." *LOHAS Journal* 3.2 (2001), 18–21

———. "Business as an Eco-System." *LOHAS Journal* 5.1 (2004), 58–60.

———. "Chopra on the Workplace: Business Must Redefine Itself." *Natural Business,* Sept 2001, 8.

———. "The Deal with Dean." *LOHAS Journal* 3.3 (2002): 34–37.

———. "Eight Questions for Amy." *LOHAS Journal* 2.3 (2001): 34–37.

———. "Mainstream Media Meets LOHAS." *LOHAS Journal* 4.1 (2003): 32–35.

———. "One Man's Crazy Ideas." *LOHAS Journal* 5. 1 (2004): 54–56.

———. "Riding the Wave toward a New LOHAS Generation." *LOHAS Journal* 5.1 (2004): 20–22.

Lampman, Jane. "Trendwatcher Sees Moral Transformation of Capitalism." *Christian Science Monitor,* 3 Oct. 2005. 18 Nov. 2009. http://www.csmonitor.com/2005/1003/p13s01-wmgn.html.

Landres, Shawn J. "Public Art as Sacred Space." In *Practicing Religion in the Age of Media.* Eds. Stewart Hoover and Lynn Schofield Clark. New York: Columbia University Press, 2002. 91–112.

Lane, Laura. Tying the Knot. *Yoga Journal,* May/June 2004, 18.

Langley, Paul, and Mary Mellor. "Economy, Sustainability and Sites of Transformative Space." *New Political Economy* 7.1 (2002): 49–65.

Lappé, France Moore. "A Call for Guts." *ODE Magazine,* Nov. 2008, 21.

Leach, William. *Land of Desire: Merchants, Power, and the Rise of a New American Culture.* New York: Random House, 1993.

Leaf, Brian. "The Eco-Doctor is In." *Conscious Choice* 17.7 (July 2004): 20–22.

Lefkowitz, Fran. "The Church of Nature." *Body+Soul,* Sept. 2004, 93.

Lindlof, Thomas R. *Qualitative Communication Research Methods.* Thousand Oaks, Calif.: Sage, 1995.

Liu, Hugo, Patti Maes, and Gloriana Davenport. "Unraveling the Taste Fabric of Social Networks." *International Journal on Semantic Web and Information Systems* 2.1 (2006): 42–71.

Louden, Jennifer. "The Rest of Your Life." *Body+Soul,* Nov.–Dec. 2004, 66–70.

Loudermilk, Linda. *LindaLoudermilk.com.* 27 Sept. 2005. http://www.lindaloudermilk.com/home.html.

Lundby, Knut. "The Web of Collective Representations." In *Rethinking Media, Religion and Culture.* Eds. Stewart M. Hoover and Knut Lundby. Thousand Oaks, Calif.: Sage, 1997. 146–64.

Mackey, John. "The Past, Present and Future of Food." *John Mackey's Blog,* 13 March 2007. 4 June 2009. http://www2.wholefoodsmarket.com/blogs/jmackey/2007/03/13/past-present-and-future-of-food.

———. "The Whole Foods Alternative to Obama Care." *Wall Street Journal,* 11 Aug. 2009. 3 Sept. 2009. http://online.wsj.com/article/SB10001424052970204251404574342170072865070.html.

Manconi, Barbara. "The New Frontier of Luxury." *Sustainable Brands Weekly,* 15 Oct. 2009. http://www.sustainablebrandsweekly.com.

Marchand, Ray. *Advertising the American Dream: Making Way for Modernity 1920–1940.* Berkley: University of California Press, 1986.

Marcuse, Herbert. *One Dimensional Man.* Boston: Beacon Press, 1964.

Martín-Barbero, Jesús. "Communication, Culture and Hegemony. From the Media to Mediations." Trans. Elizabeth Fox and Robert E. White. London: Sage, 1993.

Marx, Karl. *Capital, Vol. 1.* Trans. Samuel Moore and Edward Aveling. Ed. Frederick Engels. Online Version. Marx/Engels Internet Archive (Marxists.org) 1995, 1999. 12 Sept. 2005. www.Marxists.org/archive/marx/works/1867-c1.

———. *Grundrisse.* Trans. Martin Nicolaus. London: Penguin Books, 1973. (Orig. written 1857–61).

McDannell, Colleen. *Material Christianity.* New Haven, Conn.: Yale University Press, 1996.

McFague, Sallie. *The Body of God: An Ecological Theology.* Minneapolis: Fortress Press, 1993.

Mclaughlin, Katy. "Is Your Grocery List Politically Correct?" *Wall Street Journal,* 2 Feb. 2004, D1–D2.

Mears, Daniel P., and Christopher G. Ellison. "Who Buys New Age Materials: Exploring Sociodemographic, Religious, Network, and Contextual Correlates of New Age Consumption." *Sociology of Religion* 61.3 (2000): 289–313.

Mellor, P. A., and C. Shilling. *Re-forming the Body: Religion, Community and Modernity.* London: Sage Publications, 1997.

Meyer, Donald. *The Positive Thinkers.* Middletown, Conn.: Wesleyan University Press, 1988.

Middendorf, Bobbi. "Business with a Passion." *LOHAS Journal* 2.4 (2001): 30–32.

———. "For a Higher Purpose." *LOHAS Journal* 3.1 (2002): 50.

Miller, Perry. *Errand into the Wilderness.* Cambridge, Mass.: Harvard University Press, 1956.

Millet, Lydia. "Ecoporn Exposed." *High Country News* April 2004. *Utne Reader,* Sept.–Oct. 2004, 34–35.

Mitchell, Don. "There's No Such Thing as Culture: Towards a Reconceptualization of the Idea of Culture in Geography." *Transactions of the Institute of British Geographers, New Series* 20.1 (1995): 102–16.

Moisander, Johanna, and Sinikka Pesonen. "Narratives of Sustainable Ways of Living: Constructing the Self and the Other as a Green Consumer." *Management Decision* 40.4 (2002): 329–42.

Monte, Bonnie. "HomeEcology." *Yoga Journal, Balanced Living, Special Issue,* Winter 2004, 78, 83, 115.

Montgomery, Charles. "The Pursuit of Square Footage." *Utne Reader,* May–June 2008, 48–49.

Montgomery, Dan. "Is LOHAS the Business Culture of the Future?" March 2009. 28 March, 2011. http://www.resilient-strategies.com/2009/03/is-lohas-the-business-culture-of-the-future.

Mooney, Nan. "Reimagining the American Dream: What the Good Life Really Means and Why We Can Still Grab It." *Utne Reader,* May–June 2008, 39–41.

Moore, Lawrence. *Selling God.* Oxford: Oxford University Press, 1994.

Moore, Thomas. "A Fresh Look at Jesus." *Spirituality & Health,* Sept.–Oct. 2004, 11.

———. "The Spiritual Arts." *Spirituality & Health,* July–August 2004. 21 January 2005. www.spiritualityhealth.com/newsh/items/article/item_9102.html.

Moran, Victoria. "Enough Is Enough." *Yoga Journal,* October 2004, 63–64, 68–69.

Morley, David, and Roger Silverstone. "Communication and Context: Ethnographic Perspectives on the Media Audience." In *A Handbook of Qualitative Methodologies for Mass Communication Research.* Eds. Klaus Brhun Jensen and Nicholas Jankowski. London: Routledge, 1991. 149–62.

Murphy, Tim. "Discourse." In *Guide to the Study of Religion.* Eds. Willi Braun and Robert. T. McCutcheon. London: Cassell, 2000. 396–408.

Nachman-Hunt, Nancy. "Bill Coors: There's Nothing Like an Original." *LOHAS Journal* 2.1 (2001): 28–31.

———. "The Hunt for the Aging 78-Million Pound Elephant." *LOHAS Journal* 4.1 (2003): 26–31.

———. "Less Bad Isn't the Answer." *LOHAS Journal* 5.1 (2004): 62–64.

———. "Ray Anderson's Epiphany." *LOHAS Journal* 2.2 (2001): 16–20.

Naess, Arne. "The Deep Ecological Movement." In *Deep Ecology for the 21st Century.* Ed. George Sessions. Boston: Shambhala, 1995. 64–84.

Neimark, Jill. "Tapping into Horse Sense." *Spirituality & Health,* Oct. 2004, 511–55.

Nelson, Julie. "Cocks, Creation and Clarity: Insights on Ethics and Economics from a Feminist Perspective." *Ethical Theory and Moral Practice* 7 (2004), 381—98.

Nicholls, Alex, and Charlotte Opal. *Fair Trade: Market-Driven Ethical Consumption.* London: Sage, 2004.

Ning, Ted. "Can't Buy Me Love." Blog entry. *LOHAS.com,* 22 July 2009. 15 Mar. 2011. http://blog.lohas.com/blog/lohas-trends/cant-buy-me-love-v2.

———. "Social Media and LOHAS." Blog entry. *LOHAS.com,* 30 July 2009. 15 Mar. 2011. http://blog.lohas.com/blog/lohas-trends/social-media-and-lohas.

Norlander, Torsten, L. Gård, L. Lindholm, and T. Archer. "New Age: Exploration of Outlook-On-Life Frameworks from a Phenomenological Perspective." *Mental Health, Religion, and Culture* 6.1 (2003): 1–20.

NZHerald.co.nz. "Cadbury Caves." *New Zealand Herald,* 17 Aug. 2009. 28 Nov. 2009. http://www.nzherald.co.nz/business/news/article.cfm?c_id=3&objectid=10591340&pnum=1.

Orloff, Judith. *Reinventing Medicine.* Oasis Television. Dec. 2005.

Oxenhandler, Noelle. "Money and the Middle Way. *Utne Reader,* Sept.–Oct. 2004, 104–6.

Palmer, Louise Danielle. "Go Ahead and Make Someone's Day." *Spirituality & Health,* Nov.–Dec. 2004, 22.

Palmer, Parker J. "Finding Your Soul." *Spirituality & Health,* Oct. 2004. 19 Apr. 2011. http://www.spiritualityhealth.com/NMagazine/articles.php?id=126.

Paris, Darlene. "Spiritual Practice: Just Do It!" *Conscious Choice,* July 2004, 32.

Payne, Michael. *A Dictionary of Cultural and Critical Theory.* Oxford: Blackwell, 1997.

Peck, Janice. *In the Age of Oprah: Cultural Icon for a Neoliberal Age.* Boulder, Colo.: Paradigm Publishers, 2008.

Pelczynski, Z. A. "Solidarity and the 'Rebirth of Civil Society.'" In *Civil Society and the State: New European Perspectives.* Ed. John Keane. London: Verso, 1988. 361–80.

Perrucci, Robert, and Earl Wysong. *The New Class Society: Goodby American Dream?* New York: Rowman and Littlefield, 2007.

Pesek, Todd, Lonnie R. Helton, and Murali Nair. "Healing across Cultures: Learning from Traditions." *EcoHealth* 3 (2006): 114–18.

Petrini, Carlo. *Slow Food: The Case for Taste.* Trans. William McCuig. New York: Columbia University Press, 2004.

Pike, Sarah. *Earthly Bodies, Magical Selves: Contemporary Pagans and the Search for Community.* Berkeley: University of California Press, 2001.

Pollan, Michael. "Walmart Goes Organic, Now for the Bad News." *New York Times,* 15 May 2006. 15 Nov. 2009. http://pollan.blogs.nytimes.com/2006/05/15/wal-mart-goes-organic-and-now-for-the-bad-news/?scp=1&sq=walmart%20goes%20organic%20now%20for%20the%20bad%20news&st=cse.

"Poll Says Spirituality Not Replacing Religion." *Christian Century* 118.17 (2001): 13.

Popham, Peter. "Catholics Urged to Fight off New Age Religions." *New Zealand Herald,* 16 June 2004. 30 Nov. 2009. www.nzherald.co.nz/peter-popham/news/article.cfm?a_id=124&objectid=3573500.

Porritt, Jonathon. "As if the World Matters: Reconciling Sustainable Development and Capitalism." *OpenDemocracy Ltd.,* 30 Nov. 2005. 30 Nov. 30 2005. www.opendemocracy.net.

Powell, Bonnie. "Michael Pollan, Whole Foods' John Mackey Usher Berkeley Foodies into 'Ecological Era.'" *UC Berkeley News,* 27 Feb. 2007. 14 Oct. 2009. http://berkeley.edu/news/media/releases/2007/02/28_pollanmackey.shtml.

Promey, Sally M. "Interchangeable Art." In *Icons of American Protestantism: The Art of Warner Sallman.* Ed. David Morgan. New Haven, Conn.: Yale University Press, 1996. 148–81.

Putnam, Robert. *Bowling Alone.* New York: Simon & Schuster, 2000.

Rabinow, Paul. *The Foucault Reader.* New York: Pantheon Books, 1984.

Ray, Paul. "Who Is the LOHAS Consumer?" *LOHAS Journal* 1.1 (2000): 35–38, 52.

Ray, Paul H., and Sherry Ruth Anderson. *The Cultural Creatives: How 50 Million People are Changing the World.* New York: Three Rivers Press, 2000.

Reddy, Sameer. "It Costs More to Save." *Newsweek* 3 Nov. 2008.

Reder, Alan. "Love Thy Neighbor, Heal Thy Self." *Natural Solutions,* 1 Feb. 2006. 20 Oct. 2009. http://www.naturalsolutionsmag.com/articles-display/8005/keyword/reder/Love-Thy-Neighbor-Heal-Thyself.

Reinhardt, Angela. "Slow Food Movement Picking up Speed." *Pickens County Progress*

Newspaper, 27 May 2009. 27 Aug. 2009. http://www.pickensprogress.com/articleinfo
.asp?Link=1252.

Riches, David. "The Holistic Person; or, the Ideology of Egalitarianism." *Journal of the
Royal Anthropological Institute* 6.4 (2000): 669–86.

Rifkin, Jeremy. "The European Dream." *Utne Reader,* Sept.–Oct. 2004, 75–79.

Ritzer, George. *The McDonaldization of Society.* Thousand Oaks, Calif.: Pine Forge Press,
2004.

Robbins, Richard. *Global Problems and the Culture of Capitalism.* Boston: Allyn & Bacon,
2005.

Robertson, Roland. *Globalization: Social Theory and Global Culture.* London: Sage, 1992.

Roof, Wade Clark. *Spiritual Marketplace.* Princeton, N.J.: Princeton University Press, 1999.

Rooks, John. "A Beautiful Ambiguity." *LOHAS Journal* 9.1 (2008): 49–51.

Rosanoff, Nancy. "Embracing Chaos: A Conversation with Margaret Wheatley." *Body+Soul,*
Dec. 2004, 73–76.

Rose, Nick. "Humans, Food and Inhuman Food." *Utne Reader,* 4 May 2006. 20 Aug. 2009.
www.utne.com/2006-05-01/HumansFoodandInhumanFood.aspx.

Rosenbaum, Ron. "The Hostile New Age Takeover." *Slate Magazine,* 21 Mar. 2007. 29 Oct.
2009. www.slate.com.

Roth, Gabrielle. "Move Your Soul." *Body+Soul,* July–Aug. 2004, 69–71, 96.

Said, Edward. *Orientalism.* New York: Vintage Books, 1978.

Satter, Beryl. *Each Mind a Kingdom.* Berkeley: University of California Press, 1999.

Scammel, Margaret. "The Internet and Civic Engagement: The Age of the Citizen-Con-
sumer. *Political Communication,* 17 (2000): 351–55.

Schimke, David. "A New National Narrative." *Utne Reader,* May–June 2008. 12 April 2011.
http://www.utne.com/2008-05-01/Politics/A-New-National-Narrative.aspx.

Schlehofer, Michele M., Allen M. Omoto, and Janice R. Adelman. "How Do 'Religion'
and 'Spirituality' Differ? Lay Definitions among Older Adults." *Journal for the Scientific
Study of Religion* 47.3 (2008): 411–25.

Schlitz, M. "Child Spirit." *Body+Soul,* Oct. 2004, 12–13.

———. "A 60-Second Guide to Integral Medicine." *Spirituality & Health,* Nov.–Dec. 2004,
12–13.

Schull, Christiane. "Quantum Physics Made Easy." *Whole Life Times,* June 2004, 24.

Scott, Robert Owens. "Baby, Look at You Now." *Spirituality & Health,* Oct. 2004, 6.

Senge, Peter. "Sustainability: Not What You Think It Is." *MIT SLOAN Management Review,*
4 June 2009. 11 June 2009. http://sloanreview.mit.edu/beyond-green/sustainability-its
-not-what-you-think-it-is.

Sessions, George. Introduction to *Deep Ecology for the 21st Century.* Ed. George Sessions.
Boston: Shambhala Publications, 1995. 3–8.

Shah, Dhavan V., Douglas M. McLeod, Lewis Friedland, and Michelle R. Nelson. "The
Politics of Consumption/The Consumption of Politics." *Annals of the American Academy of Political and Social Science* 611 (2007): 6–15.

Shalmy, Paul. "The Corporation: Unmasking Today's Robber Barons." *Whole Life Times,*
July 2004, 26–28.

Shi, David. 1985. *The Simple Life: Plain Living and High Thinking in American Culture.*
New York: Oxford University Press.

Shin, Annys. "AOL Founder's Latest Lifestyle Choice." *Washington Post,* 9 Aug. 2005, D01.

Shireman, Bill. "Business Lessons from the Rain Forest." *LOHAS Journal* 3.2 (2002): 50.

Shuman, Michael H., and Merrian Fuller. "Profits for Justice." *The Nation,* 24 Jan. 2005,13.

Siklos, Richard. "Discovery to Start Channel on Green Movement." *New York Times,* 5 Apr. 2007. 5 Apr. 2007. http://www.nytimes.com/2007/04/05/business/media/05green .html?scp=1&sq=&st=nyt.

Smith, Jonathan. Z. "Religion, Religions, Religious." In *Critical Terms for Religious Studies.* Ed. Mark C. Taylor. Chicago: University of Chicago Press, 1998. 269–84.

Spayde, Jon. "20 years of Utne." *Utne Reader,* Sept.–Oct. 2004, 58–63.

Speth, James Gustave. *The Bridge at the End of the World: Capitalism, the Environment and Crossing from Crisis to Sustainability.* New Haven, Conn.: Yale University Press, 2009.

Stanczak, Gregory, and Donald Miller. *Engaged Spirituality: Spirituality and Social Transformation in Mainstream American Religious Traditions: Report Supplement.* Los Angeles: University of Southern California Center for Religion and Civic Culture, 2002.

Stark, John. "30 Years of Whole Living." *Body+Soul,* Nov.–Dec. 2004, 93–101.

Starker, Steven. *Oracle at the Supermarket: The American Preoccupation with Self Help Books.* New Brunswick: Transaction Publishers, 2002.

Sutcliffe, Steven. "The Dynamics of Alternative Spirituality: Seekers, Networks, and 'New Age.'" *The Oxford Handbook of New Religions.* Oxford: Oxford University Press, 2004. 466–90.

Sutcliffe, Steven, and Marion Bowman. *Beyond New Age: Exploring Alternative Spirituality.* Edinburgh: Edinburgh University Press, 2000.

Tábara, J. David, and Salvador S. Giner. "Diversity, Civic Virtues, and Ecological Austerity." *International Review of Sociology* 14.2 (2004): 261–85.

Teeple, Gary *Globalization and the Decline of Social Reform.* Aurora, Ont.: Garamond Press, 2000.

Thompson, John. *Ideology and Modern Culture: Critical Social Theory in the Era of Mass Communication.* Stanford, Calif.: Stanford University Press, 1990.

———. "Mass Communication and Modern Culture: Contribution to a Critical Theory of Ideology." *Sociology* 22.3 (1988): 359–83.

———. *Media and Modernity.* Stanford, Calif.: Stanford University Press, 1995.

Time Magazine. "The High Priestess of Nutrition." 18 Dec. 1972. 28 Mar. 2011. http://www .time.com/time/magazine/article/0,9171,945187,00.html.

Tomlinson, John. *Globalization and Culture.* Cambridge: Polity Press, 1999.

Trainer, Ted. "Debating the Significance of the Global Eco-Village Movement: A Reply to Takis Fotopoulos." *Democracy and Nature* 8.1 (2002): 143–57.

Traube, Elizabeth G. "Secrets of Success in Postmodern Society." *Cultural Anthropology* 4.3 (Aug. 1989): 273–300.

Turner, Bryan. "Religious Authority and the New Media." *Theory, Culture, and Society* 24. 2 (2007): 118–34.

Utne, Leif. "The Personal Goes Political." *Utne Reader,* Nov.–Dec. 2004, 90–91.

Utne, Nina. "The Flow of Intention." *Utne Reader,* Sept.–Oct. 2004, 68–70.

Van Gelder, Sarah, and Paul Ray. "A Culture Gets Creative." *Yes! Magazine,* Winter 2001. 10 Jan. 2007. http://www.yesmagazine.org/article.asp?ID=399.

Varman, Rohit, and Russell Belk. "Weaving a Web: Subaltern Consumers, Rising Consumer Culture, and Television." *Marketing Theory* 8.3 (2008): 227–52.

Verter, Bradford. "Spiritual Capital: Theorizing Religion with Bourdieu against Bourdieu." *Sociological Theory* 21.2 (June 2003): 150–74.

Vogue Australia. Apr. 2007, 135. 19 Aug. 2009. http://email.nuovon.com.au/download/files/07905/394492/nuovon_vogue0407.pdf135.

Waldman, Steven, and Valerie Reiss. "BeliefWatch: LOHASians." *Newsweek,* 5 June 2006.

Wang, Georgette. Introduction to *The New Communications Landscape: Demystifying Media Globalization.* Eds. Georgette Wang, Anura Goonasekera, and Jan Sevaes. London: Routledge, 2000. 1–18.

Warkins, Brad. "Q & A with Conscious Media." *LOHAS Journal* 5.1 (2004): 23.

Weber, Max. *The Protestant Ethic and the Spirit of Capitalism.* Trans. Talcott Parsons. Mineola, N.Y.: Dover, 2003. (Orig. pub. 1958.)

Weil, Andrew. "What Doctors Should Know." *Body+Soul,* Sept. 2004, 84–91, 122.

Wellner, Alison Stein. "Get Your Green On." *Yoga Journal,* 16 Apr. 2009. 2 Aug. 2009. http://www.yogajournal.com/lifestyle/2586?utm_source=DailyInsight&utm_medium=newsletter&utm_content=b&utm_campaign=DI_2009-04-16.

White, Lynn. "The Historic Roots of our Ecological Crisis." *Science* 155 (1967): 1203–07.

Williams, Raymond. *The Long Revolution.* London: Chatto & Windus, 1961.

Willson, Michele. "Community in the Abstract: A Political and Ethical Dilemma?" In *Virtual Politics.* Ed. David Holmes. London: Sage, 1997. 145–62.

Winne, Mark. "The Poor Get Diabetes; The Rich Get Local and Organic." *AlterNet,* 9 Jan. 2008. 11 Jan. 2008. http://www.alternet.org/environment/72417/?page=entire.

Winninghoff, Ellie. "Think Slower." *Evergreen Monthly,* June 2004, 62.

Winquist, Charles E. "Person." In *Critical Terms for Religious Studies.* Ed. Mark C. Taylor. Chicago: University of Chicago Press, 1998. 186–204.

Wolfe, Cary. "Nature as Critical Concept: Kenneth Burke, the Frankfurt School, and Metabiology." *Cultural Critique* 18 (1991): 65–96.

Woodhead, Linda. "Post-Christian Spiritualities." *Religion* 23.2 (1993): 117–26.

York, Michael. "New Age Commodification and Appropriation of Spirituality." *Journal of Contemporary Religion* 16.3 (2001): 361–73.

———. "Wanting to Have Your New Age Cake and Eat It Too." *Journal of Alternative Spiritualities and New Age Studies* (2005): 15–34.

Zukin, Sharon, and Jennifer Smith Maguire. "Consumers and Consumption." *Annual Review of Sociology* 30 (2004): 173–97.

Zuniga, Marielena. "Hold This Thought in Your Dreams." *Spirituality & Health,* Sept.–Oct. 2004, 26.

Index

MONICA M. EMERICH is a research afflilate at the
Center for Media, Religion, and Culture at the University
of Colorado, Boulder, and the president of Groundwork
Research & Communications in Lafayette, Colorado.

The University of Illinois Press
is a founding member of the
Association of American University Presses.

—————————————————————————

Composed in 10.5/13 Minion Pro
by Celia Shapland
at the University of Illinois Press
Manufactured by Sheridan Books, Inc.

University of Illinois Press
1325 South Oak Street
Champaign, IL 61820-6903
www.press.uillinois.edu